D1129792

IMPERIAL CONTROL OF COLONIAL LEGISLATION
1813-1865

IMPERIAL CONTROL OF COLONIAL LEGISLATION

1813–1865

*A Study of British Policy
towards Colonial Legislative Powers*

BY

D. B. SWINFEN, M.A., D.PHIL.

DEPARTMENT OF MODERN HISTORY,
UNIVERSITY OF DUNDEE

CLARENDON PRESS · OXFORD

1970

Oxford University Press, Ely House, London, W.1

GLASGOW   NEW YORK   TORONTO   MELBOURNE   WELLINGTON
CAPE TOWN   SALISBURY   IBADAN   NAIROBI   DAR ES SALAAM   LUSAKA   ADDIS ABABA
BOMBAY   CALCUTTA   MADRAS   KARACHI   LAHORE   DACCA
KUALA LUMPUR   SINGAPORE   HONG KONG   TOKYO

PRINTED IN GREAT BRITAIN
BY BUTLER AND TANNER LTD
FROME AND LONDON

TO ANN

ACKNOWLEDGEMENTS

IF I were to name all the individuals and institutions upon whose aid and advice I have so heavily relied in preparing this book, serious doubts would arise as to whether my name should appear at all, except, of course, as the scapegoat for any remaining mistakes. I must, however, acknowledge a special debt to my friends in Oxford, Dr. A. F. Madden and Mr. D. K. Fieldhouse, who provided both the initial inspiration and continuing encouragement, and my friend and colleague in Dundee, Dr. Donald Southgate, who has saved me from the worst of my errors.

I should like to pay tribute also to the staffs of the Public Record Office, London, The Privy Council Office, the British Museum, Rhodes House Library, Oxford, and the University Library in Dundee, all of whom have catered for my research needs with customary efficiency and forbearance.

Lastly I should like to thank Miss Jessie Milne for her help in preparing the typescript, and especially my wife, who typed the first draft and who has also, throughout the whole process, offered her unfailing sympathy and understanding.

D. B. S.

Dundee, 1970

CONTENTS

ABBREVIATIONS

Am. Hist. Ass.	American Historical Association
Bull. of Inst. of Hist. Res.	*Bulletin of the Institute of Historical Research*
Can. Bar Rev.	*Canadian Bar Review*
Can. Hist. Rev.	*Canadian Historical Review*
C.H.B.E.	*Cambridge History of the British Empire*
C.O.	Colonial Office
Economic Hist. Rev.	*Economic History Review*
H.A.	House of Assembly
Knapp	*Privy Council Appeal Cases*, compiled by Edward Knapp, in *English Reports*, vol. 12 (London, 1901).
L.C.	Legislative Council
N.L.S.	National Library of Scotland
P.C.	Privy Council
P.P.	(English) *Parliamentary Papers*
Proc. of Am. Antiquarian Soc.	*Proceedings of the American Antiquarian Society*
Proc. of Royal Geog. Soc. of Austr.	*Proceedings of the Royal Geographical Society of Australia*
S.A.P.D.	*South Australian Parliamentary Debates*
S.A.P.P.	*South Australian Parliamentary Papers*

INTRODUCTION

EVERY student of British colonial policy after 1783 is now well aware that the breach with the thirteen American colonies did not immediately produce a radical change in the basic principles of that policy. Change there was, but it was a gradual process, influenced by developments in the economy and political institutions within the colonies and by reform movements and the adoption of Free Trade principles at home. These pressures, together with other external factors, such as events in the Spanish and Portuguese empires, helped to produce, in time, a new attitude towards empire. It began to be recognized, in the half century after 1815, that it might be to the mutual benefit of Britain and her overseas possessions if the bonds of empire were relaxed.[1] This feeling affected not only politicians like Gladstone and Disraeli, but also senior officials like Sir Frederic Rogers, who remarked in 1854 upon 'What we are, I suppose, all looking to, the eventual parting company on good terms'.[2]

At the same time there was a definite reluctance on the part of the British Government to let this trend get out of hand. The maintenance of an empire was still thought a desirable object. In this very period no dependencies were lost and many were gained.[3] No two colonies were at the same stage of political development or economic viability—the fruit must be allowed to ripen before it could fall from the tree.

Humanitarian movements, among other influences, persuaded the Government that there was still important work to be done. Many politicians, writers, and officials continued to feel a strong sense of responsibility towards the maturing communities overseas.

The problem of the Colonial Office in this period was twofold, in that it had both to devise policy and to administer an empire.[4]

---

[1] Cf. Williamson, J. A., *A Short History of British Expansion*, vol. II, 3rd edn. (London, 1947), pp. 17 et seq., and Burt, A. L., *The Evolution of the British Empire and Commonwealth from the American Revolution* (Boston Mass., 1956), pp. 207–11.

[2] Quoted in Williamson, op. cit., p. 57.

[3] Cf. Robinson, R., and Gallacher, J. A., 'The Imperialism of Free Trade', *Economic Hist. Rev.* (1953).

[4] The C.O. did not, of course, become a separate department of state until

With the formation and administration of imperial policy in general, however, we are not here concerned. The purpose of this study is to consider one aspect only of the problem—the process of colonial law review.

The term 'review process' requires some explanation, if only because of its comparative neglect, with one or two important exceptions, by historians of the British Empire.[5] In its widest sense this meant the process whereby colonial laws could either be ratified, amended, or rejected by the Crown or have their constitutional validity tested by the courts, colonial and imperial.

Constitutionally, the Crown's power of veto over colonial legislation was derived from the fact that the colonial legislatures occupied an essentially subordinate position.[6] Historically, the right of disallowance had been exercised from the earliest years of the British colonial system.[7] A procedure developed whereby all laws passed by colonial legislatures were reviewed, and a decision taken upon them, by the appropriate government department—in the seventeenth and eighteenth centuries the Privy Council with its Board of Trade, in the nineteenth century the Colonial Office. The Secretary of State for the Colonies (until 1854, War and the Colonies) was the official reponsible for this process and it did not matter in the least that the decisions were made, in form, by the King-in-Council, or that they were embodied in an Order-in-Council. Nor was the direct intervention of Parliament involved, except in the rare cases where laws on certain subjects were required to be laid before both Houses under the authority of an imperial statute.[8]

The Colonial Office and the Secretary of State were therefore

---

1854. But apart from sharing a Secretary of State with the War Office since 1801, the Office between 1813 and 1854 may be considered for our purposes as a self-contained institution.

[5] e.g. Manning, H. T., *British Colonial Government after the American Revolution* (New Haven, 1935), and Young, D. M., *The Colonial Office in the early Nineteenth Century* (London, 1961).

[6] Todd, A., *Parliamentary Government in the Colonies*, p. 155; Merivale, H., *Colonisation and the Colonies*, p. 664 et seq.

[7] Andrews, C. M., 'The Royal Disallowance', *Proc. of Am. Antiquarian Soc.* N.S. 24. 342.

[8] e.g. 3 & 4 Vict., c. 35 required that Canadian Acts for the sale of public lands be laid before Parliament for thirty days. The Duke of Newcastle refused, in 1853, to waive this formality, but agreed that the statute should be amended at the first opportunity. C.O. 323/75, Canada; Murdoch and Wood to Merivale, 21 Dec. 1853; Minute by Newcastle.

in possession of considerable authority over colonial legislatures. The question arises of what value were these powers, and how far were the authorities prepared to make use of them?

The amount of dull, slogging, hard work required to operate the system was formidable, and there were times when even those officials most directly concerned doubted its necessity. James Stephen[9] reckoned in 1840 that 'among all the duties which are to be discharged here, the most unwelcome has always been that of revising our Colonial Legislation. On a rough estimate I take at 21,000 the number of laws on which in my time I have had to report my opinion. Such a mass of uninteresting details it would be difficult to bring together from any other quarter.'[10] Stephen suggested to Hope (Parliamentary Under-Secretary to Lord Stanley) in 1841 that his only reason for continuing to write reports on acts after his appointment as Permanent Under-Secretary in 1836 was 'to keep up the continuity of records in this Office'.[11] Apart from this there was always the unpleasant suspicion that, where a conflict arose within a colony over which law, imperial or colonial, was to be obeyed, the local law would almost certainly prevail.

If these misgivings had been permanent, rather than occasional, the system might have been allowed to lapse or the colonial department might have been content to act in this matter as little more than a registry office for colonial statutes. In practice, almost the contrary was true. All laws passing through the Office were carefully scrutinized and many were reported on in detail. Colonial laws were approved, amended, and even disallowed.

Throughout the period, opinion within the Office clearly favoured the retention of this important means of control over the colonies. In 1828 Stephen deplored the action of the Van Diemen's Land Legislature in passing acts for such short periods of time that they had expired before reaching home. This practice (pro-hibited in the older colonies, like the West Indies, by Royal Instructions) was bound to lead to a situation where the 'control of His Majesty's Government, over the proceedings of the local legislature will be little more than nominal'.[12] In such cases the

[9] Legal adviser to the Colonial Office, 1813–46.
[10] C.O. 318/148, Russell Memorandum, 10 Oct. 1840; Minute by Stephen, 17 Oct.
[11] C.O. 323/56, fol. 236, Stephen to Hope, 6 Sept. 1841.
[12] C.O. 323/45, Van Diemen's Land; Stephen to Murray, 28 Nov. 1828.

abuse and conflict of laws could be prevented only by 'the most watchful superintendence by some authority common to both'[13] colony and Imperial Government (i.e. the governor). But even the local governor could not be entrusted with authority to give final assent to colonial bills; and colonial laws which attempted to give him such authority were open to the strongest objections. 'I would submit to you', wrote Stephen to the Colonial Secretary Sir George Murray in August 1830, 'that there is no good reason why the check, imperfect though it may be, which the transmission of laws for the Royal Assent provides, should be dispensed with.'[14]

The members of the Office thus insisted that their power to review should not be allowed to lapse. They were equally convinced that the power of disallowance of colonial laws should be used sparingly and with discretion. On this point they adopted a much less extreme position than that of their colleagues at the Board of Trade. When their Lordships suggested that the proper security against the passing of colonial acts imposing discriminatory duties on British goods lay 'in the power of the Secretary of State to recommend the disallowance by the King of any Acts which may impugn this principle',[15] the Colonial Office took a very different view. 'Although', wrote Stephen, 'the power of disallowing Colonial Acts unquestionably exists, and is frequently enforced, yet it is a remedy the use of which is attended with such extreme inconvenience as to forbid the recourse to it except in extreme cases.'[16] Nor was disallowance necessarily to be used, even in those cases where the Governor of the colony might have been justified in withholding his assent.

Colonial Office officials in this period were therefore agreed that the powers of control over colonial legislatures, implicit in the review process, should be retained. Even in colonies having 'responsible government' the power of disallowance was most important to preserve imperial interests.[17] But disallowance was an 'extreme remedy', and the number of acts actually disallowed in the period dwindled significantly towards the end.

It is one thing to note that contemporaries believed in the importance of the review process; it is quite another to establish

[13] C.O. 323/46, Nova Scotia; Stephen to Murray, 19 June 1829.
[14] C.O. 323/47, Ceylon; Stephen to Murray, 28 Aug. 1830.
[15] C.O. 323/219, Lack to Hay, 7 May 1835.
[16] C.O. 323/60, St. Vincent; Stephen to Stanley, 9 Sept. 1845.
[17] C.O. 323/87, New Brunswick; Rogers to Merivale, 23 Sept. 1858.

that it was in fact important in the context of contemporary British colonial policy.

A number of points should be borne in mind in this connection. The first is a general one, relevant to any imperial system or similar structure. In any such system, where one or more dependencies are controlled by some central authority, some kind of machinery must exist whereby the relative powers of each are defined and conflict between them resolved.[18] In some systems the resolution of any such conflict may be entrusted to the courts. In the United States the Supreme Court has frequently exercised its powers of 'judicial review' where a conflict has arisen between states or federal legislation and the Constitution. The process of judicial review has also operated within the British imperial system, though in this case the courts, colonial and imperial, have had powers over colonial legislation only. The main disadvantage of this system is that it can only operate to correct anomalies after the offending colonial law has come into force.

The process of 'administrative review', on the other hand, combined the advantages of the judicial system with other important advantages. It was possible, in many cases, to scrutinize colonial laws for conflict with imperial laws and for other defects *before* the former came into operation. In this way, the inconvenience of having laws already in force disallowed, amended or declared repugnant could be avoided. While it is true that most colonial laws to be reviewed had in fact already come into force, the provisions of the Royal Instructions requiring the reservation of certain classes of bills for the assent of the Crown meant that those bills most likely to raise legal and political problems were reviewed first, and passed into law afterwards.

One of the most important functions of the 'administrative' review process, therefore, was to apply to colonial laws existing legal rules, such as they were, in order to avoid future inconvenience. Just what these legal rules were was not always as clear as it might have been. The best contemporary exposition had been that of Lord Mansfield in *Campbell* v. *Hall*, 1774. In his judgement his Lordship had considered the question as to what laws should obtain in the two types of colony, conquered or ceded on the one hand and settled on the other, and had laid down that in the former the existing system of law was retained until altered by the Crown.

---

[18] Cf. Schuyler, R. L., *Parliament and the British Empire*, pp. 204–5.

Settlers in new and previously uninhabited colonies, however, took with them the Law of England, in so far as it was applicable to their situation.[19] These rules were obviously important when it came to deciding how far new laws passed in these colonies could be held to conflict with an imperial statute dealing with the same subject.

Nevertheless there was often considerable confusion in the colonies as to which laws were in fact in force at any one time.[20] Once again the review process could be helpful here, by pruning colonial laws of any provision or provisions which might be, probably inadvertently, repugnant.

The officials who operated the review process might have gone further and tried so to mould colonial laws as to produce general uniformity throughout the Empire. There were some suggestions that such a policy might be tried, but no serious attempt was made to implement it—indeed opinion within the Office was generally against any such unpractical experiment. There were, however, individual cases where uniformity of law was obviously desirable, and was encouraged.

Finally, the review process, or at least that part of it which was operated by the Colonial Office, could also be used as an instrument of political control. Colonial laws which conflicted in some way with imperial policy or which encroached upon imperial interests could be quickly dealt with, before too much damage had been done. The legal adviser to the Office, who was supposed to give his opinion on colonial acts 'in point of law', deemed it his duty also to draw his superiors' attention to political implications, and indeed by the mid-thirties had dropped the distinction from the adviser's reports.

Colonial Office attitudes to colonial laws were generally empirical, broadly in line with contemporary liberal policies, and greatly influenced by colonial desires and the relative impotence of Downing Street to interfere decisively in the face of strong colonial opposition. But these attitudes were still based on the assumption that the position of the colonial legislatures was essentially subordinate. The powers of control implicit in the re-

[19] *Campbell* v. *Hall*, 1774. Lord Mansfield's judgement is presented in full in Shortt, A., and Doughty, A. G., *Documents relating to the Constitutional History of Canada*, 2nd edn. (1918).

[20] Cf. Report of the Commissioners of Enquiry into the Administration of Justice in the West Indies, *P.P.* 1825 (157), XV. 233.

view process were retained, though their use varied from colony to colony and in general gradually diminished towards the end of our period. Thus the Colonial Laws Validity Act of 1865, intended as a liberating rather than as a restrictive enactment, still retained certain limitations upon the freedom of colonial legislature. And as time went on these limitations, especially as they affected the Dominion legislatures, became irksome.

The part played by 'judicial review' of colonial laws in this period was of mixed importance. As far as the British courts were concerned, and the Judicial Committee in particular, no cases came before them in our period involving the exercise of the power of review, and there is no evidence to suggest that there was any connection between their decisions and governmental policy. It was, however, suggested on a number of occasions that in colonial courts judgements concerning the validity of colonial acts had been influenced by non-legal prejudices. The most famous examples of these were the judgements of Mr. Justice Boothby in the Supreme Court of South Australia between 1859 and 1867. While his decisions were in no way influenced by Colonial Office policy, they *did* have an influence upon that policy and a vital influence upon the formulation of the 1865 Colonial Laws Validity Act.

There are three main reasons, therefore, why a study of the processes of colonial law review should be of value to the student of British imperial affairs.

In the first place, the workings of the process are of intrinsic interest for the light they throw upon the administrative organization of the Office itself. They may help to illustrate, for example, how efficient this organization was and where real responsibility for the formulation of policy lay. Secondly, a study of the opinions and action taken upon colonial laws offers valuable information upon specific points of colonial policy, as well as upon general trends and principles. Finally, by analysing governmental attitudes to the legal relationship between Britain and her colonies, in conjunction with an appraisal of the 'Boothby Affair' in South Australia, we may arrive at a fuller understanding of the origins of the Colonial Laws Validity Act.

Part I

THE REVIEW PROCESS

I

THE MACHINERY OF REVIEW

BY 1813, the date of James Stephen's first appointment on a part-time basis as counsel to the Colonial Office, the review process was already a well-established part of imperial administrative machinery.[1] Laws passed by the first assemblies in the American colonies were recognized as being subject to the approval of their respective Companies in England, although the first case of an actual disallowance did not take place until 1664.[2] Governmental control over colonial legislation was first entrusted to the Committee of the Privy Council for Trade and Plantations in 1660, a duty which passed to the Board of Trade twenty-five years later. Even after the reapportionment of colonial business in 1768, and the abolition of the old Board of Trade in 1784, the Privy Council Committee for Trade and Plantations continued to intervene in the review process—a circumstance which goes some way to explain the cumbersome and roundabout nature of the review machinery. Not until the latter part of our period was that process purged at last of the most striking of its inconveniences and anomalies.

For the purpose of clarity it is probably best to divide up the process into two parts: the overall procedure followed by colonial laws from colony to metropolis and back again, and the procedure followed within the Colonial Office itself.

In 1825, the year of Stephen's permanent appointment as counsel, the Commission of Enquiry into the Administration of Justice in the West Indies presented its Report. In this Report was included a very full (though not altogether accurate) account of the various stages through which colonial acts were obliged to pass.[3]

---

[1] For a discussion of the review of colonial laws in the seventeenth and eighteenth centuries, see Russell, E. B., *The Review of American Colonial Legislation* (New York, 1915).

[2] Andrews, C. M., 'The Royal Disallowance', *Proc. of Am. Antiquarian Soc.* (1914).

[3] *P.P.*, 1825, XV. (157), 233 et seq.

On arrival from the colony these acts were referred by the Secretary of State to the legal counsel for the colonial department, whose duty was to 'report his opinion on them in point of law'. This 'old and established form of expression' was considered to mean that counsel was to report whether the acts were such that the governor was authorized by his Commission and Instructions to pass them; whether, in terms of 7 & 8 Wm. III, c. 22, s. 9, they were repugnant to any law made in the kingdom 'so far as such law may mention or refer to the plantations'; and whether each act was so framed as to give 'full and entire effect to the purposes with which the colonial legislature may have passed it'.

Counsel's report was delivered to the Secretary of State, and transmitted by him, together with the acts and a covering letter, to the President of the Council, to be laid before the King-in-Council for His Majesty's consideration. At the next meeting of the Council the acts were referred again, this time to the Privy Council Committee for Trade and Plantations, with directions that their Lordships should report to the King-in-Council 'their opinion what proceedings it may be proper to take in relation to them'.

The Committee for Trade then went on to pick out from the acts any which might present some point of 'peculiar novelty or importance', or might give rise to any questions of legal difficulty. These selected acts, together with all private acts, were again sent on their travels—this time to the Law Officers of the Crown. On receipt of the Law Officers' report, the Lords of the Committee considered all the acts of the session together, it being a 'settled rule' that their Lordships were assisted in their deliberations by the Secretary of State for the Colonies, in his capacity as a member of the Committee.

In the Committee's final report to the King-in-Council, all the acts were classified into three sections: those to be disallowed, in which case the report contained a full statement of the objections to the act; those which, by virtue of their 'peculiar importance and interest' were to be specially confirmed by Order-in-Council; and thirdly the great majority of acts which, 'being usually little more than business of routine and continual recurrence', the King-in-Council would be advised to 'leave to their operation'.

Once the King-in-Council had adopted the report, the necessary Orders were drawn up with regard to acts in the first two classes. (No colonial act could be disallowed, the West Indian Commissioners noted, without such an Order-in-Council.) The decision taken on each of these acts was then transmitted to the Secretary of State by the Council Clerk, together with the original Orders. The Secretary of State in turn informed the respective colonial governors, including in his dispatch a list of those acts which were neither confirmed nor disallowed and which were, therefore, to be 'left to their operation'.

Most colonial acts, then, had to go through some ten or eleven stages before being returned to the hands of the governor. Nor does this account include the procedure which they followed within the colonial department itself. It is hardly surprising that the delay involved was considerable; yet remarkably few mistakes were made or acts lost on this formidable trek from department to department.

Under their terms of reference, the Commissioners were particularly interested in the fate of acts from the West Indian colonies. They noted that 'comparatively few of the statutes passed in the West Indies receive either direct confirmation or disallowance of the King', and that 'so long as this prerogative is not exercised, the act continues in force, under the qualified assent, which is given by the governor in the colony itself, on behalf of the King'. 'It is also,' they reported, 'received as a maxim that the King may at any time, however remote, exercise his prerogative of disallowing any colonial act which he has not once confirmed by any Order-in-Council.' This power, they agreed, had lain dormant for many years, nor were they able to cite a single instance 'in modern times', of the disallowance of any colonial statute after the notification to the governor that it would be 'left to its operation'.

The Commissioners, continuing their report, drew attention to an Order-in-Council of 15 January 1806 which declared that 'in all cases when His Majesty's confirmation shall be necessary to give validity and effect to any Act passed by the legislatures of any of His Majesty's colonies or plantations, unless His Majesty's confirmation shall be obtained within three years of the passing of such Act in any of the said colonies or plantations, such Act shall be considered as disallowed.' This Order, they pointed out, had sometimes been supposed to lay down a rule applicable to all types of colonial enactments. A study of the wording and circumstances of the Order had convinced them, however, that this was neither its intention nor its effect. The order in question referred to one type of colonial statute only—namely those which contained a clause suspending their operation till the pleasure of the King was known. 'Without the assistance of such a general rule, it would have been impossible to know, in any particular case, whether the statute would or would not, at some future time, be called into operation; an uncertainty peculiarly embarrassing, in reference to private acts, which invariably contain a suspending clause.'

This section of the Report concludes with a paragraph interesting as much for what it does not say as for what it does. The Commissioners agree that it is not within their terms of reference to 'investigate minutely the reasons which may have induced your Lordship and the other members of His Majesty's Government, in so large a proportion of cases, to advise the King to abstain from the exercise of his prerogative, by leaving colonial acts to their operation, instead of expressly confirming them'. Had such an investigation been required of them, it might not have been difficult to 'discover the policy and motives which led to such results'. Even without such instructions, they feel capable of putting forward one or two suggestions. 'There are', they point out, 'a multitude of cases in which it would be equally inconvenient to confirm or disallow the acts transmitted from the colonies.' Moreover, there must be still more cases 'in which the act has expired, or become obsolete, or has been repealed, before the period arrives for pronouncing the decision of His Majesty in Council on it'.

The Report of the West Indian Commissioners thus tells us a great deal, but does not pretend to tell us all. Nor was their account of the procedure regarding the review of colonial laws strictly accurate, either for the mid 1820s or later.

In the first place, on a number of points of detail they were either silent or misleading. They made little mention, for instance, of what happened to the acts before they reached this country. Nearly all acts, before they left the colony of origin, had received the assent of the governor, acting as the King's representative under the authority of his Commission. This assent had the effect of bringing the acts into immediate operation (subject, of course, to eventual disallowance), with the exception of those which included a suspending clause. No action could be carried out under these latter acts until the King's pleasure was known. The necessity of giving this assent sometimes involved the governor in inconvenience or embarrassment. It was decided, for instance, when the matter was brought up by the Governor of Antigua, that, if a governor was unable to give his assent to a bill before the close of a session, the bill must be reintroduced in the following session.[4] One colony at least avoided this problem by passing an act which enabled the governor to give his assent out of session.[5] There were occasions also where the governor deliberately reserved bills because he personally disliked them, but, by sending them home for His Majesty's consideration, he might be able to avoid an open clash between himself and influential local interests. In 1830 the Governor of Dominica took this course with regard to a bill (eventually disallowed) which sought to introduce discriminatory duties to the prejudice of foreign traders. Stephen could see no objection, in theory, to such a proceeding, and suggested that in practice it might prove very convenient. He could discover no precedent for such an action other than in Canada, where it was constantly done, but under the express conditions of the Canada Act of 1791.[6]

The writers of the Report laid much greater stress on the part played by the Lords of the Committee for Trade and Plantations than on that of the colonial department and its legal adviser. While there might have been some constitutional justification for this view, there was none in practice. Counsel's reports were confined, they asserted, to an opinion 'in point of law'. Though this phrase was included in the counsel's reports into the thirties, it had long been only a formality, and as time went on the strictly legal content of the opinion became overshadowed by advice on policy. As Stephen explained to Hope in 1841, 'it is something of a fiction to regard as mere legal opinions Reports which embrace or advert to every topic which seems to me to demand the notice of the Secretary of State in reference to the Acts of Assembly'.[7]

There were other similar 'fictions'. For instance, in theory, the Lords of the Committee for Trade and Plantations should have provided the King-in-Council with a report on each of the acts

---

[4] C.O. 323/64, Antigua; Wood, 29 Mar. 1848.
[5] Tobago.
[6] C.O. 327/47, Dominica; Stephen to Twiss, 22 May 1830.
[7] C.O. 323/56, St. Vincent; Stephen to Hope, 6 Sept. 1841.

submitted to them by Order-in-Council. In practice, it was not usual for any such report to be made, 'except when it is necessary that any Act should be disallowed or expressly confirmed. In these cases, a report is made to His Majesty, and an Order-in-Council is thereupon issued disallowing or confirming the Act. In general, however, *their Lordships make no report at all upon the reference to them*. The usual course was for them to communicate through their secretary to the Secretary of State such observations as they are pleased to make on the subject. In many recent cases, this communication from their Lordships is confined to the remark that they are not officially competent to express an opinion on the Acts thus referred to them.'[8]

During their deliberations on a reference from the King-in-Council, the Secretary of State, as a member of the Board of Trade, was supposed to be present. 'In point of fact,' wrote Stephen, 'he does not go there. Instead of personally attending, he sends a Minute (not an official letter) stating how he would have each Act disposed of. Those Minutes are kept at the Board of Trade, and constitute in reality the basis of their reports to the Queen-in-Council.'[9] Stephen evidently approved of this distinction between theory and practice. 'It is a proceeding which has been in use here for many years, and as the fiction of the Secretary of State's presence at the deliberations of the Board aptly expresses the principle, and as the substitution of a Minute for his actual attendance saves him a great deal of unprofitable trouble, I apprehend that although it be a fictitious it is also a reasonable or unobjectionable mode of proceeding.'[10] Furthermore, this Minute was invariably based upon, if not exactly in accordance with, the original report prepared by departmental counsel. Thus Stephen's explanation of the workings of inter-departmental machinery helps to reinforce the claim that it was round the report of the legal adviser, and not that of their Lordships, that the whole process of review revolved.

The Report of the West Indian Commissioners further gives the impression that legislation from all the colonies was subject to this intricate procedure. This, of course, was not the case. At the beginning of our period, the laws of the older colonies only

---

[8] C.O. 324/146, Horton to Lack (Board of Trade), 23 June 1826. Draft in C.O. 323/205 under 'Stephen'.

[9] C.O. 323/56, St. Vincent; Stephen to Hope, 6 Sept. 1841.   [10] Ibid.

had to be reviewed in this way, although by 1865 a number of others had been added to the list.[11] In the newer colonies the pleasure of the King was signified through the Secretary of State. Stephen considered the constitutional distinction between the two classes of laws to be both 'obvious and plausible'. 'The Acts of a Legislative Assembly assented to by the Governor and his Council in a country governed by English law may properly exact a more solemn form of proceeding for their confirmation or disallowance than Ordinances emanating entirely from the representatives of the King, the Governors or Lieutenant-Governors of conquered colonies, assisted only by Councils nominated by H.M.'[12]

The procedure for reviewing colonial acts was, therefore, highly complex, though that complexity was to some extent tempered in its operation by common sense. By 1826 the system had so broken down that the Board of Trade made no report on those acts to be left to their operation, and no Order-in-Council respecting them was prepared. This state of affairs, Stephen asserted, placed the Secretary of State in an embarrassing position: he was unable to inform the colony of the decision of His Majesty-in-Council, as no decision had been made. He did not have the authority to decide the matter himself, and he could not bring the acts to the notice of the Privy Council a second time without 'manifest impropriety'.[13] The result was that 'in a great many cases the Acts remain at the C.O. without any measure being taken upon them'. The contingency envisaged by the West Indian Commissioners, that the decision on some acts would not be taken until the acts themselves had expired, was frequently a real danger. In fairness, however, it should be pointed out that when this situation did occur, it was often as much the fault of the local authorities as that of the colonial department. Some governors, particularly in the West Indies, persisted in giving their assent, against Instructions, to laws of limited life; while others occasioned 'serious inconvenience to the colonies, by waiting until the close of a session before sending home authenticated copies of Acts passed within it'.[14]

[11] For a complete list of colonies whose laws passed through the Privy Council in our period see Appendix C.

[12] C.O. 323/205, Minute by Stephen, 26 Sept. 1826.

[13] C.O. 324/146, Horton to Lack, 23 June 1826.

[14] C.O. 323/69, Canada; Wood to Merivale, 18 Sept. 1850; Minute by Blunt.

The system came in for violent criticism from contemporaries, most notably Charles Grant[15] who, as a junior minister in 1826, jibbed at being 'required by his sacred Majesty gravely to address him and advise him on subjects on which he is misled if he thinks it is in our power to offer an opinion'.[16] Grant considered that the only way to avoid the 'absurdities, artifices, anomalies and inconsequences' of the present system was to abandon the system and start again. His proposal was for a new Committee of the Privy Council to be appointed expressly for the purpose of reporting to the King on colonial laws; this committee to be composed of the Secretary of State and other Privy Councillors. 'In this case', he hoped, 'the responsibility will ostensibly rest where it really does.'[16a]

As with so many systems which have evolved over a long period the existing procedure of review could not be swept aside and replaced as easily as Grant suggested. Any change in the existing Board would have required a Cabinet decision, probably unobtainable without the consent of the Lord President and the Colonial Secretary. Lord Bathurst, who had been the responsible minister since 1812, declared himself unable to agree with Grant that the Board of Trade had no means of knowing, any more than any other body, what related to the colonies—the Secretary of State himself was a member of the Board.[17] Indeed it is difficult to see what real change, if any, Grant's proposed scheme would have brought about. On the other hand, there were some, including Bathurst and, as we have seen, Stephen who were satisfied with the system as it was, because it could be made to work. In 1848, the 3rd Earl Grey (Colonial Secretary, 1846-52), wishing to put forward a scheme whereby the Committee for Trade would help in the administration of the British colonies, reminded them of their past connection with colonial affairs, not only as regards commercial policy affecting the colonies 'but also for advising the sovereign in council as to the course to be taken on all Acts passed by the colonial assemblies, whether such Acts relate to commercial interests or not'.[18] Although, Grey admitted, such an arrangement might seem to be objectionable in theory as 'obliterating to some

---

[15] Vice President of the Board of Trade; later Lord Glenelg.
[16] C.O. 323/205, Grant to Horton, 22 Aug. 1820.
[16a] Ibid.
[17] C.O. 324/15, Minute by Bathurst, 25 Aug. 1826.
[18] P.P. 1847-8 (371), p. 5.

extent the lines of demarcation which should separate from each other the functions of the two departments', none the less it was one 'to which no practical objection of any moment exists'. He further applauded the ease and practicability of the two departments occupying, to a certain extent, the same sphere of action.

In these circumstances it is hardly surprising that the only changes that were made were designed to make the existing system more efficient, and not to replace it entirely by another. The changes were, nevertheless, important. In 1828 the Lords of the Privy Council represented to the King-in-Council that it 'would conduce to the more speedy despatch of business', if they were authorized to refer all colonial acts to the Committee for Trade without first obtaining an Order-in-Council.[19] Their request was granted, and so a minor modification of the system was put into practice. For a more radical reform the Colonial Office had to wait a further twenty-eight years, when Merivale (Permanent Under-Secretary, 1847-59) received permission from the Lord President to make a number of significant alterations.[20] The details of these changes Merivale set out in a draft dispatch dated 8 October 1856.[21] In the first place, 'the practice of referring to the Board of Trade the colonial acts received from certain colonies is hence forth to cease altogether, except in such cases where the subject of such acts concerns the Board of Trade in its ordinary functions'. Secondly, the Secretary of State was to refer acts to the Board and to the Treasury only 'when these Acts relate to matters of Trade or of Treasury superintendence, and simply by letter, in the same manner as Acts concerning other functions of the Government are referred to the Admiralty, the Board of Health and so forth'. Finally, 'when the Secretary of State shall have thus prepared himself by communicating with the proper departments to determine the course to be pursued in regard to each Colonial Act, he will transmit such Act to the Council Office, advising the Lord President by letter what Orders-in-Council should be passed thereon.'

While still remaining outwardly cumbersome and complex, the system of review in practice achieved considerable efficiency.

[19] P.C. 2/209, Representation of the Lords of the Privy Council respecting the referring of colonial acts to the Committee for Trade, 28 May 1828.
[20] C.O. 323/247, Grenville to Merivale, 19 Sept. 1856.
[21] C.O. 323/247, Merivale to Wood and Rogers, 8 Oct. 1856.

There were mistakes and delays, and occasionally acts were mislaid for long periods. But generally decisions were arrived at quickly. The elimination of unnecessary stages made for increased efficiency, while at the same time the old connection with the Board of Trade was reduced to that enjoyed by any other government department. The Colonial Office was now officially recognized, as it had been for many years in practice, as the department best suited to carry out an authoritative review of laws from the colonies under its jurisdiction.

2

THE LEGAL ADVISER

IN a room in the late Colonial Office building, Great Smith Street, there used to hang a list of legal advisers who had held the position since 1866. The omission of all mention of Colonial Office legal counsel before that date may serve to emphasize the 'rather haphazard and imprudent fashion'[1] in which the Office had been accustomed to take legal advice in previous years. Between 1834 (the year of Stephen's appointment as Assistant Under-Secretary) and 1866 there was no one official entrusted solely with the legal business of the Office. Nevertheless, it was clearly intended that, as far as colonial review was concerned, there should be no break in the continuity of the reports.[2]

Continuity of policy was assured by the fact that, although four or five names appeared at various times on counsel's reports, the effective reviewers were two: Sir James Stephen[3] and Sir Frederic Rogers.[4]

Stephen owed his original appointment in 1813 to the Secretary of State Lord Bathurst, whose attention he had attracted by a scholarly compilation of colonial acts. To begin with he combined the post with his private practice, being paid on a fee basis at the rate of three guineas per report.[5] By 1825 precarious health and the pressure of work obliged him to give up private practice in favour of the permanent appointment as counsel to both the Colonial Office and the Board of Trade, who shared his services

[1] Knox, B. A., 'The Provision of Legal Advice to the Colonial Office', *Bull. of Inst. of Hist. Res.* (1962), 179.

[2] C.O. 323/56, fol. 236, Stephen to Hope, 6 Sept. 1841, 'I have ever since 1836 persevered in writing reports of this kind on such Acts, as I wrote them before, in order to keep up the continuity of records in this Office.'

[3] James Stephen junior (later Sir James). First appointed part-time counsel in 1813; given permanent appointment 1825; Assistant Under-Secretary, 1834; Permanent Under-Secretary, 1836–47.

[4] Sir Frederic Rogers (later Lord Blachford). Appointed to the Colonial Land and Emigration Board in 1846, with particular responsibility for reviewing Colonial acts; Permanent Under-Secretary, 1860–71.

[5] Beaglehole, J. C., 'The Colonial Office, 1782–1854', *Historical Studies of Australia and New Zealand*, 1, 178, n. 27.

and their cost.[6] At the time, the appointment aroused a good deal
of opposition, notably from Joseph Hume. Hume's main objection
to Stephen arose out of the fact that he was the son of the ardent
abolitionist James Stephen senior, 'the person whom the colonists
supposed to be their greatest enemy; and to put him in an office
in which every communication to and from the colonies must pass
through his hands' was 'highly objectionable'. The appointments
had 'outraged the feelings of the colonists more than any act of
the government'.[7] Wilmot Horton, the Permanent Under-
Secretary, denied that there was any sort of understanding between
father and son, and offered as proof the fact that James Stephen
senior had published a pamphlet in which he described an Order-
in-Council drawn up by his son as a 'parcel of trash'. Stephen,
Horton declared, was merely an executive officer and 'could do
no more than obey the instructions of the head of the department'.[8]
In spite of Horton's defence, Stephen continued to suffer criticism
from the public; so much so that in 1830 he felt driven to complain to Sir George Murray (then Secretary of State) that, in
accepting the post, he had made a 'most improvident and foolish
contract, if my interests and comfort only were to be considered'.[9]
   Evidently he did not feel sufficiently strongly about the matter
to resign. In 1834 he became Assistant Under-Secretary in the
Office, though he continued to act as counsel and received no
extra salary.[10] Two years later he was given the Permanent Under-
Secretaryship, and ceased to draw his salary as counsel, though
he 'never did cease to consider himself as holding that particular
office'.[11] However, by 1841, apart from reporting on colonial laws
he had 'scarcely any duty to perform as counsel'.[12] At the same
time his connection with the Board of Trade was severed, and
the Board made its own arrangements for legal advice.
   Even with the reduction in his duties Stephen's health, never
good, rapidly deteriorated under the double burden. In 1845
Gladstone, then President of the Board of Trade, sought to relieve

[6] Pugh, R. B., *The Colonial Office, 1801–1925* (*C.H.B.E.*, vol. III), p. 711.
[7] *Hansard*, N.S., XIV 1081, 3 Mar. 1826.
[8] Ibid., 1081 et seq.
[9] N.L.S., Murray Papers, Statement by Stephen, 16 Feb. 1830, vol. 171,
fol. 55; quoted by Young, D. M., op. cit., p. 113.
[10] Knox, op. cit., p. 180.
[11] Ibid.
[12] C.O. 323/56, fol. 236, Stephen to Hope, 6 Sept. 1841.

the strain both on Stephen and on the Board's Legal Secretary, Shaw Lefevre, by appointing a legal assistant to the Board.[13] This new official was given the job of reporting on colonial laws, but the arrangement lasted barely a year. Once Gladstone had become Secretary of State for the Colonies, he realized the great inconvenience of legal advice being given to the Under-Secretary by an official not under the control of the Secretary of State. Accordingly, he proposed to the Treasury that an additional Under-Secretary of State be appointed to the Colonial Office who would also be a member of the Board of Colonial Land and Emigration Commissioners. An Order-in-Council of 18 May 1846 duly appointed Frederic Rogers, then a Fellow of Oriel, to the Board, and he was told that 'in future all colonial laws will be referred to you for your report in the same manner that business connected with the management of Colonial Lands and Emigration now is.'[14] The post of counsel remained on the establishment of the Colonial Office, though neither Rogers nor anyone else was appointed to it. However, he continued to act, as he put it, as 'legal cad to Stephen'.[15]

In 1847 Stephen left the Colonial Office for good, though he was appointed to the Privy Council Committee for Trade and Plantations and continued to give advice on colonial affairs when asked. The state of his health had been giving cause for anxiety for some time, and his work was suffering. Before he handed over to Rogers, his reports on colonial laws had been growing thinner and thinner, and he had tended, where possible, to refer acts directly to other government departments, without going into detail himself. Characteristically, in the year before his retirement, his minutes on Rogers's reports were frequently as long or longer than his own reports had been. When at last continued illness made his return to work impossible, the Secretary of State was at a loss to find a suitable replacement. Grey wrote to the Lords of the Treasury in November 1847,[16] reminding them of the 'unrivalled zeal, energy and ability with which Mr. Stephen, during a period of thirty-five years, has afforded his assistance to

[13] Knox, op. cit., p. 181.
[14] Quoted by Hitchins, F. H., *The Colonial Land and Emigration Commission* (Philadelphia, 1931), p. 71 (no reference is given).
[15] Marindin, G. (ed.), *Letters of Lord Blachford*, p. 132, Rogers to Mrs. Rogers, 20 Dec. 1846.
[16] *P.P.* 1847–8, XLII (42). Earl Grey to Treasury, 27 Nov. 1847.

successive Secretaries of State'. It would be impossible, he felt, to make good the loss of Stephen's services by any new appointment, since 'even if a successor equally able and zealous . . . could be found, the acquaintance with colonial subjects, and with the conduct of the business of this department which Mr. Stephen had acquired during that long period, could be possessed by no other person'. The only remedy would be for the Treasury to sanction the appointment of two assistant Under-Secretaries.

In the event, the gap left by Stephen's departure was filled by reviving the posts of Précis Writer and Assistant Under-Secretary;[17] while the work of reporting on acts was, as we have seen, entrusted to Rogers, with the assistance of another member of the Board, Alexander Wood. Wood, also a lawyer, had been appointed in November 1843, with the consideration of legal questions and documents as his special duty.[18] A number of the reports were also drawn up by T. C. W. Murdoch, the third member of the Board. An able man, he had particularly distinguished himself as Civil Secretary to Lord Sydenham in Canada, but neither his, nor Wood's contribution to imperial policy towards colonial laws was sufficiently large to merit more than passing attention.

There were obvious objections to this arrangement. A select committee in 1848 expressed doubts as to whether the officers of the Board were 'peculiarly fitted for the consideration of colonial laws' and stated their preference that any excess legal work from the Colonial Office should go to the Board of Trade.[19] But Grey, in this and the following year, defended the existing arrangement, asserting that without the help of the Commissioners it would be impossible to carry on Colonial Office business.[20] Nothing was done at this stage.

From 1847 to 1866 there was, as the Colonial Office informed the Attorney-General in March 1858, 'no counsel properly so called in this Office',[21] and Rogers continued to deal with most of the legal business. In the rearrangement following Rogers's appointment as Permanent Under-Secretary in 1860, the post of counsel disappeared from the establishment.[22] In dividing up the work of the Office with T. F. Elliot, Rogers took responsibility,

---

[17] Knox, op. cit., pp. 181–2.   [18] Hitchins, op. cit., p. 71.
[19] *P.P.* 1847–8, XVIII. Pt. 1, 528 et seq.
[20] Ibid.   [21] Knox, op. cit., p. 183.   [22] P.C. 2/252, fol. 399.

among other things, for 'legal business everywhere',[23] though he wondered at the time how long the arrangement would last. It lasted in fact for six years, when the double burden proved too much for Rogers, as it had for Stephen.

In 1866 Rogers wrote, on Carnarvon's behalf, to the Treasury to suggest certain changes in the Colonial Office establishments.[24] He reminded them how, in 1860, Merivale had removed to the India Office and the Secretaryship of the Emigration Board had been abolished. In consequences, 'the duty of revising colonial laws, and of dealing with various legal questions, from time to time referred to the Legal Member of that Board, was adopted by the Colonial Office.' In Lord Carnarvon's opinion, this arrangement did not work well; it added too much to the Permanent Under-Secretary's existing work. It would be more suitable, he suggested, for a barrister to be appointed to take over all the legal work from Rogers. The new appointment was made, and Holland became the first full-time legal adviser since Stephen took up the Assistant Under-Secretaryship in 1834.

The most striking characteristic of the legal advisership in this period is continuity, not of office, but of personnel. In contrast to the frequent change of Secretary of State (Molesworth lasted in office only four months, and Gladstone barely a year) Stephen and Rogers between them filled the position for the whole period with scarcely a break, except for occasional help from the Land and Emigration Commissioners. The impact of Stephen and Rogers upon the policy behind the review process was not, however, simply a matter of long service. Both were able and conscientious men, with decided personal views on colonial affairs.

James Stephen was a man well suited, by training and temperament, to carry out the duties of legal adviser.[25] He was a lawyer, continuing in private practice until 1825, with a particular interest in colonial law. He was immensely industrious, with an academic turn of mind, matched by a donnish sense of humour.[26]

[23] Marindin, G. E., op. cit., p. 226, Rogers to Miss Rogers, 4 May 1860.
[24] Knox, op. cit., pp. 182–3.
[25] Stephen's opinions on colonial laws will be frequently referred to throughout this study.   For an illuminating, if uncritical, appraisal of his beliefs and qualities see Knaplund, P., *James Stephen and the British Colonial System 1813–1847*, (Madison, Wisc., 1953), pp. 17–35.
[26] It is significant that Stephen accepted the Regius Professorship in Modern History at Cambridge in 1849.

As a member of the Clapham Sect, and connected through his father, James Stephen senior, with the abolitionist movement, he displayed a genuine concern for the colonial communities with whose affairs he had to deal. His worth as an administrator may be open to criticism. His contemporary, Henry Taylor, remarked on his failure to delegate work, preferring to 'engross it into his own hands, and not be much helped'.[27] Although Stephen was continually complaining of procrastination and confusion in other departments, notably the Treasury, he has been criticized for introducing in his own department, cumbersome procedures, involving long minutes and a rigid, formal system of work, which slowed down the processes of colonial business.[28] While these may have been substantial defects in a Permanent Under-Secretary, they were of much less importance in a legal adviser.

The value of Stephen's contribution to the review process comes out most clearly when it is compared with that of his two predecessors, William Selwyn and William Baldwin. Selwyn was appointed counsel after the reorganization of colonial business in 1782,[29] and continued to write reports on colonial laws until he retired in 1796. Between 1784 and 1796 he reported on nearly 1,050 acts, of which only 21 drew from him any critical comment beyond remarking on clerical errors. Baldwin, counsel from July 1796 to his death in September 1813, reported on more than twice as many acts, but with comments in proportion. The reports of both men were usually brief, and it is consequently difficult to arrive at any very detailed conclusions as to their general opinions on colonial affairs. Like Stephen before 1825, they combined their official duties with private practice, and evidently did not feel required to spend too much time and energy on the former. It is worth mentioning, however, that even at this early stage the reviewers felt able to comment on the expediency, as well as the legal basis, of colonial laws, even if they were careful to refrain from explicit suggestions on matters of policy.

The sudden death of Baldwin in the late summer of 1813 was not altogether inopportune, either for the Colonial Secretary, Lord Bathurst, or Stephen himself. Bathurst needed a competent

---

[27] Taylor, Sir H., *Autobiography* (London, 1885), I. 233.
[28] Pugh, R. B., *The Colonial Office* (*C.H.B.E.*, vol. III), p. 711.
[29] The earliest report we have from Selwyn is to Lord Sydney, 15 Nov. 1784, C.O. 323/34, fol. 5.

lawyer who would be able to cope with the growing volume of colonial laws. Stephen was able to supplement his income from his chancery court practice with the three-guinea fee for each act reported on. By 1825 he was to be grateful for the opportunity to exchange the uncertainty of private practice for the security of an official salary. Admittedly, by 1830 he had come to doubt the wisdom of his choice, contrasting his present salary of £1,500 p.a. with the £6,000 or £7,000 to which he would have been entitled 'were I to bring a bill against the Public drawn out upon the same principles as that of a common attorney's Bill'.[30]

From this point of view the arrangement was clearly in the Office's favour. Stephen brought to the business of the Office his phenomenal gift for unremitting hard work which, on several occasions, gravely undermined his health.[31] The number of acts requiring his report (104 in 1814) rose by nearly 500 per cent by 1846. In addition there was his work in drafting Orders-in-Council and other legal work, together with, after 1834, his duties as a member of the administrative staff of the Office.

Stephen's whole approach to his duties as counsel was much more thorough and painstaking than that of his predecessors. His comments were frequent, lengthy, well informed, and wide rang-ing. Clearly in command of the legal knowledge required, he was also prepared to be explicit in his criticism of the practical effect of defective laws. Particularly in the early years, he would allow himself to be carried away by his own enthusiasm and interest; for example his reports on the various West Indies Slave Registra-tion Acts were unnecessarily detailed. After twenty pages of minute examination of the Bermuda Act, he admitted that many of the points he had raised were of small importance and that on the whole the Act was no worse than the corresponding acts of the other islands. In the event, all these acts were confirmed without alteration.[32]

As the years passed and the burden of work increased, Stephen became more and more wearied by the monotonous and laborious

---

[30] N.L.S., Murray Papers, Statement by Stephen, 16 Feb. 1830, vol. 171, fols. 56–7.

[31] Possibly the best-known example is Stephen's feat in drafting the Order-in-Council for the abolition of slavery within three days, making himself seriously ill as a result. See Mathieson, W. L., *British Slavery and its Abolition* (London, 1926) p. 240.

[32] C.O. 323/41, fols. 240–50, Bermuda; Stephen to Bathurst, 25 Aug. 1821.

task of reviewing colonial laws, for which he seemed to be repaid only by public criticism. In 1830 he was stung by the attacks made upon him to point out to the Secretary of State, Sir George Murray, just how hard he was being required to work.[33] 'I trust it is not necessary to prove', he protested, 'that I am sedulously engaged in my public duties. I can with strict truth declare that I begin my business daily at 6 o'clock, and continue it till night, with no deduction of any part of my time for amusements, or for studies of a different nature. It is in truth a very laborious as well as a very invidious calling.'[34] The wearisome nature of the work was a feature to which he was always returning. As we have seen, he complained in 1840 of the 'mass of uninteresting details' with which he had had to deal in revising colonial laws. In particular 'the routine through which each law has to pass in order to decide on the final measure taken on each is wearisome in the extreme. Four or five copies must be made of all the Titles, and about as many letters must pass between different Departments, each of which approaches the subject reluctantly, and stands in need of continual flapping, and when all this is done, there is still a correspondence with the Governor—explanatory admonitory, not seldom coaxing—but almost always unprofitable. The Governors dislike it, and the Assemblies still more, and there is a constant struggle in the shape of passive resistance to get the better of Downing Street criticisms and critics!'[35]

These occasional outbursts of annoyance and disillusion should not be taken as characteristic of his usual outlook. He developed a technique of rapid reading which minimized the burden of reviewing, and although his reports continued, until the last few months before he handed over to Rogers, to be extremely thorough, he was very tolerant of minor mistakes in drafting, provided no material injury to individuals or classes might result.

His attitude throughout was one of pragmatism and common sense: whatever his private feelings on the unity of empire, he recognized very early that the central authority had its limitations,

[33] After 1836 Stephen appears to have dropped all legal work but the reporting on colonial acts. For a full account of his various duties as counsel see Young, D. M., op cit., pp. 100–1.

[34] N.L.S., Murray Papers, Statement by Stephen, 16 Feb. 1830, vol. 171, fols. 56–7.

[35] C.O. 318/148, Russell Memorandum, note by Stephen, 17 Oct. 1840.

and that the demands for autonomy from the colonies would become more insistent as the colonies developed their internal strength. In his address to the National Association for the Promotion of Social Science in St. George's Hall, Liverpool, in 1858 he summed up the results of his own experience, stating his belief that the colonies 'are bound to us by alliances which they will hold sacred and inviolable, as long as we ourselves continue to be true and faithful to them'. On the other hand, he was quite prepared for the day 'when our Canadian and our native dependencies will calmly and deliberately insist upon being dependencies no longer, but on being as independent in form as they are already in truth and reality.'[36]

The overriding characteristic of Stephen's thought was his concern for the underprivileged and the victimized, in particular the slaves and ex-slaves of the West Indies and the Cape. 'It being the most anxious, if not the first duty of a government', he wrote in 1843, 'to consult for the permanent interests of Society, as opposed to the immediate interests of the most active and powerful of its members; and to watch over the welfare of the many, rather than the present advantage of the few; and to protect those whose only property is the power of labour against the rapacity of the rich . . .'[37]

Fortunately for Stephen a number of his superiors in the Office, notably Bathurst and Glenelg, were sympathetic towards his humanitarian views. This did not mean, of course, that his advice was always accepted, on this or any other issue. It would be remarkable if it had been. Quite apart from the fact that Stephen was less successful in establishing a close relationship with some colonial secretaries, notably Stanley, than with others, his duty was to bring to the Secretary's notice *all* points which might be important. It was the task of the Secretary and his senior officials to decide whether the points raised by Stephen were important enough to warrant action which might offend colonial opinion. Nevertheless, Stephen seldom met with outright opposition from his superiors, who were well aware of his value as an expert on colonial law and the difficulty they would have to find a replacement when he came to retire. Lord John Russell in October

[36] Stephen, J., 'The British Colonies and Colonisation', pp. 3 et seq.
[37] Minute of 2 May 1843 on coolie immigration to New South Wales, quoted by H. L. Hall, *The Colonial Office*, p. 85.

1840 could 'see no chance of our having anyone to follow Mr. Stephen in his comprehensive view of all the legislation of our Colonies'.[38]

Fears that Stephen's long experience and vast knowledge of colonial law would be irreplaceable were shown to be groundless. Sir Frederic Rogers, though best known for his work as Permanent Under-Secretary after 1860, should be given credit for his contribution as legal adviser for the two decades after 1846. Stephen's equal as a hard and conscientious worker, he suffered from the same kind of public criticism as had Mr. Mother-country. The colonies, declared George Higginbotham, the Australian politician, in 1869, have 'been really governed for the last fifteen years by a person named Rogers'.[39] Though their social backgrounds differed, Rogers was a man very much in the Stephen mould in training and temperament. 'Thoughtful, clear headed, and humane; a devout churchman;'[40] he is revealed by his private letters as at once liberal, but distrustful of the 'populace', believing above all in the moral responsibility of government. Where he differed from Stephen was in his greater capacity to put up with irksome detail, and, at least in later years, his acceptance of the inevitability of colonial independence. The matters which came before the Colonial Office, he once wrote, 'are by the nature of the case in great part official details and controversies even of the most petty kind'.[41] What, to Rogers, gave interest to these small cases was the necessity for the Colonial Office at all times to 'maintain a reputation for justice, as an accessible Court of Appeal'. What he found much more enthralling, however, was to be a witness to the development of general principles of colonial policy. Looking back over his long connection with colonial affairs, Rogers picked out as the chief of these principles the establishment of colonial self-government.

It would be going too far to describe Rogers as the champion of colonial independence. In his attitude to colonial policy he was not an idealist, but a realist. He understood very well the power of colonial demands for self-government, and criticized Lord Grey for the naïve assumption that it was possible to grant

[38] C.O. 318/148, Russell Memorandum, 19 Oct. 1840.

[39] *Dictionary of National Biography*: Rogers, Sir Frederic.

[40] Hargreaves, J. D., 'Colonial Office Opinions on the Constitution of 1863', *Sierra Leone Studies* (Dec. 1965), p. 4.

[41] Marindin, G. E. (ed.), *Letters of Lord Blachford*, pp. 295–7.

representative institutions to the developing colonies of white settlement, yet stop short of responsible government. Briefly summarizing the evolution of colonial independence over the half century before 1885, he concluded that 'this great establishment of colonial independence cannot (as I think) be wisely or possibly arrested'. 'I had always believed', he went on, '. . . that the destiny of our colonies is independence; and that in this point of view the function of the Colonial Office is to secure that our connection, while it lasts, shall be as profitable to both parties, and our separation when it comes, as amicable as possible.'[42]

Neither Stephen nor Rogers was a mere spectator of this process. Although as Permanent Under-Secretaries they were obviously in a stronger position to influence events than they were as legal counsel, they could still, in the latter role, make significant contributions. Stephen built up the office of counsel from one of minor significance to one that became the key to the review process, and injected into his reports his own brand of early Victorian liberalism. Rogers followed Stephen's lead, displaying in the exercise of his office similar capabilities and principles. The experience he had gained as legal adviser was of great value to him as Permanent Under-Secretary. In the early 1860s it was Rogers the lawyer as well as the administrator who served as the architect of the Colonial Laws Validity Act, an act which, as we shall see in a later chapter, arose both out of immediate political circumstances and out of long Colonial Office experience of colonial legislation.

[42] Ibid., pp. 299–300.

3

REVIEW PROCEDURE WITHIN
THE COLONIAL OFFICE

THE failure of the Colonial Office to provide replacements for Stephen in 1834, and then for Rogers in 1860, may be explained in part by contemporary demands for economy in government departments. Equally important must have been the extreme difficulty of finding a suitable candidate able to meet the exacting requirements of the post. The legal adviser had, of course, to be an able lawyer. He had to possess a thorough knowledge of colonial law and affairs. He had to understand the intricacies of colonial policy, and in particular to be conversant with the rules, precedents and procedures of the Office in dealing with colonial laws.

Basically, there were two alternative courses which might be followed in dealing with any given act. Either a preliminary decision was made on it within the Office, or it was referred to another government department for comment before a final decision could be reached. Stephen generally wrote a report on all acts which he considered should be brought to the attention of the Secretary of State, even if he felt obliged to add that a reference to another department would be necessary. But in 1845 Lord Stanley suggested to him that in future he should extract from the list of acts those which had to be directed elsewhere, without waiting for his general report on those which he alone had to consider.[1] Stephen complied.

The general principle upon which such reference to other departments was made was obvious enough. The Home Office would be sent acts relating to convict discipline, the Queen's Advocate matters of ecclesiastical law, the Foreign Office acts involving the interpretation of treaties. Some departments, the Treasury in particular, had established rules which required that all acts of a certain type should be sent to them as a matter of course. Stephen told Lord Stanley in 1842[2] that six Canadian Banking Acts would

[1] C.O. 323/60, Canada; Stephen to Stanley, 25 July 1845; Minute by Stanley.
[2] C.O. 323/57, Canada; Stephen to Stanley, 12 Jan. 1842.

have to go to the Treasury, as that department had some time before insisted on the general rule that all such bills should be reserved. A question arose in 1851 whether certain Ordinances from Turks Island relating to finance should also be sent to the Treasury. In this instance, Lord Grey felt able to avoid the reference, on the ground that, although 'in all Crown Colonies the assent of the Treasury is necessary to measures of finance', it was 'not so when the legislature is of a representative character, and in Turks Island the Legislative Council is partly elected'.[3] Grey was a notable champion of the right of the Colonial Office to decide its own affairs. He strongly dissented from the view of Rogers and others that a Sierra Leone ordinance levying a tax on land and houses should be sent to the Treasury because it raised revenue. 'I do not think', he wrote, 'that it has been the established practice of this office to refer to the Treasury colonial acts and ordinances for the imposition of internal taxes, and if not, it would be highly inconvenient that such a practice should be established.'[4]

Stephen, then, was not alone in his unwillingness to bring in other departments unnecessarily. The main argument against so doing was the inevitable delay which this involved. In the first place, there was delay over procedure. As Grey explained to Merivale in 1848, 'all Acts passed in the colonies having representative constitutions are referred to the Board of Trade, because the Queen's decision on them is always made in Council, and the Privy Council always in such matters proceeds upon the report of the Committee for Trade and Plantations.'[5] Thus, 'when other departments require to be consulted the proper form . . . is to suggest to the Board of Trade to make the necessary reference.' Further delays generally took place within the department referred to. Here again, the Treasury incurred severe criticism. Stephen once complained to Stanley that 'in such references many months are usually consumed, for it is the habit, I suppose the unavoidable habit, of each of these Boards to move at a very slow pace, especially on matters . . . which do not immediately and perceptibly involve

[3] C.O. 323/70, Turks Island; Rogers to Elliot, 23 Oct. 1851; Minute by Earl Grey.

[4] C.O. 323/69, Sierra Leone; Rogers to Merivale, 18 Nov. 1850; Minute by Earl Grey.

[5] C.O. 323/64, Jamaica; Wood to Merivale, 15 Apr. 1848; Minute by Earl Grey to Merivale.

any domestic interest.'[6] Still worse, their conclusions 'usually proceed on grounds which seem to me to be altogether of secondary importance, in reference to such questions as the present'. The war against departmental incompetence and delay was one which Stephen continued to wage to the last. On a report sent to him by Rogers in 1847, referring various acts to the Treasury, the Railway Board, and other departments, he commented somewhat plaintively, 'the only remark I have to make to this report is that it would seem very necessary that the different departments to which it is proposed to refer these reserved laws should be requested to expedite them, and would not be allowed to forget that request.'[7] 'This is the only department of the government', he grumbled, 'which ever hears anything of the inconvenience and of the complaints induced by dilatoriness in disposing of such laws as these.'[8]

There were other interests to be considered besides the convenience of the Colonial Office officials. It was fully recognized that the colonists themselves had some claim to consideration, if only because the government on the spot was more likely to understand the domestic situation than were officials in Downing Street. Wood, reporting to Merivale in 1853 on twenty-nine Canadian Acts to do with the building of railways, suggested that the usual practice of referring such acts to the Railway Board should be dispensed with, partly because no object of imperial interest would be gained by such a reference, but also because 'as there must now be considerable local experience in the construction of Railways, it is more than probable that any suggestions would not be appreciated in the Colony'.[9]

Delay in assenting to local acts could be positively harmful in at least two ways. It could, as might have been the case with the Canadian Banking Acts of 1842, lead to the 'prevention of measures of the highest local interest on grounds which, to the colonists themselves, appear either trivial or unfounded'.[10] There were cases like the St. Lucia Ordinance of 1852 making provision for the immediate taking of a census. Delay here would have been fatal to the whole enterprise, though Lord Grey agreed that a

[6] C.O. 323/57, Canada; Stephen to Stanley, 12 Jan. 1842.
[7] C.O. 323/63, Canada; Rogers to Stephen, 14 Sept. 1847; Minute by Stephen.
[8] Ibid.   [9] C.O. 323/75, Canada; Wood to Merivale, 13 Dec. 1853.
[10] C.O. 323/57, Canada; Stephen to Stanley, 12 Jan. 1842.

distinction was to be drawn between enactments of this kind and prospective acts providing for a census to be made at such a distance of time as to allow for improvements. These last were to be sent to the Registrar-General.[11]

A second danger, especially to be avoided in relations with the North American colonies, was that of needlessly offending the local population. 'There is scarcely any amount of bad legislation about provincial Banks,' Stephen wrote in 1842, 'of which the mischief is to be compared with that of offending the legislature and the whole population (especially the commercial population) of Canada, first by a long delay on matters of the deepest interest to them, and then by disquisitions on their projected laws which, however just in themselves, are received as the rebukes of a superior and distant authority.'[12]

Finally, the members of the Office had to consider their own proper pride, their confidence in their ability to decide colonial questions unaided, and their natural belief that they, of all government departments, were most conversant with local circumstances in the colonies. T. F. Elliot objected to Rogers's view in 1850 that a West Australian Convict Act should be referred to the Home Office, 'partly because I have little doubt that we can arrive at an opinion on it ourselves, and partly because we might have to refer to the Home Office too often for the convenience of either department, if we introduced a precedent of consulting them on colonial laws about convicts'.[13] He followed a similar line nine years later, when Rogers suggested reference to the Foreign Office over a Victorian Act regulating Chinese immigration which appeared to involve the question of treaties with foreign powers. Elliot here protested that the Foreign Office could not be expected to understand the extreme difficulty of controlling the Australian legislature upon a subject of this kind, in which 'the feelings of the people, and, in truth, the permanent interests of the European race, are so much involved'. If, as might well happen, the Foreign Office advised allowing unfettered immigration, it would mean entering into a contest with the Australians 'with the tolerable certainty of being worsted, but exciting hostility that would endure long

[11] C.O. 323/70, St. Lucia; Wood to Merivale, 2 July 1851; Minute by Earl Grey.

[12] C.O. 323/57, Canada; Stephen to Stanley, 12 Jan. 1842.

[13] C.O. 323/69, West Australia; Rogers to Merivale, 9 May 1850; Minute by Elliot.

beyond that defeat'.[14] The general tendency then was for the number of references to be cut to a minimum, in the interests both of the Office and of the colonies which it had to administer.

To refer, or not to refer, was only the first, and perhaps the least important, of the decisions which had to be taken upon the acts within the Colonial Office. We have seen that however many stages colonial acts had to pass through, and however many reports were written about them by various departments, the real responsibility for a final decision lay effectively with the Secretary of State for the Colonies, upon whose Minute the King-in-Council invariably acted. This decision was not limited only to a choice between allowance or disallowance, but could be expressed by one of a number of different formulas. Which form was to be used depended variously on the type of act involved, the type of colony from which it came, and the attitude which the Colonial Office chose to take towards the particular enactment.

Of all the acts which had to be dealt with by Order-in-Council,[15] the vast majority were 'left to their operation'. A much smaller number each year were 'specially confirmed', whilst some underwent outright disallowance.[16] Although no comparable figures exist for the remaining colonies, the impression to be gained from the legal advisers' reports would suggest similar proportions.

Acts which were 'left to their operation' were those which had already received the governor's assent and were already in force. If the Secretary of State recommended 'leaving to their operation', rather than 'special confirmation', they could, in law be subsequently disallowed by the Crown within a limited space of time, but no instance of such an act being later disallowed has emerged in this period. So Clarke, commenting on Merivale's suggestion in 1854 that Australian acts should no longer be 'confirmed' but 'left to their operation', suggests that the use of the latter form was intended to emphasize that the assent given by the governor was not provisional, in the old sense of requiring imperial approval, but final, subject to the remote contingency of disallowance.[17]

[14] C.O. 323/89, Victoria; Rogers to Merivale, 10 June 1859; Minute by Elliot.

[15] i.e. the acts of the older colonies and of the newer settlement colonies in Australia and New Zealand. For a full list of colonies whose acts were dealt with in this way see Appendix C.

[16] For a table of 'specially confirmed' and 'disallowed' acts see Appendix B.

[17] Clarke, D. P., 'The Attitude of the Colonial Office to the Workings of Responsible Government, 1854–68', London Ph.D. thesis (1953), p. 266.

There was, however, a more concrete reason for the sparing use of 'confirmation'. Once an act had been confirmed by Order-in-Council, any amendment or repeal of its provisions would also be required to be confirmed in the same way, thus inflicting a restriction upon the powers of the local legislature. Such a case arose in 1849, over an Ordinance from St. Lucia amending two clerical errors in a previous enactment. Sir Frederic Rogers pointed out that the original Ordinance had been confirmed by an Order-in-Council and that therefore an amending ordinance ought to go through the same process, but he suggested that, in the case of a mere clerical error, this formality might be relaxed. At the same time he drew Merivale's attention to the fact that, since the Judicial Constitution of St. Lucia (like Trinidad and British Guiana) had been established by Order-in-Council, then even the most minute amendment to it had to be confirmed likewise, under the provisions of the original Order of June 1831. Accordingly, Lord Grey gave instructions for a new Order to be prepared giving the colonial legislative powers to alter this, and previous, Orders.[18]

There were only two classes of acts which *had* to be specially confirmed: those as mentioned above and acts containing a suspending clause. There were, however, a number of occasions when the colonial authorities themselves asked for special confirmation. The Colonial Office was generally reluctant to do this, on the ground that unnecessary confirmation only cast doubts on the usual mode of proceeding. Stephen made this point in 1846 when Chief Justice Peterson of St. Vincent asked that the local act providing for his salary be given this treatment.[19] Three years later, when the Governor of British Guiana asked for special confirmation of an Ordinance to extend the elective franchise so as to remove any doubts as to its operation, Wood suggested that the only effect of so doing would be to impute doubts as to the validity of the enactment before the Order could be passed.[20] In neither case were these objections pressed.

In 1852 Sir George Grey, then Governor of Jamaica, brought to light the half-forgotten Treasury practice concerning special

[18] C.O. 323/56, St. Lucia; Rogers to Merivale, 4 Aug. 1849; Minute by Earl Grey.
[19] C.O. 323/61, St. Vincent; Rogers to Grey, 16 Nov. 1846; Minute by Stephen.
[20] C.O. 323/66, British Guiana; Wood to Merivale, 3 Dec. 1849.

confirmation. He had sent home an Act to provide for the erection
of a lighthouse at the entrance to Port Royal, and had, some time
before, asked for a loan to enable him to carry out the intention of
the Act. If the loan were approved, he stated, then the Act ought
properly to be specially confirmed. Wood was completely be-
wildered by the remark. As far as he knew, only acts with a
suspending clause had to be dealt with in this way. Some other
member of the Office (probably Elliot) informed Wood that Sir
George was referring to an old Treasury procedure, whereby, if
they had lent money on an act, they liked that act to be specially
confirmed, so that it could not be amended in future by another
act without a suspending clause.[21]

It was not unusual for minor technicalities of this nature to be
ignored in dealing with acts from the more advanced settlement
colonies in Canada and Australia. The acts of the Canadian
legislature in particular, Merivale told Lord Desart in 1852,
'stand on a somewhat different footing from those of ordinary
charter colonies, under the provisions of the Canada Union Act.
They require no confirmation by the Crown, except in cases where
they are specially reserved for the Crown's assent.' The ordinary
course was for Canadian acts to be sent home in separate batches,
one of reserved acts, the other those which were already in operation. These last required no confirmation, although they could,
in theory, be disallowed by the Crown within two years.[22]

The acts of politically advanced colonies like Canada (and, as
we have seen, Australia) did not require confirmation because
of that very political status.[23] At the other end of the scale were
ordinances from the tiny settlement of Honduras (not formally
annexed until 1862). For diplomatic reasons, to avoid a clash with
Spain, the government of Honduras was not recognized by His
Majesty's Government. It was therefore not usual to confirm the
acts of the Public Meeting of Honduras,[24] but to bring them to
the notice of the Crown only when reserved, or when they were

[21] C.O. 323/72, Jamaica; Wood to Merivale, 9 Oct. 1852; pencil note [by
Elliot?].

[22] C.O. 323/23, Canada; Rogers to Merivale, 19 Feb. 1852; Minute by
Merivale to Lord Desart, 6 Mar. 1852.

[23] It should be emphasized that the grant of 'responsible government' to the
colonies of white settlement involved no *legal* change.

[24] C.O. 323/74, Honduras; Rogers to Merivale, 5 July 1853; Minute by C.
Talbot, 6 July.

to be disallowed. Otherwise it was enough for receipt of them to be acknowledged by dispatch. Merivale, while acquiescing in this procedure in 1854, did not appear to be aware of the reasons for it. He considered it anomalous that a different procedure should be employed for Honduras when their Constitution Act used the same form of words (that the Governor is empowered to 'give the assent of the Crown') as the Imperial Acts granting constitutions to Australia, Canada, and New Zealand.[25]

What amounted to 'tacit allowance' for Honduras acts could also be used for acts from the colonies proper, but for different reasons. Where the object of an act was felt to be impolitic or mistaken, but the officials were unwilling either to disallow, or to imply Crown approval by confirming or 'leaving it to its operation', the governor might be told that the Crown would take no direct action in the matter. The effect of this was much the same as if the act had been left to its operation. In 1845 Stephen found himself faced with two Canadian Acts of Incorporation to give corporate privileges to two firms with obviously insufficient capital. While he felt that it was very difficult to 'reconcile such legislation with the Principles usually observed on this subject', he was sure that the Secretary of State 'would not think it worth while to reverse their [the Canadian authorities'] decision, at the expense of the great inconvenience of disallowing these Enactments'. Tacit allowance would be the best course, he suggested, and Lord Stanley agreed.[26]

There was at least one other way by which the Colonial Office could show its disapproval of a colonial act, without actually disallowing it. An extreme step might be to refuse assent until the desired amendments were made. Grey and Stephen were agreed that this was, as Grey wrote in 1846, 'a power to be used with very great caution, and not in those cases in which the only effect of at once confirming the law will be some inconvenience to the colonists themselves, which need only last until an amending Act is passed.'[27] In the following year, Stephen took much the same line over an Act from Antigua, which would have superseded the

---

[25] C.O. 323/76, Honduras; Wood to Merivale, 17 Aug. 1854; Minute by Merivale.

[26] C.O. 323/60, Canada; Stephen to Stanley, 25 July 1845; Minute by Stanley.

[27] C.O. 323/61, New South Wales; Rogers to Grey, 15 July 1846; Minute by Grey, 21 July.

necessity for Masters of Vessels to enter into a penal bond that they would comply with the fugitive laws. Wood and Rogers objected that it failed to compensate the Colonial Secretary for the loss of his customary fees, and they suggested holding over a decision pending amendment. Stephen flatly disagreed. Suspension, he wrote, 'is an indirect and implied, and therefore an offensive menace, that the Act will be disallowed altogether if the necessary amendments are not made'.[28]

Despite these qualms, there were a number of occasions when suspension was felt to be necessary and justified. In 1834 the Jamaican legislature passed an Act to enable ordinary magistrates to take cognizance of petty assaults and misdemeanours. The circumstances of the time, as we shall see in a later chapter,[29] made it imperative that such acts, however apparently innocuous, be carefully scrutinized. Stephen pointed out that the effect of this one would be to allow two justices to exercise summary and irreversible jurisdiction over all misdeameanours, and he was being unusually tactful in suggesting that this effect might be unintentional.[30] Here was a clear case for insisting on an amendment before assent could be given. Exactly the same course was followed nearer the end of our period over a Dominican Act to extend the franchise, which provided no means of registering voters or determining their qualification to vote, beyond requiring them, at the time of the election, to swear to their qualifications according to prescribed forms of oath. The Governor agreed that the Act was defective, but pleaded that the 'irritated state of public feeling' had prevented any thorough consideration of details. On the advice of Henry Taylor, confirmation was suspended until the legislature had had time to consider the measure afresh.[31]

Many other examples could be cited. The suspensive power was very useful in securing amendments to objectionable acts without the inconvenience and annoyance which would inevitably follow outright disallowance. Nevertheless, as Stephen had said, its use implied a rebuke, and was only called for when circumstances demanded.

[28] C.O. 323/62, Antigua; Wood and Rogers to Stephen, 12 Mar. 1847; Minute by Stephen.
[29] See Chapter 9.
[30] C.O. 323/60, Jamaica; Stephen to Wellington, 5 Dec. 1834.
[31] C.O. 323/70, Dominica; Wood to Merivale, 7 May 1851; Minute by H. Taylor and Earl Grey.

If suspension was to be used sparingly, then disallowance was to be pronounced only as a last resort. The general reluctance of the authorities to make use of this weapon was expressed early in the period by Glenelg, though a considerable number of West Indian acts suffered this fate during his term of office. Disallowance of the acts of the 'responsible government' colonies was particularly infrequent. 'It need hardly be said', wrote Merivale in 1852, 'that the power to disallow Canadian Acts is one which has been very rarely indeed exercised of late years.'[32] The figures given in the Appendix indicate that disallowances reached a peak in the late thirties and dwindled to almost nothing by 1865.

In 1852 an important point of principle arose about the disallowance procedure, which might have resulted in a severe limitation of the powers of the Crown over colonial legislation. At the end of a long dispute over the Mauritius liquor laws, the Governor reported that he had delayed the promulgation of the royal disallowance of a liquor Ordinance, because experience had shown that the Ordinance had not had the effect, as feared, of raising the incidence of intemperance in the colony.[33] The Governor evidently assumed that disallowance could not take place until he chose to announce it—with this assumption Rogers, if reluctantly, felt obliged to agree. For disallowance to take effect from the date of the dispatch conveying it, or from the date of its arrival in the colony, without a formal promulgation and without affording the subject any means of knowing the law to which he had become liable, would, he considered, be 'contrary to every rational principle of jurisprudence'.[34] Merivale, writing to Lord Desart, remarked on the singular fact that on a point of such importance there should be no written law to appeal to.[35] Failing this, he had consulted Stephen, who was quite sure that disallowance should take effect from its arrival in the colony, and in support of this Merivale noted that the Governor's Instructions contained no clause requiring him to publish disallowance in any authentic manner. It was thus difficult to say 'on what legal principle the notion of disallowance having effect from promulgation can rest, however convenient and reasonable a doctrine it may be'. The

[32] C.O. 323/73, Canada; Rogers to Merivale, 19 Feb. 1852; Minute by Merivale to Desart, 6 Mar.
[33] C.O. 323/72, Mauritius; Rogers to Merivale, 4 Nov. 1852.
[34] Ibid.
[35] Ibid., Minute by Merivale to Desart.

Colonial Secretary Sir John Pakington agreed,[36] and approved Merivale's plan that the Governor be told to pass an ordinance legalizing acts done under the disallowed Ordinance, but not extending it. The Governor was to be reproved for disregarding clear instructions, and a point of some importance for the effectiveness of the review process was thus settled.

[36] C.G. 323/72, Mauritius; Rogers to Merivale, 4 Nov. 1852; Minute by Sir John Pakington.

4

THE COLONIAL OFFICE AND
JUDICIAL REVIEW

THE review of colonial legislation carried out by the Colonial Office, though by far the most important part of the process, was not the whole of it. There remained a further and final stage at which a colonial law, which had duly received the assent of the Crown, could still be declared inoperative—not by the Crown itself but by the courts.

This process of 'judicial review' was described at some length by Alpheus Todd, in his *Parliamentary Government in the British Colonies*, published in 1880.

It is [wrote Todd] a primary condition of all legislation by subordinate and provincial assemblies throughout the British Empire that the same 'shall not be repugnant to the law of England'.[1] This condition is enforced in two ways: firstly . . . by the right and duty of the Crown to disallow any Act that contravenes this principle; secondly, by the decision of the local judiciary in the first instance and ultimately of Her Majesty's Imperial Privy Council, upon an action or suit of law duly brought before such a tribunal, to declare and adjudge a colonial, dominion or provincial statute, either in whole or in part, to be *ultra vires* and void, as being in excess of the jurisdiction conferred upon the legislature by which the same was enacted, or at variance with some Imperial law in force in the colony, or otherwise, by a similar decision, to confirm or approve of the legality of the act, the validity of which has been impugned. The power of interpreting colonial statutes, and of deciding upon their constitutional effect and validity, is a common and inherent right appertaining to all Her Majesty's courts of law before which a question arising out of the same could be properly submitted for adjudication.

As this was essentially a judicial process, the Colonial Office naturally had little direct connection with it. One late-eighteenth-century writer has suggested that the process of review by the Privy Council was regarded by the British Government as an

[1] See below, p. 53 et seq.

important instrument of control over the colonies.[1a] This argument is untenable. Very few of the appeals from the colonies brought before the Privy Council raised the question of the constitutionality or validity of colonial laws. Of the 265 cases brought on appeal to the Privy Council from the American colonies in the last century of British rule, only four involved the exercise of judicial review. More to the point, there were, in the period covered by this book, *no* relevant cases heard by the Privy Council. Writers who have criticized the Judicial Committee of the Privy Council for appearing to allow political prejudice to enter into their legal judgements have, in general, based their views upon the latter's interpretation of the British North America Act, in such cases as *Attorney-General for Ontario* v. *Attorney-General for Canada* (1896).[2]

In the period under consideration, therefore, there can be no truth in any suggestion that the Privy Council's power of review was used to further imperial policy. And there is no evidence to suggest such a 'political' bias in the normal process of hearing appeals from the colonial courts on matters which did not involve the exercise of judicial review. The oft-repeated insistence that colonial appeals should be judged, wherever possible, according to the *lex loci*—the law obtaining in the colony in question— was mere commonsense. This attitude ran parallel to, but was probably not influenced by, the Colonial Office policy of the devolution of power to the colonial governments. There was, in any case, no tangible connection, either personal, constitutional, or political, between the Judicial Committee and the Colonial Office; indeed, the non-political nature of the Committee was clearly recognized by members of the Colonial Office itself. Herman Merivale, after transferring to the India Office in 1860, made this point clear. Writing in 1863 to the Secretary of State for India, Sir Charles Wood, on the case of the Carnatic and the interpretation of treaties generally, he remarked 'As I understand, it has been suggested to refer this and similar cases, where rights

---

[1a] e.g. Bryan Edwards in his *History of the West Indies* (vol. II, p. 431) claimed that the reason for allowing appeals from the colonies to the King-in-Council was that, failing this system, the rules and practice of colonial law might gradually deviate from that of the mother country, and so lead to a diminution of her superiority.

[2] e.g. Macdonald, V. C., 'The Privy Council and the Canadian Constitution', *Can. Bar Rev.* (1951), pp. 1–21 et seq.

guaranteed by treaty are in question, either to the Judicial Committee, through the general powers reserved to the Crown by Act of Parliament, or to some body to be created *ad hoc*. It seemed to me that objections to the first course are very strong, both as regards England or India. As regards ourselves, the mischief would be this: judges are appointed to try cases of right, Civil or Criminal. *They have no peculiar qualifications for deciding questions of public expediency.* The Executive is better qualified for this. But questions on treaties must and will continually involve questions of public expediency.'[3] A number of cases involving questions of repugnancy, constitutionality, or the application of English law to the colonies came before the colonial courts, but did not filter through to the Judicial Committee. Sir Harrison Moore, in his study of Victorian law over the past century, noted in 1934 that of the 300 cases in Legge's *Selection of Supreme Court Cases in New South Wales*, between a quarter and one third involved the question of the applicability of English law to the colony.[4]

Courts sitting within a colony must have found it difficult to disassociate themselves completely from popular feeling or public policy. On the two occasions that this happened, the Colonial Office was inevitably drawn into the dispute, and forced to make clear its attitude to the review powers of the colonial courts.

The first such clash arose in Van Diemen's Land in 1847–8, and revolved around the exercise of judicial review by the colonial Supreme Court in the case of *Symons* v. *Morgan*.[5] At first glance, the case appears to be supremely insignificant. The defendant, a prominent local newspaper proprietor, was being prosecuted for his refusal to pay a £2 fine imposed upon him in a Police Magistrate's Court—a fine which he had incurred for failing to take out a licence for his dog, as required by the local Dog Act.

It soon becomes clear, however, that the implications, both political and legal, of this case were very far from being insignificant. Morgan had, in fact, deliberately refused to take out a licence or pay the fine, as a protest against the recent proliferation of acts designed to raise revenue to support the influx of convicts from New South Wales. He therefore hoped that, by challenging

[3] India Office MSS. EUR F79, Wood Collection, India Office Correspondence, India Box 6/90.

[4] Moore, Sir W. H., 'A Century of Victorian Law', *Journal of Comparative Legislation* (1934).

[5] C.O. 280/224, Denison to Grey (confidential), 18 Feb. 1848.

the validity of the Dog Act, he would also bring down various other similar acts. These tactics paid off. The judges, Chief Justice Sir John Pedder and Mr. Justice Montague, accepted his plea that the Dog Act was repugnant to the Imperial Statute 9 Geo. IV, c. 83, and therefore invalid, and his conviction was quashed.

The grounds of the decision to declare the Act invalid were open to question. They rested partly on the interpretation of 9 Geo. IV, c. 83 and partly on the nature of the Dog Act itself. By the 25th section of the Imperial Statute it was required that 'the Governor and Council shall not impose any tax or duty, except such as it may be necessary to levy for local purposes . . . and the purpose for which every such tax or duty may be so imposed . . . shall be particularly and distinctly stated in the body of every law or ordinance imposing every such tax or duty.' The judges, rightly or wrongly, took these provisions to be not directory but imperative. The Dog Act, they held, although its main purpose might be otherwise, did impose a tax, by requiring owners of dogs to buy a licence at the rate of 5s. per dog and 10s. per bitch. And although it was clearly stated in the appropriation clause of the Act that the revenue thus accruing was to be applied to the general revenue of the colony, they did not consider that this section was sufficiently specific to satisfy the requirements of the Statute, and was therefore repugnant to it.

Whether or not this decision was correct in law need not concern us. It was, however, abundantly clear to all concerned that the principle involved could be extended to other local acts, with disastrous consequences. The Solicitor-General's report detailed fifteen acts (among them the Customs and Police Acts) which would be invalidated by the application of a similar process, and twenty-nine others whose validity might be questioned.[6]

The Governor, Sir William Denison, was naturally alarmed and anxious to do what he could to remedy the situation. But by attacking the judges for their part in the affair he had clearly put himself in the wrong. Writing to the Secretary of State, Earl Grey, in February 1848 he alleged that the recent crisis had been 'caused altogether by the conduct of Judges of the Supreme Court in assuming to themselves a power [i.e. the power of judicial review] neither warranted by express words, nor by any fair construction of the statute 9 Geo. IV, c. 83 upon which the

---

[6] *P.P.* 1847/8, p. 93, Report of local Solicitor-General, 17 Feb. 1848.

existence of the Supreme Court and that of the Legislative Council alike depends.'[7]

Denison was evidently relying here upon the advice of his Attorney-General, who in *Symons* v. *Morgan* had argued for the prosecution that the Court had no power to say that an act of the Council was illegal, except by certifying to its repugnancy *before* it became law, since both Supreme Court and Legislative Council alike were creatures of the Constitution Act, 9 Geo. IV, c. 83. For the Court to assume this power, was to exceed the jurisdiction exercised by the Queen's Courts at Westminster.

Chief Justice Pedder, however, giving judgement, denied the parallel between the colonial and British structure. The colonial Legislative Council was an 'inferior legislature', bound by the 20th, 21st, and 25th clauses of 9 Geo. IV, c. 83, whereas 'that Act conferred on the Court [i.e. the Supreme Court] the united powers and authorities of all the Queen's superior Courts in England'. 'If', he concluded, 'in any case before the court, the question arose whether a given Act of Council was one which the Council had not the power to enact, or whether it was repugnant to the Act of Parliament and therefore void, it was not only competent to the court, but it was our duty to decide on it.'[8]

The Colonial Office had been brought into the matter by Denison's plaintive dispatch of 18 February 1848. The Office's attitude to the points raised were expressed in a dispatch to the Governor based upon a minute written by Herman Merivale in June. While the latter was doubtful of the correctness of Pedder's judgement on the repugnancy issue, he was convinced that the Court was well within its rights in the matter of judicial review. Denison was firmly criticized for his part in the affair, and he was given no support for his views as to the constitutional position of the Court, *vis-à-vis* the Legislative Council.[9]

In this case, the views of the Colonial Office regarding the review powers of colonial courts were clear, if not very fully stated. Some fourteen years later, in the similar but more far-reaching crisis in South Australia, the home authorities were forced to be rather more explicit.

[7] C.O. 280/224, Denison to Grey, 18 Feb. 1848.

[8] *P.P.* 1847/8, XLIII, p. 75, Account by [Pedder, C.J., of his judgement in *Symons* v. *Morgan*, 29 Nov. 1847.

[9] C.O. 280/224, Merivale to Hawes, 19 June 1848.

The South Australian crisis, as we shall see in a later chapter,[10] involved more than one case and more than one point of law. But once again, at the centre of the whole affair, lay the question of the respective positions of colonial legislature and colonial courts, and the power of the latter to pass judgement on the validity of the former's acts. Just as Governor Denison of Van Diemen's Land had argued that in that colony the Legislative Council and the Supreme Court were on an equal footing, so various South Australians reviewed their own crisis as an attempt on the part of the Supreme Court to upset a supposed balance between court and legislature. 'We believe', declared one of the local newspapers, 'that their Honours are jealous of the powers of the Parliament; that they are struggling to aggrandise their own authority; and that, like many other men in high positions, they are desirous of making themselves absolute.'[11] 'The real question', the Legislative Council was informed by one of its members, 'was whether the Supreme Court or the Parliament was to be supreme.'[12]

A Select Committee of the Legislative Council of South Australia set up to inquire into the recent disturbing Supreme Court Judgements, took the view that the Court had no power to set aside the acts of the Legislature, and argued that colonial legislatures, though undoubtedly subordinate to the Imperial Parliament, were nevertheless supreme within their own colony.[13] But this opinion was opposed on all sides. Mr. Justice Boothby, the central character in the affair, was convinced that 'the Judges of the Supreme Court have cast upon them by Imperial Statute the function of deciding on the validity or otherwise of all legislation by the Parliament of this Province, when any question as to such validity arises between suitors of the Queen in her Supreme Court.'[14] R. D. Hanson, leader of the colonial bar and soon to become Chief Justice, pointed out that if the judges did not have the power to decide on the validity of the laws which they were called upon to administer, they might be obliged to give judgements which they knew would be reversed on appeal to the Privy Council.[15] Even Governor MacDonnell, who was particularly embarrassed by Mr. Boothby's inconvenient judgements and dicta, supported him on this point. In a dispatch accompanying the

---

[10] See Chapter 11.   [11] *South Australian Register*, 19 July 1865.
[12] *S.A.P.D.*, L.C. (1861), para. 940.   [13] *S.A.P.P.*, 141 L.C. (1861).
[14] *S.A.P.P.*, 128 L.C. (1861).   [15] *S.A.P.P.*, 141 L.C. (1861), para. 94.

Report of the Legislative Council, he drew attention to the 'grave error' included in it 'of supposing that the Judges cannot impugn the validity of any Act passed by the Legislature, and left to its operation by the Crown'.[16]

The authorities in England were quite clear as to the powers of the local courts, and their position relative to that of the local legislature. The Law Officers and the Colonial Office disagreed with many of Boothby's findings, but were sure they must resist the demand by the South Australian Parliament for the judge's removal. What might happen, it was asked, if both Houses of the legislature, supported by public opinion, decided that colonial law would in no way be affected by imperial law, and demanded the removal of all judges who failed to agree? 'The defence of the Judicial independence', wrote Sir Frederic Rogers, 'is the defence of (among others) Imperial interests.'[17] In their Report, accepted by the Colonial Office, the Law Officers expressed themselves convinced that a 'Colonial Court is bound to satisfy itself of the legal validity of any Act of the Colonial Legislature, the provisions of which it is called upon to administer'.[18]

Thus, in the course of these two colonial crises, the Colonial Office and their advisers had shown themselves to be in complete support of the judicial independence of colonial judges, and of their full power to review the acts of their local legislatures.

This is not surprising. In the early 1860s the Colonial Office was not yet prepared to concede to colonial parliaments the power to override imperial law altogether and to use the Crown as a passive instrument in the removal of judges who opposed them. But to see this as an attempt to hold back, let alone reverse the constitutional development of the colonies, is to take the matter quite out of its proper context. In the first place, it was inconceivable that the Office should have agreed to reject what was a generally accepted corollary of the subordinate position of colonial legislatures, that is, the controlling effect of imperial law, and the duty of colonial judges to review colonial laws in the light of imperial law. Secondly it should be pointed out that the general attitude of the Colonial Office to the South Australian crisis was essentially liberal and devolutionary. Within the limits of the law,

16 *S.A.P.P.*, 48 H.A. (1862).
17 C.O. 13/106, MacDonnell to Newcastle, 25 Oct. 1861, Minute by Rogers.
18 C.O. 13/110, Law Officers' Opinion, 12 Apr. 1862.

colonial governments and legislatures, especially within the colonies of white settlement, were to be encouraged to handle their own problems and cure their own mistakes.

The Colonial Office attitude to judicial review reveals, therefore, that curious dichotomy faced by all such institutions in a period of progressive change. Sympathetic to colonial aspiration towards political autonomy, it was nevertheless bound by the constitutional framework of the Empire—a framework which, though dissolving, was not yet dissolved. The necessary existence of the process of judicial review was still an accepted part of that framework, and it would take more than a few isolated cases of inconvenience and colonial irritation to remove it altogether.

Part II

IMPERIAL LAW AND COLONIAL LAWS

5

CONFLICT WITH IMPERIAL LAW

CONFLICT between a colonial act and an imperial statute or statutory instrument is generally termed 'repugnancy'—a concept implicit in the constitutional relationship between the Imperial Parliament and the subordinate colonial legislatures, and explicit in the constitution acts which denied to these legislatures the right to pass acts 'repugnant to the laws of England'.[1] This much was clear in the early nineteenth century, and none of the authorities involved, either at home or in the colonies, would have denied that what was repugnant in a colonial act was *ipso facto* void and of no effect. Unfortunately, the concept of repugnancy still left a great deal undecided and undefined, and doubts as to its meaning persisted, if mainly in the colonies rather than at home.

Confusion arose on three main counts. First of all it was not clear whether 'repugnancy' meant a fundamental conflict of principle, or whether it covered also the mere alteration of words or forms of procedure. Secondly, it was open to question whether the repugnancy of a single clause or provision invalidated the whole of an otherwise irreproachable enactment.

The main source of confusion, however, lay in the phrase 'the laws of England'. To which laws did this refer? Did it include the whole of the English common law, or perhaps only certain ill-defined 'fundamental principles' of common law? Similarly, did it include all statutes passed by the Imperial Parliament not expressly excluding the colonies from their operation, or only certain statutes, selected according to some legal rule?

So far as the operation of the common law was concerned, the answer to these questions depended to a large extent upon a legal distinction which had evolved over the centuries—a distinction between 'conquered or ceded' colonies and 'settled' colonies. In his judgement in *Campbell* v. *Hall* (1774), Lord Mansfield held that the laws of a conquered or ceded country continue in force,

[1] e.g. 5 & 6 Vict., c. 76, s. 29, New South Wales and Van Diemen's Land. This section was applied to South Australia by 13 & 14 Vict., c. 59, s. 14.

until altered by the conqueror, and that Englishmen in such a colony could enjoy no special privileges.[2] The Crown, by virtue of its prerogative, has power to alter old laws or introduce new ones, subject of course to the overriding authority of the King in Parliament, and also to the condition that the Crown can make no alteration contrary to fundamental principles. But, once such a colony was granted an assembly of its own, the Crown lost the power to legislate, unless such a right had been expressly reserved.

In the case of a conquered colony, therefore, English common law did not apply until expressly introduced. In colonies by settlement, however, the case was rather different. In the eighteenth century it was generally held that Englishmen in such a colony took with them the common law of England, together with all statutes passed *antecedent* to the setting up of the colony in affirmation of the common law.[3] This principle was usually modified to read 'let an Englishman go where he will, he carries as much of law and liberty with him, as the nature of things will bear'.[4] As Lord Mansfield declared, 'it is absurd that in the colonies they should carry all the laws of England with them. They carry only such as are applicable to their situation.'[5]

Moreover, an imperial statute passed *after* the setting up of a settlement colony did not apply to it, unless that colony, or colonies generally, was specifically mentioned, or unless the statute was introduced by an act of either the Imperial Parliament or the local legislature. The only other possible ground for applicability, ignored by most commentators, was that of long usage—suggested by Attorney-General Yorke in 1729.[6]

The clearest expression of contemporary opinion was that given by Clark in 1833, when he stated that 'the common law of England is the common law of the plantations [i.e. colonies other than ceded colonies retaining their former laws] and all statutes in affirmance of the common law passed in England antecedent to

---

[2] *Campbell* v. *Hall* (1774) in Shortt, A., and Doughty, A. G., op. cit., I. 522–31. For a qualification of Lord Mansfield's opinion see *Sammut* v. *Strickland*, discussed in Hood Phillips, O., *Leading Cases in Constitutional Law* (London, 1952), p. 429.

[3] Chalmers, G., *Opinions of Eminent Lawyers . . . concerning the colonies of Great Britain* (2 vols., London, 1814), p. 194.

[4] Ibid., p. 195.

[5] *Campbell* v. *Hall*.

[6] Chalmers, op. cit., p. 194. Yorke held that 25 Geo. II, c. 6, s. 10 applied to Maryland, though passed after Maryland had gained its charter.

the settlement of any colony are in force in that colony, unless there is some private Act [i.e. Act of the Imperial Parliament] to the contrary, though no statutes made since these settlements are there in force, unless the colonies are therein mentioned.'[7]

Clark's statement obviously has to be read in conjunction with Lord Mansfield's remarks on the absurdity of carrying *all* English laws into a settled colony. And in dealing with imperial statutes passed *after* settlement, he makes no mention of statutes which might apply to the colonies by implication, as opposed to by express words. Clark was obviously following the wording of 7 & 8 Wm. III, c. 22, s. 9, which forbade any colonial legislature to pass laws repugnant to laws made by the English Parliament 'so far as such may mention or refer to the plantations'. It was highly un- likely that any judge would have failed to construe this phrase to include laws which clearly applied to the colonies, though making no specific mention of them. The point was made more happily in both the Canadian Act of Union and the Colonial Laws Validity Act by the phrase 'express words or necessary intendment'.

There is ample evidence of confusion, at the colonial level, as to the practical effect of the principles noted above. In 1825 the Commissioners of Enquiry into the Administration of Justice in the West Indies found wide variations in the extent to which the different West Indian islands were accustomed to accept English law.[8] In Barbados the Solicitor-General agreed that the laws of the mother country that were acknowledged and in force in the colony included the common law of England and 'such Acts of Parliament as passed before the settlement of the island, and are applicable to its condition'. He excepted, however, certain acts passed prior to the date of settlement, such as the Bankruptcy, Poor Law, and Mortmain Acts, which inflicted forfeitures or dis- abilities. On the other hand, of statutes passed subsequent to the settlement, he considered that, in addition to those which expressly named the colony, 'all navigation acts, and acts of revenue and trade, and acts respecting shipping, are obligatory, though the colonies are not mentioned in them'. While similar principles were followed by other West Indian colonies, some made no mention of English law, whilst others appeared uncertain as to the actual date

---

[7] Clark, C., *A Summary of Colonial Law* (1834), p. 8, n. 4; see also Blackstone, W., *Commentaries on the Laws of England*, 23rd edn. (London, 1854), I, p. 108.
[8] *P.P.* 1825 (157), XV, p. 233.

at which English Law became operative. The Commissioners themselves received a general impression of uncertainty and ignorance, not helped by the haphazard methods of recording used by colonial government officials. In their final report they felt obliged to state that 'unfortunately the principle upon which certain laws of the mother country are operative and held binding in her colonies, far from being clear and precise, as is desirable in presenting rules of action which all men are required to obey, is involved in considerable obscurity, and often found very difficult of operation.'

Confusion about the rules concerning the application of English law to the colonies inevitably led to confusion about repugnancy, since until one knew what laws applied, one could not know whether or not a colonial law was in conflict with English law. If further evidence of colonial confusion is required, it is to be found in the numbers of colonial laws which had to be disallowed, simply because they were obviously repugnant.

An examination of the fate of such acts passing through the process of review is much more valuable, however, than just as an illustration of this one point. It also throws a good deal of light on the attitudes and opinions of the Colonial Office officials towards the applications of the repugnancy doctrine—opinions which were often more liberal than those of contemporary lawyers.

Stephen, in his early years as counsel, appeared to favour an interpretation whereby 'repugnancy to the law of England' might involve conflict not just with specific provisions to English statutes, but with the 'fundamental principles' of the English common law. In 1825 he objected to a Barbados Act to regulate proceedings at the Court of Grand Sessions, because it seemed to put an end to the power of entering a *nolle prosequi* in all cases—'a provision manifestly repugnant to a fundamental principle of the law of England'.[9] Two years later he recommended the disallowance of another act from the same colony, on the ground that it would have made aliens of a native's children if born outside the colony. 'Now it is an undoubted maxim of the law of England', he observed, 'that children of Englishmen, wherever born, have an English birth right.'[10]

It is open to doubt, however, whether Stephen ever really believed that conflict with such fundamental principles inevitably

[9] C.O. 323/43, Barbados; Stephen to Bathurst, 13 Oct. 1825.
[10] C.O. 323/44, Barbados; Stephen to Bathurst, 12 Feb. 1827.

involved repugnancy. If he did, then it is clear that by 1834, the year of his appointment as Assistant Under-Secretary, he had completely discarded this view. By using the expression 'repugnant' he argued, 'Parliament meant only to forbid the enactment by the subordinate legislature of any laws which, in their operation, would clash with any laws established in the colony by Parliamentary authority.'[11] Where two legislatures existed with co-ordinate and concurrent powers, 'it was necessary that the superior should limit, by such a Rule as this, the exercise of the privileges it conferred upon the inferior, not only with a view to the maintenance of the supreme authority, but also that, in the event of a legislative collision, the Judges and the People at large, might have a safe rule for their guidance. *To have required, on pain of nullity, an adherence to the fundamental principles of English legislation would, I think, have involved more than one absurdity*. It may very reasonably be doubted whether these principles have any real and definite existence, and even if, by a great effort of abstraction and subtlety, our written or unwritten law could be made to yield a body of fundamental maxims pervading the whole mass, it would have been strange if Parliament had required a rigid observance of those maxims in a society of which all the material circumstances, and the whole elementary character differ essentially from what has ever been known in the Parent State.'[12]

If Stephen's attitude had indeed undergone a change between 1825 and 1834, it is easily explained. In the intervening period he had been brought much more directly into contact with colonial affairs than he had been as part-time legal adviser before 1825. Experience had begun to change him, from being a lawyer, into a practical administrator with expert legal knowledge. Although examples did arise after 1834 when he and his successors made use of the 'fundamental principles' argument, they appear to have done so as much for political as for strictly legal reasons. In 1838, for instance, Stephen reported to Lord Glenelg that a St. Vincent Act, which authorized any Justice of the Peace to effect forcible entry at any time of night or day, involved 'a very serious departure from the principles of our own law'.[13] His real objection to the Act, however, was essentially practical: the defence of the unrepresented

---

[11] C.O. 323/50, Van Diemen's Land; Stephen Memorandum, 16 June 1834.
[12] Ibid., my italics.
[13] C.O. 323/53, St. Vincent; Stephen to Glenelg, 20 July 1838.

plantation labourer against victimization by the planter-dominated legislature. Similarly, when Rogers and Merivale agreed in 1854 to advise the disallowance of a Honduras Ordinance disqualifying members of the Jamaican and Irish bars from judicial office 'contrary to a fixed principle of British legislation', they did so more out of concern for the welfare of the colonial legal profession than for the maintenance of any fundamental principle of the English common law.[14]

By the late 1840s Herman Merivale, for one, was prepared to carry the argument that Englishmen took only so much of the common law with them as was applicable to their situation to its logical conclusion. 'My own certainty is', he wrote in 1858, 'that whenever the matter shall be thoroughly examined and discussed, it will be found that colonial legislatures can alter, to any extent and in any particular, the law which they carry with them.'[15] This was an opinion, he was obliged to admit, which was unlikely to recommend itself to lawyers. As he pointed out, it had not been long since Sir R. Bethel, one of the Law Officers, had advised Colonial Office that the Legislature of Hong Kong could not make perjury punishable if committed on an unessential allegation, because this would be repugnant to the law of England. But Merivale felt convinced that 'colonial laws would in fact rest on a most insecure foundation, if the limiting doctrine were carried so far as Sir R. Bethel proposed to carry it'.

In view of Merivale's senior and influential position in the Colonial Office, this was a most important, if controversial, statement of principle. What he was suggesting was that colonial legislatures in practice had the power to alter the common law of England within their own sphere of jurisdiction. He was justified in his belief that not all lawyers would find this idea acceptable— neither did all of his colleagues. In 1858 Sir Frederic Rogers maintained that conflict with the fundamental principles of English law would involve repugnancy, and the Law Officers agreed with him.[16] But Rogers was also an administrator, and the principles which he considered to be fundamental were of such a kind that it was highly unlikely that any colonial legislature then

[14] C.O. 323/76, Honduras; Rogers to Merivale, 6 Jan. 1854; Minute by Merivale.
[15] C.O. 323/87, South Australia; Rogers to Merivale, 5 May 1858; Minute by Merivale.
[16] Ibid.

in existence would contemplate passing laws in conflict with them.[17] In any case, Rogers had already made it clear that he was in broad agreement with Merivale's views—that the general tendency was to regard a colonial legislature as legally competent to pass almost any law, provided that it did not conflict with an imperial statute intended to be binding on the colony. If any conflict with 'fundamental principles' did arise, then it could be dealt with through the normal exercise of the power of disallowance. In essence, this was the doctrine ultimately written into the Colonial Laws Validity Act, which limited repugnancy to conflict with an Imperial Statute applying 'by express words or necessary intendment' to the colony, and which made no mention at all of any fundamental principles of English law.

While the reviewers were not prepared to insist that colonial legislatures could not pass any law in conflict with fundamental principles of the English common law, they were less indulgent towards laws which conflicted with imperial statutes passed before the settlement of a colony. Merivale, in his 'Lectures on Colonisation and the Colonies' delivered between 1839 and 1841, declared that 'where the function of a colonial legislature is defined by the ordinary words of a governor's commission "to make laws for the good government of a colony", its power within its local jurisdiction has no limit, except that its enactments cannot alter existing laws, and are subject to future imperial laws.'[18] Throughout our period, there were several instances of colonial acts being declared repugnant because they conflicted with imperial acts passed before the colony in question was settled or before it became a British possession. A St. Kitts Act which enabled a body of persons acting as a corporation to deal with property by way of trade without incurring individual responsibility was, Stephen considered, by virtue of the statute 7 & 8 Will. III, c. 22, s. 9 'actually null and void'.[19] A Grenada Act which prohibited Roman Catholic priests from carrying out their clerical functions except under certain conditions, was held to be 'opposed to the Statute 1st Eliz', and 'its disallowance', remarked Horace Twiss,

---

[17] e.g. denying the sovereignty of the Queen, prohibiting Christianity, allowing slavery, polygamy, or punishment without trial.

[18] Merivale, H. M., *Lectures on Colonisation and the Colonies*, published in book form in 1861, pp. 663–7.

[19] C.O. 323/43, St. Kitts; Stephen to Bathurst, 27 Apr. 1825.

'will of course take place'.[20] A South Australian Ordinance to amend the alien law so as to give German settlers naturalization on easier terms, was undoubtedly repugnant to one of the provisions of 12 & 13 Will. III, c. 12, and would require an Act of Parliament before it could be put into operation.[21]

Similarly, there appears to have been no doubt in the minds of the reviewers that colonial acts conflicting with imperial statutes passed *after* the date of settlement must be held to be repugnant where those statutes either applied to the colony in question, or dealt with imperial matters in general. Two Bahamas Acts passed in 1826 were adjudged repugnant and disallowed, because they conflicted with the Imperial Customs Act, 6 Geo. IV, c. 114, the nature of which necessitated its application to all colonies.[22] Any number of West Indian Acts, both before and after the formal abolition of slavery and the establishment of the apprenticeship scheme, conflicted with imperial legislation on the subject, and assent was consequently refused. In 1831 the St. Kitts Legislature sought to authorize the restriction of fugitive slaves to foreign colonies, but this was declared by the Governor himself to be repugnant to 5 Geo. IV, c. 113, in which Parliament had 'in the most direct and unequivocal terms' prohibited the principle which the local legislature were trying to uphold. 'It follows, of course,' Stephen reported, 'that the Act must be disallowed, because even if allowed it would have no legal efficacy, and would be merely a trap for the ignorant and unwary. Perhaps, under such circumstances, the Governor would have judged better by refusing his assent altogether, than by imposing on H.M. the disagreeable office of disallowing this Act.'[23] Lord Goderich concurred.

Clearly the automatic invalidation of any colonial act which conflicted with an act of Parliament directly extending to the colony was not even a matter for discretion. Even the King-in-Council could not lawfully give his assent to any such act, and no peculiarity of circumstance could justify its allowance.[24] In 1834 the recognition (by a Lower Canada Act) of the Roman Catholic

---

[20] C.O. 323/47, Grenada; Stephen to Murray, 11 May 1830; Minute by Horace Twiss.

[21] C.O. 323/63, South Australia; Wood and Rogers to Stephen, 28 Apr. 1847.

[22] C.O. 323/43, Bahamas; Stephen to Bathurst, 2 Nov. 1826.

[23] C.O. 323/48, St. Kitts; Stephen to Goderich, 20 Apr. 1831.

[24] C.O. 323/50, Barbados; Stephen to Stanley, 24 May 1834. Also C.O. 323/57, Jamaica; Stephen to Stanley, 28 May 1842.

Bishop of Quebec as an officer known to the law was held to be directly opposed to the Elizabethan Act of Supremacy, which had been expressly declared to be in force there by 14 Geo. III, c. 83, s. 5.[25] Stephen regretted that 'however widely the principles of that statute deviate from the maxims of toleration or of the latitudinarian indifference at present prevailing in society, it would be impossible to admit that a law which fifty years ago was distinctly declared in force in the Province, can by desuetude or mere lapse of time have become obsolete.'

No relaxation of the rule that colonies must not enact laws in conflict with imperial statutes extending to that colony *by name* can be discovered in our period. However, it was not always the case that colonial laws conflicting with imperial statutes extending to the colonies *in general* could not be allowed, if circumstances appeared to warrant it. A good example is that of the Queensland Act of 1862, which required doctors with English qualifications to register them before practising in the colony. This was in direct conflict with an imperial Act[26] authorizing them to practise throughout the British dominions. Rogers took the view that although the Queensland Act was repugnant, it was reasonable, and best left to come into operation unnoticed. Its repugnancy would lay it open to challenge in a court of law, but until that was done, it must remain in force.[27] The same principle was implied in a marginal note by Merivale on one of Wood's reports in 1853, where Wood had asserted that 'any enactment of the Montserrat Assembly which is repugnant to the law of England would be absolutely void'. 'I think not', noted Merivale. 'Only to Acts in which the particular colony is mentioned.'[28]

The most explicit statement of the state of opinion regarding repugnancy before the enactment of the Colonial Laws Validity Act came not from Merivale, but from Rogers. In May 1858 Rogers composed an elucidating report on a South Australian Act, intended to legalize the marriage of a man with his deceased wife's sister. Rogers avoided a detailed discussion as to whether the act was in itself justifiable or not.[29] Instead he turned his attention to

[25] C.O. 323/50, Lower Canada; Stephen to Stanley, 7 Feb. 1834.
[26] 21 & 22 Vict., c. 90.
[27] C.O. 234/6, Bowen to Newcastle, 10 July 1862; Minute by Rogers.
[28] C.O. 323/74, Montserrat; Wood to Merivale, 30 Mar. 1853; Note by Merivale.
[29] C.O. 323/87, South Australia; Rogers to Merivale, 5 May 1858.

two legal points: first, whether it was repugnant to the law of England in such a sense as to be void, and secondly whether it was repugnant in such a sense as to require that Her Majesty should refuse her assent to it. This distinction alone is worthy of our attention. Rogers felt obliged to state his own view of what constituted repugnancy at the time of writing.

The legal doctrine respecting repugnancy between Colonial and Imperial laws is in a very uncertain, perhaps I should say a shifting state. When an Imperial Statute is binding on any colony, because the Imperial Legislature has declared expressly or by implication that it shall be so binding, nothing of course can be clearer than that any colonial legislation contrary to that Statute will be illegal, and of no effect. I apprehend it to be equally clear that where the Law of England is binding in any colony merely because it was imported with the persons of the first English settlers, or adopted by the Act of the Colonial Legislature, it is not therefore unalterable by that Legislature. There is indeed a recorded opinion of an Attorney General of Barbados [Chalmers' Opinions ii §1] which seems to imply the contrary, but I do not know that this opinion has any remarkable authority, and it is certainly so contrary to the stream of practice that it could not now be asserted without producing a confusion and resistance which would necessitate the interference of Parliament.

But a question not infrequently occurs whether there are not, in the English law, certain fundamental enactments of statute or principles of common law of so binding a nature that the legislation of all British Dependencies must be conformable to them, and that colonial laws which are not so conformable are void; either in virtue of the general relations between a British colony and the Mother Country, or as being at variance with some positive Instructions or Acts of Parliament which require that Colonial Laws shall not be 'repugnant to the laws of England'. This seems to have been the doctrine of former times, and as late as 1843, doubts seem to have been entertained whether a colonial law passed to admit unsworn testimony would not be repugnant to the law of England, and therefore null and void. But in practice the tendency has long been to consider Colonial Legislatures as legally competent to pass almost any law, which they are not precluded from passing by some Imperial Statute intended by Parliament to be binding in the colony—the Crown remaining at liberty to intervene by way of disallowance or otherwise in order to prevent the enactment of laws manifestly at variance with the fundamental principles of English legislation. In the larger colonies, the prevailing, if not universal opinion is said to be (as might be expected) that most favourable to the pretensions of their own Legislature. This I am aware is a very vague statement, but I do not know that the present state of the law can be laid down with greater precision.

It would be difficult to find a clearer and more explicit analysis of contemporary law and practice than this 'vague statement'. Apart from this, its particular significance must lie in the change of attitude it reflects, from that of an earlier period. In effect, it declares that the only case in which repugnancy can be insisted upon for legal reasons is where a colonial law conflicts directly with an Imperial Statute clearly intended by Parliament to apply to the colony. This was exactly the principle enacted by the first three clauses of the Colonial Laws Validity Act.

The prime object of the reviewers was to avoid any such conflict, not only because disagreements led to poor relations between colony and imperial authority, but also because there was good reason to suppose that in practice, it would often be the local law which would prevail. As Stephen once remarked, it was 'rather to the practical than to the theoretical question that it is really important to advert'.[30] Where the justifiable needs of the colonists conflicted with the rule of law, the latter must bend, as far as practicable.

[30] C.O. 323/49, Barbados; Stephen to Stanley, 3 Sept. 1853.

6

LEGAL UNIFORMITY

SOME of the confusion about the application of English law to
the colonies might conceivably have been avoided if individual
colonies had merely taken over and re-enacted existing English
statutes. In some cases this was done, especially in Victoria, where
attempts to preserve uniformity between English and Victorian
law were attributable, not so much to a fondness for tradition,
symmetry, or the influence of 'imported' judges as to a general
desire for certainty.[1] The adoption of English law as a model gave
to Victoria the guidance and authority of English textbooks and
precedents. Furthermore, a number of colonies passed local acts
adopting the body of English common and statute law as it stood
at a given date, though in many cases these enactments were
superfluous.

Professor Knaplund has suggested that, in general, the Colonial
Office was against the literal transcription of English laws into the
colonial statute books, and there is a good deal of evidence to
support this.[2] It was particularly true in cases where a colony
sought to apply English statutes of an early date to contemporary
conditions. Stephen wrote disparagingly of a Virgin Islands Act
to prevent the forcible entry and detainer of Lands or Tenements,
that 'this Act has the singularity of being taken from the statutes
of Richard II and Henry VI. The authority of the Legislature of
the Mother Country . . . is relied on by the lawyers in the colony
as almost conclusive in favour of it. I need, however, scarcely
observe that the parental relation between Great Britain and her
colonies is a metaphor which loses all, or nearly all significance,
when applied to the case of England during the reign of the
Plantaganets, and that the presumption at the present day is not
in favour of, but against the wisdom of Acts transcribed from the

---

[1] Moore, Sir W. H., 'A Century of Victorian Law', *Journal of Comparative
Legislation* (1934), p. 178 et seq. The Victorian Companies Act of 1864, for
example, was a virtual copy of the English Act of 1862.

[2] Knaplund, P., *James Stephen and the British Colonial System*, Ch. 9.

English Statute Book of the Fourteenth and Fifteenth Centuries.'
In particular, he objected, the use of obsolete phraseology will
'arm every colonial J.P. with a kind of absolute authority over all
the occupiers of small Tenements and will be taken as a precedent
for imitations in other colonies'.[3]

There was a constant and justifiable fear that even where recent
Acts of Parliament were adopted, the different circumstances of
the colony would result in a different and possibly injurious interpretation. Stephen suggested the tacit allowance only of a Montserrat Act to adopt 1 & 2 Vict., c. 74, because of the 'difficulty, on
the one hand, of objecting to the transference into the colonial
statute book of a recent Act of Parliament, and, on the other hand,
the apparent probability that the administration of the law in a
small West Indian island, and by colonial J.P.'s, would entirely
change the character and effect of it'.[4] Even if the local authorities
could be trusted to administer the borrowed laws in the spirit in
which they had been enacted, there might be other differences
of circumstances which would render the transcription undesirable.
For example, for a small colony like Nova Scotia, whose choice of
candidates for the Assembly was already limited, to pass an Act
disqualifying the Master of the Rolls and the Admiralty Judge
from sitting in the House, was 'plainly one of those cases in which
an exact correspondence between the Law of the Mother Country
and the Law of the Province is neither necessary nor desirable'.[5]

There were other occasions also when the comprehensiveness
of the colonial statute was bound to lead to uncertainty in the law.
In 1855 the Legislature of Honduras sought to introduce the
common law of England, as declared or limited by statute, together with, so far as they could be applied to Honduras, all
criminal statutes of universal application, present and *future*, and
all statutes respecting the most important subjects of civil legislation. The Act was objected to as involving 'the usual and inevitable
uncertainty as to what is so applicable'. Still worse, the 'importation of *future* criminal laws subject to the same limitations and
concurrently with local legislation', was, it was considered, 'likely
to prove in the highest degree perplexing'.[6]

[3] C.O. 323/57, Virgin Islands; Stephen to Stanley, 25 Feb. 1842.
[4] C.O. 323/56, Montserrat; Stephen to Russell, 21 July 1841.
[5] C.O. 323/51, Nova Scotia; Stephen to Aberdeen, 23 Mar. 1835.
[6] C.O. 323/79, Honduras; Rogers to Merivale, 10 Apr. 1855.

Stephen and his colleagues were obviously very well aware that colonial circumstances often differed materially from conditions in Britain, and that allowances for this must be made. Hence they were often willing to approve, or even encourage, the passing of laws which differed from the English model, but which would be better suited to the needs of a colonial society. Thus a Prince Edward Island Act for the summary conviction of persons wilfully committing trespass clearly went very much further than English law, in that it authorized a single Justice of the Peace to commit an alleged offender on the oath of the injured party. This departure, however, was considered excusable in that 'it was not unreasonable to suppose that, in such a society, trespass on property may form a grievance of such magnitude and of so frequent an occurrence, as to require a much stronger remedy than is necessary elsewhere'.[7] Stephen was even more explicit with regard to a Nova Scotia Act which enabled 200 or more persons concurring in any religious belief to nominate trustees to hold land to the value of £2,000, and personal property to the value of £10,000 for the support of a minister. 'That this Act is entirely at variance with the law of England', he reported, 'cannot be disputed. But I apprehend that this departure from English law is required, and is therefore justified by the different circumstances of society in the two countries. It is, I presume, vain to attempt to secure to the Church of England on the North American continent that species of monopoly of secular privileges which it enjoys in this country, nor does it seem probable that the real interest of the Church would be promoted by maintaining any such exclusive principle.'[8]

In 1842 Stephen wrote a long memorandum to Lord Stanley in which he expressed a classic opinion on the inadvisability of the wholesale adoption by a colony of large sections of English law.[9] The document illustrates particularly well Stephen's pragmatic approach to the question; he made it quite clear that, in his opinion, the long-term interests of a colony were generally best served by the enactment of an entirely new body of law, unrestricted by a slavish copying of English models.

The point arose when he received a dispatch from the Governor of New Zealand enclosing copies of nineteen separate ordinances,

[7] C.O. 323/43, Prince Edward Island; Stephen to Bathurst, 9 Dec. 1825.
[8] C.O. 323/45, Nova Scotia; Stephen to Murray, 29 Nov. 1828.
[9] C.O. 209/14, fols. 360–7, Stephen to Stanley, 29 Sept. 1842.

covering a wide variety of legal and procedural subjects, from the establishment of a Supreme Court to the registration of land titles and the solemnization of marriages. Stephen rejected a suggestion that in passing so many important and novel acts over a period of only three months, the local legislature 'had been actuated by a morbid propensity to interfere with everything'. As he pointed out, 'in the infancy of a Colony, the choice must be made between the adoption of an old and inapplicable Code, or a new and immature Code. Both are evils, but, in my mind, it is much safer to begin with a vigorous effort to lay the foundations of law on a right and durable basis, than to build on a basis which must be wrong, and which can never possess any stability.'

'Englishmen colonizing new Countries', he went on, 'are often said . . . to carry the law of England with them. So far as this means that they are to live under a system of government, and in the enjoyment of Franchises as like to those of England as the dissimilarity of the cases will allow, it is at once a maxim intelligible and wise. But when the meaning is carried so far as to imply the adoption of all our Laws regarding the acquisition, tenure, and alienation of property . . . the result invariably is utter confusion.' As an example, he quoted the case of Jamaica which for two centuries 'has been oppressed with a Law of Real Property, and a system of Conveyancing, which have enriched many generations of lawyers, and have impoverished as many generations of Proprietors'. The Legislature of New Zealand, he felt, deserved high praise for their efforts to 'arrest this mischief at its birth'. The laws they had passed were in many ways defective, and would certainly have to be amended in the light of experience. Nevertheless, Stephen considered that 'they will constitute a basis to work on in the way of amendment, far less difficult than if the old precedent had been followed of adopting the Law of the England in the mass "so far as it might be found applicable to the circumstances of the Colony". This has the appearance of laying down a Rule. In reality it is the throwing down of all Rules.'

It has to be remembered, of course, that New Zealand was a comparatively young settlement colony, with no existing legal code derived from a foreign imperial power. In the case of conquered colonies which did possess such a code, it was often felt to be preferable to replace that code with the wholesale adoption of English law. In 1846 Sir Frederic Rogers raised a number of objections to a St. Lucia Ordinance for 'assimilating Criminal Punishments in St. Lucia to those inflicted in the case in England'. The criminal law in force in St. Lucia at the time was the old law of France, by which the nature of the punishment was frequently determined by the rank of the offender. Stephen agreed that the ordinance was defective in many ways, but suggested a more constructive response than mere disallowance. He pointed out that legal reforms of this kind could only be carried out effectively by a competent body of men, which should include professional lawyers. 'The evil is that no persons can be found on St. Lucia to execute such a work. The choice lies between going on with the existing system, and innovating with a rough hand, e.g. establishing at once the French or English penal code. It is my own belief that the latter course is the right one.'[10] In Lower Canada, in Dominica, in Tobago, and in Grenada, the introduction of the English penal law had been effected by a single clause of a statute, and no real inconvenience had followed.

Grey accepted the opinion unreservedly. The Ordinance was to be disallowed, but the Governor was to be instructed to report 'whether he sees any unsurmountable objection to the substitution of the English penal law as a whole for that now in force in St. Lucia'. Nor was this an isolated example. English law was suggested as a model to Jamaica in 1846,[11] and to Gibraltar in 1848.[12]

The Colonial Office, therefore, was not doctrinaire in its policy of discouraging colonies from the adoption of English law. In certain cases, to do so might provide just that element of certainty and stability which Stephen had denied would be the case in New Zealand. The adoption of English law was not objected to *per se*, but only when it seemed likely that the colonists would suffer by it. We can see this quite clearly if we consider a Jamaican Act of 1842 which transferred to the colony several provisions from the English statutes dealing with relations between Master and Servant. In many ways the Act was open to objections similar to those raised by Stephen against the Montserrat Act noted earlier. Here he took a different view, very largely because of the difference

[10] C.O. 323/61, St. Lucia; Rogers to Grey, 31 July 1846; Minute by Stephen and Grey.

[11] C.O. 323/61, Jamaica; Stephen to Gladstone, 7 Apr. 1846.

[12] C.O. 323/64, Gibraltar; Rogers to Merivale, 7 Feb. 1848.

in circumstances between the two West Indian colonies. In Jamaica, unlike Montserrat, the system of magistracy had been brought under the restraining superintendence of the Quarter Sessions, presided over by a salaried chairman. The abuses which might have been expected to have taken place in Montserrat were less likely to occur in Jamaica.[13]

Even where the circumstances of a colony were not, then, completely analogous to those of the mother country, colonial ordinances adopting English legal provisions often went unmolested, provided that no obvious harm would ensure from such assimilation.

If responsible officials within the Colonial Office did not come out clearly for the establishment of some sort of uniform legal code for the whole Empire, it must not be assumed that the idea was never considered, or was not felt to be desirable so far as certain branches of the law were concerned. Lord Carnarvon, writing to the Governor of South Australia in June, 1859, remarked that 'it appears to me that there can be few subjects of greater importance to the entire body which is united under the government of the British Crown, than the maintenance of uniformity of legislation, as far as possible, in matters of social and domestic interest.'[14] In some cases such uniformity was essential, in order to avoid confusion. The Colonial Office took great exception, in 1859, to a proposed South Australian Bankruptcy Law, which would have given rise to considerable inequality between the remedies afforded to creditors in South Australia and those in Great Britain. It was particularly objected that 'any principle of legislation admitted in the case of one colony might be claimed by every other colony of Great Britain possessing a local legislature, and that hence might arise such conflict and confusion of laws as would render necessary great caution in any legislation on the subject'.[15]

A singular example of an attempt by the Colonial Office to establish some sort of uniformity of law throughout the Empire is provided by its policy towards colonial marriage laws. The provisions of English law on the subject were to be taken as the

[13] C.O. 323/57, Jamaica; Stephen to Hope, 10 June 1842.
[14] C.O. 13/99, fol. 92, Carnarvon to MacDonnell, 1 June 1859.
[15] C.O. 13/100, fol. 352, MacDonnell to Newcastle, 8 Oct. 1859; Minute by Newcastle.

model, and deviations were openly discouraged. Sometimes this policy led to the Colonial Office exhibiting a more liberal attitude than that of the colonists. Quite early in our period a New Brunswick Act extending the privilege of solemnizing marriage to ministers of certain religious congregations in the Province was criticized because it did not go far enough. It was inequitable, thought Stephen, that these privileges should be accorded only to those who had no real objection to the Church of England ceremony. What about the Unitarians?[16] In his opinion, it would be better to lay down the requirements of the civil ceremony, and leave the rest to conscience, allowing all teachers of all revealed religion, having no secular calling, to solemnize marriage. But there was an important distinction drawn between the civil and religious aspects of marriage law. When a New Zealand Act in 1852 confused these two aspects, and sought to confide the power of issuing marriage licences, not to the Governor but to 'every officiating minister', Merivale was quick to point out the error. In trying to ensure religious equality as to solemnization, the Legislature had come to ensure it for registration also. It was his opinion, with which Lord Grey concurred, that if unauthorized marriages were the evil to be guarded against, it would be difficult to imagine provisions less likely to have any such effect. Wood took the same view of a similar South Australian Act of the following year, and drew a further distinction 'between allowing constituted authorities to continue a practice which they exercise under the authority of Ecclesiastical law, and consequently subject to control, and conferring a like privilege upon irresponsible persons, claiming to be officiating ministers, whose only necessary qualification is the recommendation of twenty householders'. In an attached note Merivale stressed the fact that the importance of the marriage law went further than the boundaries of individual colonies. 'With every desire to respect the independence of the colonial legislatures', he was firmly of the opinion that 'the law of marriage is really too important and almost too Imperial in its character to allow such enactments to pass without full examination'.[17]

[16] C.O. 323/49, New Brunswick; Stephen to Stanley, 31 Aug. 1833. Cf. Clarke, op. cit., p. 303; Clarke takes 1858 as the date by which the British Government had admitted the right of colonists to empower ministers of any sect to solemnize marriage.

[17] C.O. 323/75, South Australia; Wood to Merivale, 18 Apr. 1853; Minute by Merivale, 22 Apr.

Merivale was evidently of the opinion that, in the matter of marriage law, it would have been desirable to have one law universally applicable throughout the Empire. Failing this, the colonies might be sent a draft act and be encouraged to copy it. Lytton, the Colonial Secretary, disagreed. 'Private and domestic relations such as divorce, etc., should', he felt, 'be left as much as possible to the communities which had formed their own politics and know their own social grievances.'[18] This was too large a concession to be followed in practice. South Australia was unsuccessful in its bid to legalize the marriage of a man with his deceased wife's sister. This case, besides calling forth Rogers' lengthy exposition of the repugnancy doctrine, also caused him to defend the right of the Crown to intervene where necessary. 'I would submit', he wrote, 'that whatever be the technical powers of a colonial legislature and the received doctrine of "responsible government", the British Crown has not parted with the right and duty of interfering to protect its dependencies from ill advised legislation which affects the foundations either of Government or of Society.'[19]

This is not to say that deviations from the English model were not permitted at all. But they were generally of minor importance, or passed for a strictly limited period. In 1852 the Bay Islands produced a Marriage Act which included a provision enabling children born out of wedlock to be legitimized by the marriage of the parents within twelve months. The provision was 'open to the obvious objection that it is calculated to encourage concubinage by practically removing one of the chief penalties upon it'. Rogers, however, recommended that it should not be interfered with, as it was limited in its duration. Merivale agreed, but felt that there was no need, as Rogers had suggested, to inform the Governor that under no circumstances would sanction be given to its further extension. He pointed out in a marginal note that 'there is no reason to suppose that they intend to make the law perpetual, and unnecessary threats of opposition are apt to irritate.'[20] Similarly, no objection was raised to South Australia's

---

[18] C.O. 309/43, Barkly to Labouchere, 7 Dec. 1857; Minute by Merivale, 17 Feb. C.O. 42/613, Head to Labouchere, 14 May 1858; Minute by Lytton, 8 June.

[19] C.O. 323/87, South Australia; Rogers to Merivale, 5 May 1858.

[20] C.O. 323/72, Bay Islands; Rogers to Merivale, 7 Dec. 1852; Minute by Merivale.

action in making the condonation of adultery a bar to divorce within the discretion of the court, instead of, as in England, an absolute bar, as this was felt to be a deviation of only minor importance.[21]

In the following year, however, the same colony received rather less encouragement for its spirited attempt to

> . . . prick that annual blister,
> Marriage with deceased wife's sister.

This was, of course, a current political issue at home, upon which Gladstone for one had strong feelings. The Colonial Secretary, Newcastle, in common with other Anglo-Catholic Peelites, held decided views about the validity of the ecclesiastical law and the impropriety of parliamentary legalization of 'heresy'. Thus for the legislature of a colony to adopt a law of such an advanced character was to invite adverse criticism. A recent decision in the English courts in the case of *Brooke* v. *Brooke*[22] emphasized that such a marriage was at that time considered contrary to God's law, and could be considered valid only if it were valid in the country where it had taken place, and if that country were also the domicile of the couple. In the Duke of Newcastle's opinion, it was not clear 'that the judges would allow any force whatever to a law enacted in a British possession and permitting what was authoritatively declared by English laws to be *contra bonos mores*'. Persons married under the proposed South Australian law might well find themselves in an awkward situation if they returned to England, and it was felt that in this case a strict correspondence between English and colonial law must be maintained.[23]

Another area of the law in which a general uniformity throughout the Empire was clearly desirable—and was for a time pursued—was that to do with naturalization and the status of aliens. It must be admitted, however, that many of the objections to colonial laws on these subjects were based less on the desirability

---

[21] C.O. 13/99, MacDonnell to Lytton, 20 Jan. 1859; Minute by Merivale. For more details of Colonial Office policy on marriage and divorce legislature see Clarke, op. cit., pp. 302–7.

[22] It is not clear to which case this referred. The only case of *Brooke* v. *Brooke* to be decided at about this time had to do with maintenance payments to a separated wife; *English Reports*, vol. 53. 25 Beav. 342 (1858).

[23] C.O. 13/103, Newcastle to MacDonnell (draft dispatch), 7 Nov. 1860.

of uniformity, than on the inequity of the particular laws in question.

The concern felt by the home authorities about this subject was evidenced to some degree by the inclusion in almost all Royal Instructions of a clause requiring the reservation of any local law dealing with naturalization. The home officials found themselves faced with the task of striking a balance between acts which imposed too great disabilities on aliens, and those which were too liberal.

Instances of the former were few, though a Jamaican Act of 1838 which refused aliens entry without licence, authorized deportation on suspicion, and permitted aliens to be kept in custody until deported was disallowed outright, as being 'a statute far more inhospitable than any which prevails in this Kingdom or generally in any part of the civilized world'.[24] If this was generally accepted West Indian policy in the thirties, the situation had radically changed by the early 1850s when, as a consequence of the abolition of slavery, the need for labour to work the plantations had become pressing. Lord Grey suggested in a circular to the West Indian governors that immigrant labour might be attracted by the offer of a bounty and the chance of naturalization.[25]

This suggestion was taken up by the Legislature of the Bahamas in a way that neither the Secretary of State nor Governor Gregory had envisaged. An Act was passed in 1852 to enable subjects of friendly states to hold land for twenty-one years, with all the privileges of naturalized subjects except the right to vote or hold public office. Wood could find no legal objection to the Act which the Legislature were constitutionally entitled to pass. But on grounds of policy, it had little to recommend it. Its effect, thought Gregory, would be to encourage the introduction of republicans from the United States, who could be relied upon to stir up trouble, and expose the locals to the risk of 'imbibing a spirit of discontent with their own monarchical institutions'.[26] Colonial Office officials took an even stronger line: 'It seems to me', wrote one, 'that to give to aliens the privileges of British subjects without any

[24] C.O. 323/53, Jamaica; Stephen to Goderich, 12 Mar. 1838.
[25] C.O. 323/72, Bahamas; Wood to Merivale, 5 June 1852. Wood refers to Grey's circular in detail.
[26] C.O. 23/140, Bahamas; Gregory to Grey, 27 Mar. 1852.

obligations of allegiance is bad enough. But it is worse when these privileges are only to last twenty-one years, as it divests the recipients at once of any permanent interest in the welfare of the community of which they form a part. I think this (as far as the Bahamas are concerned) may be more serious than it at first seems'. The Colonial Secretary, Sir John Pakington, ordered the Act to be disallowed.[27]

This severity was not relaxed, at least in the early years, even in the case of the politically most advanced of the British colonies. When Canada sought, in 1842, to extend to all aliens who had completed seven years' residence and taken the necessary oaths the privileges of natural-born subjects, Stephen expressed grave doubts as to the right of the colonial legislature to enact such a statute.[28] Parliament had already expressly declared how foreign Protestants were to be naturalized on the North American continent, and in this case the Canadian authorities had established a law essentially different from the British Acts, and probably repugnant to them. In particular, the rights of naturalization were given absolutely, with no exclusion from public trusts and offices, an exclusion invariably contained in all English Bills of naturalization. The Act was disallowed.

One rather curious instance seems to demonstrate a change of attitude towards the powers of the Canadian Legislature. In 1845 the Colonial Office was required to decide upon a Canadian Bill for the quieting of title of naturalized persons. Despite the general terms of the title of the Bill, it was clear to everyone concerned that it was designed quite simply to settle a particular case— *Donegani* v. *Donegani*—on which there had already been several judicial decisions, and which was eventually to reach the Judicial Committee.[29] The Law Officers of the Crown were of the opinion that 'it would not only be unjust, but of mischievous consequence if, upon any notion of hardship in the particular case, the repeated solemn decisions of the legal tribunals of the country should be overturned by this species of legislation.'[30] Despite these cogent objections, and after a four years' delay, it was decided that the

[27] C.O. 323/72, Bahamas; Wood to Merivale, 5 June 1852; the initials on the attached Minute are unfortunately undecipherable; Minute by Sir J. Pakington, 11 June.
[28] C.O. 323/57, Canada; Stephen to Stanley, 10 Jan. 1842.
[29] 3 Knapp 63.
[30] C.O. 42/529, Canada; Law Officers to Stanley, 7 Aug. 1845.

wishes of the Canadian Legislature in the matter should not be interfered with, and the enactment should be acquiesced in, however reluctantly.[31]

The whole question of the state of the law regarding aliens was the subject of some correspondence between the Colonial Office and the Board of Trade in 1846. On 26 February Stephen wrote to Shaw Lefevre enclosing a memorandum setting out the state of the alien law throughout the colonies.[32] He drew the attention of the Board of Trade in particular to the lack of uniformity existing between different colonies, and pointed out that this uncertainty had been greatly increased by 7 & 8 Vict., c. 66 which, by expressly conferring on aliens rights which they had previously been supposed to possess by common law, had thrown doubt on the position of persons previously entitled to the privileges of naturalization. Stephen suggested the enactment of an imperial law to establish a uniform practice throughout the Empire. Their Lordships broadly agreed, singling out for special consideration the confused state of the law regarding the right to be owners and masters of British shipping. For the existing multiplicity of regulations, they suggested the substitution of an enactment giving to all colonial dependencies the power of admitting foreigners to the right of becoming masters and owners, without by so doing depriving such shipping of the privileges of British Registry.[33]

Whatever the value of the decisions arising out of this correspondence, the precedent set by the Canadian Act of 1849 (No. 519), that any alien was to have the same powers to take and transmit real estates as a natural-born subject, seems to have had more immediate impact. It was this precedent which persuaded the home authorities not to obstruct the passage of a Nevis Act of 1850 which conferred on aliens the right to hold and transmit every description of real property.

The legal powers of the colonial legislature were somewhat more clearly defined in the case of South Australia. That colony passed an Act to amend and consolidate the law regarding aliens—most of its provisions being taken from the previously mentioned Imperial Statute 7 & 8 Vict., c. 66. To this Act the colonial legislature had made a number of significant alterations—among

[31] C.O. 323/67, Canada; Rogers to Merivale, 2 Aug. 1849.
[32] C.O. 324/148, fol. 269, Stephen to Lefevre, 26 Feb. 1846.
[33] C.O. 323/231, fol. 39, Lefevre to Stephen, 3 Apr. 1846.

them the omission of the House of Hanover from the oath of allegiance, and the provision that naturalized aliens might become members of the Executive Council and Colonial Parliament after five years' residence. Governor MacDonnell had sent it home with a suspending clause, because he had been informed that it might, in theory, infringe upon the prerogative. He felt confident, however, that the Secretary of State would agree that it simplified existing arrangements for naturalization and afforded an additional guarantee against abuse.[34] In point of fact, there appeared to be little cause for concern. Rogers and Carnarvon were agreed that the Act was within the powers granted by 11 & 12 Vict., c. 83 which authorized the colonies to pass laws 'importing to any person or persons the privileges . . . of naturalization to be . . . enjoyed with the limits of any such colonies'.[35]

Uniformity of law within the Empire was, therefore, only encouraged in certain matters of personal status, and there was never any intention on the part of the British authorities to erect a common body of law for the Empire as a whole. Such a project would have been wholly unrealistic, and attempts to force uniformity on colonies of such differing origins as, say, the Cape and Lower Canada would certainly have failed if only, as Lord Stanley explained to Mr. Horsfall in 1858, on account of the opposition which would certainly arise within the colonies themselves.[36] The most that could be hoped for would be that legislation enacted since the colonies' inclusion in the Empire would conform to the English model.

There is scant evidence, however, of any expectation that colonial legislatures would, or should, follow this latter course. The main criterion was simply how might the interests of the Empire as a whole, or of the particular colony involved, be best served. On balance, the bias within the Office was against uniformity, and against the literal translation of English laws on to the colonial statute book, except in those few cases where uniformity was clearly desirable in order to avoid confusion, or where no obvious harm would ensue. Officials within the Office were always well aware of the material differences between their own country and the various colonial societies, differences which

[34] C.O. 13/97, South Australia; MacDonnell to Labouchere, 28 Jan. 1858.
[35] C.O. 323/87, Rogers to Labouchere, 27 Apr. 1858.
[36] *Hansard*, 3rd Ser., vol. 149, cols. 422–3, 19 Mar. 1858.

made any hoped-for certainty in adopting English laws a mere illusion. They were also aware, and becoming increasingly so, that a healthy, stable society is one which frames its laws to suit its own situation, without any slavish attachment to obsolete and irrelevant codes of law.

7

ROYAL INSTRUCTIONS AND
COLONIAL LAWS

THERE had always been in the eighteenth and nineteenth centuries a strong connection between Royal Instructions and the passing of colonial laws. A sizeable proportion of all such Instructions was taken up with commands to the Governor as to how he should deal with colonial laws, either prescribing a procedure or imposing certain restrictions on his power of assent. Thus in the Instructions the imperial authorities appeared to possess a powerful instrument of political control. Colonial governors could be, and were, instructed to refuse their assent to, or to reserve, bills on a wide variety of subjects.

The important point here, however, is the effect of these Instructions, and the attitudes adopted by the Colonial Office reviewers towards them. As with all laws which came before them, they had to consider two basic questions: was there any legal objection to a law which conflicted in some way with an Instruction? Did it conflict with avowed Colonial Office policy?

The question of the legal status of Royal Instructions (and therefore the legal validity of laws which conflicted with them) was raised in our period. As we shall see in a later chapter,[1] the judgement of Mr. Justice Boothby in the case of *McEllister* v. *Fenn* in South Australia in 1861 was based on the assumption that Instructions had the force of law, and that therefore a colonial act to which the Governor had given his assent against his Instructions was *ipso facto* invalid. As a direct result of this opinion, a clause was included in the Colonial Laws Validity Act which laid down in express terms that no colonial law, past or future, should be considered 'void or inoperative, by reason only of any Instructions with reference to such law or the subject thereof, which may have been given to the Governor by any Instrument other than the Letters Patent, or Instrument authorising such Governor . . . to

[1] Chapter 11.

assent to laws for the peace, order and good government' of the colony. After 1865, therefore, conflict with Royal Instructions could not invalidate a colonial law, unless the Instructions were contained in Letters Patent or the governor's Commission. As far as the provisions of the Instructions dealing with colonial laws were concerned, they could not, after 1865, be considered to have the force of law.

One recent commentator suggests that, as a general rule, Instructions *did* have the force of law, and that the Colonial Laws Validity Act constitutes a statutory exception to this rule.[2] It would follow from this view that, before 1865, conflict with Instructions would be on a par with conflict with an imperial statute, and that Boothby's interpretation of the law was correct. But it seems very doubtful if, in fact, Royal Instructions *did* have the force of law, even before 1865.[3] Certainly the officials most concerned, whether members of the Colonial Office or Crown Law Officers, wrote and acted as if the Instructions had no such legal status. Stephen indeed, in one of his more cynical moods, seemed to suggest at one point that the Instructions were worthless pieces of paper. When the question arose, in the early 1840s, of the possible revision of the Instructions, he argued strongly against it.[4] To be effective, he pointed out, revision would have to be total, since 'a partial correction would seem to imply that what was not corrected was to be taken as reasonably consonant with the meaning'. In any case the undertaking would only serve to arouse many dormant controversies. It would be best, on the whole, to keep the old forms unchanged, since the 'truth is that no one ever looks at them. A page from Robinson Crusoe would answer the purpose quite as well, if it had been but customary to employ it, for all this mass of paper really amounts to is this—"Be you Governor of Jamaica, and govern according to the law!"' Even if this particular outburst is not altogether characteristic of Stephen's real attitude towards the value of the Instructions, it is significant. It is difficult to reconcile the contemptuous nature of these remarks with the view that Royal Instructions had the force of law.

[2] Roberts-Wray, Sir K., *Commonwealth and Colonial Law* (London, 1966), pp. 146–9.

[3] For a fuller discussion of this point, see Swinfen, D. B., 'The Legal Status of Royal Instructions to Colonial Governors', *Juridical Review*, Apr. 1968.

[4] C.O. 380/21, Stephen to Hope, 18 Feb. 1842.

Certainly Stephen would never have agreed that colonial laws which conflicted with Instructions were, for that reason, invalid. In 1839, a New Brunswick Act was passed concerning the issuing of certain Treasury debentures. When the Governor drew the attention of the Colonial Office to the opinion of his Attorney-General that the Act was repugnant to a clause of the Instructions, and therefore null and void, Stephen stated emphatically: ' . . . with regard to the supposed invalidity of a law by reason of its repugnancy to a Royal Instruction, my conviction is so clear that this is an error, that I cannot affect to express myself doubtfully upon it.'[5]

Stephen here was writing in general terms, and was presumably considering the legal effect of only the most usual kind of Instructions—as issued to each governor at the time of his appointment, under the Royal Sign Manual and Signet. Where Instructions were issued, or obedience to them enforced, by other authority, some members of the Colonial Office were less sure of their ground. Two cases in point arose in 1850, one from Natal and one from New Zealand.

When the settlement of Natal had been first established, the ordinary powers of legislation over it had been given, by Letters Patent, to the Legislature of the Cape, and this body enacted that the Roman Dutch law in force there should also obtain in Natal. But by further Letters Patent of March 1847, a Legislative Council was set up for Natal with powers to make laws, subject to Royal Instructions. Among the provisions of these Instructions was included Article 28, whereby the Lieutenant-Governor was required to issue a Proclamation stating that the Crown had not interfered with or abrogated any native laws or customs except those repugnant to general principles of humanity. The issuing of this Proclamation, with the approval of Lord Grey, was delayed. But the Secretary of State recommended that steps should be taken to legalize the administration of native law as it had been carried out by the Political Agent, Mr. Shepstone; the Public Recorder, Mr. Cloete, had publicly denounced Mr. Shepstone's administration as unlawful. Accordingly, the Proclamation was now issued, and the present Ordinance passed.

This might have settled the matter, had it not been for the local Attorney-General who objected that any attempts to control native

[5] C.O. 323/54, New Brunswick; Stephen to Lord Normanby, 27 Dec. 1839.

law must conflict with the 28th Article of the Instructions set out above, these Instructions themselves having, so he argued, equal force in law with the Charter setting up the government of Natal. The only way out of the difficulty, he suggested, would be the special confirmation of the Ordinance by Order-in-Council.

Rogers accepted the Attorney-General's argument, and proposed that steps be taken to revoke the inconvenient clause in the Instructions.[6] Merivale and Grey concurred. Although this may well have been the course most likely to avoid confusion and argument in the future, it is doubtful if it was based upon a correct reading of the law. As has been argued elsewhere,[7] Royal Instructions in general did not have the force of law, one of the few possible exceptions being Instructions issued by the Crown for a 'conquered or ceded' colony, before the grant of a legislature, and the consequent abrogation by the Crown of its right to legislate. In this case, a legislature had been granted to Natal by the Letters Patent of March 1847.

Sir Frederic Rogers must have had this case in mind when he had to deal with a very similar example from New Zealand in the same year (1850).[8] Here the question had to do with the perennial problem of titles to land in the province of New Ulster. The granting of land titles in the early years of the New Zealand settlement had been carried on in such a disorganized and haphazard fashion that many Crown grants had been made of doubtful extent and validity. Consequently, it had been left to the Governor to settle land titles abitrarily, on the ground that in strict law the original grants were bad. Apart from the obvious legal objections to this practice, the position of the Crown had been further undermined by the decision in *Regina* v. *Taylor* by which the Crown had lost the power of dictating terms to the grantees. Characteristically, Governor Grey sought to settle the matter by means of a local ordinance, though even he feared that a reference to the Imperial Parliament might be necessary. Rogers felt the disadvantage of such a course very keenly, but raised an interesting objection to the Ordinance as it stood. If, he suggested, the 44th clause of the Instructions of 1840 were still in force, it might perhaps be held to invalidate any local ordinance which authorized

[6] C.O. 323/69, Natal; Rogers to Merivale, 25 Apr. 1850.
[7] Swinfen, D. B., op. cit., *passim.*
[8] C.O. 323/69, New Zealand; Rogers to Merivale, 7 June 1850.

the disposal of land otherwise than by sale at the prescribed price.
Some weight was added to this argument by the fact that under
New Zealand's Charter of 16 November 1840 and the Letters
Patent of 24 November 1840 it was declared that 'any Ordinance
repugnant to or inconsistent with the above Charter or Instructions should be absolutely null and void, to all intents and purposes'.[9] In this case, however, Rogers's opinion that the validity of
a colonial ordinance might be affected by the Instructions was not
upheld. T. F. Elliot had no hesitation in recommending that the
Ordinance be confirmed at once, without even waiting for a report
from the Law Officers.[10]

The most that one can say is that some doubts existed within the
Colonial Office itself as to whether Instructions referred to in
either Letters Patent or a similar instrument had legal force, and
that therefore colonial acts or ordinances which conflicted with
such Instructions were invalid. Certainly after 1865 this was not
the case. The 4th clause of the Colonial Laws Validity Act made
it quite clear that no colonial law was to be held invalid by reason
of any Instructions issued to the governor, even if these Instructions were referred to in Letters Patent or the governor's Commission.

Although the legal status of the Instructions was an issue
implicit in Boothby's argument in *McEllister* v. *Fenn*, the main
point upon which that argument rested was rather different from
the one discussed above. Here Boothby was contending that the
failure of Governor MacDonnell to adhere to the Instruction
requiring him to reserve certain classes of bills for the Royal
assent had the effect of invalidating the South Australian Real
Property Act of 1860. As we shall see in a later chapter,[11] neither
the Colonial Office nor the Crown Law Officers agreed with him,
and clause 4 of the 1865 Act put a final end to the discussion.

In general then, opinion within the Colonial Office appears to
have been that Instructions could not be considered as legally
binding, and that acts and ordinances which conflicted with them
should not for that reason be considered invalid.

Given this opinion, and Stephen's contemptuous reference to

[9] *P.P.* 1841 (311), p. 31.
[10] C.O. 323/67, New Zealand; Rogers to Merivale, 7 June 1850; Minute by
Elliot.
[11] Chapter 11.

the Instructions in 1840, it would not be very surprising to find
that little notice of any kind was taken of them by the reviewers.
As is well known, the form of the Instructions had, over the years,
become stereotyped. They changed very little either chronologically, as governor succeeded governor, or geographically, from
colony to colony. It frequently occurred that one governor was
issued with an exact copy of the Instructions given to his pre-
decessor, the name of the governor himself being the only alteration. Similarly, the difference between Instructions in one
colony and another were frequently of wording only. Instructions
to the governors of the various West Indian islands scarcely
differed at all. This characteristic sameness might in itself provide
an argument against their being taken too seriously. Just as
Stephen had argued against the revision of the Instructions in
1840, so Merivale, in 1854, disagreed with Mr. Booth of the Board
of Trade that a particular clause habitually included in the
Instructions should be amended. While he agreed that the new
clause would be a great improvement, he thought that it 'admits of
a question, how far the soundest policy is promoted by enforcing
it on colonial legislatures, and a new clause in the Instructions
would of course be considered as inserted in earnest, while an old
one is quietly ignored'.[12] Although a textual revision was under-
taken in the 1860s (the exact date differed from colony to colony),
it seems to have been carried out as part of a tidying up process,
and does not of itself reflect any new determination to bring the
Instructions up to date or make them easier to enforce.

This rigidity of the Instructions was no doubt a factor in making
it extremely difficult to force colonial governors to comply with
them. Since the early eighteenth century, attempts by the Home
Government to enforce adherence had been continually thwarted.
A Bill with this intention failed to get through the British Parliament in 1744. In 1752 a Board of Trade circular sent to all colonial
governors exhorted them 'to have a proper regard to the regulations contained in your instructions', but at the same time the
Board was obliged to concede that deviation would be permissible
'upon evident necessity, justified by the particular circumstances
of the case'.[13] What had been a problem throughout the eighteenth

---

[12] C.O. 323/242, J. Booth to Merivale, 25 Jan. 1854; C.O. 324/151, fol. 210,
Merivale to Booth, 8 Feb. 1854.
[13] Labarée, L. W., *Royal Government in America*, pp. 33–4.

century, remained one in the nineteenth; although some Instructions, like those to Governor Ross of the Leeward Islands,[14] contained penalty clauses, there is little evidence that these were ever invoked. Only one governor in our period was actually recalled for repeated disobedience to his Instructions—Robert Fitzroy of New Zealand (in 1845).[15]

Despite all this, when we come to examine the attitude of the Colonial Office to colonial acts connected with particular Instructions, the results are not entirely negative. Conformity with Instructions was occasionally insisted upon and even when it was not, this fact can tell us something about the details and general trends of official policy.

Most of the Instructional provisions dealing with the passing of laws fall into one of two categories: those which required the governor to follow a certain course of procedure, as when the governors of the West Indian islands were ordered to transmit by the first available boat copies of all acts passed in a session; and those which imposed some sort of restriction upon his assent to acts on certain specific subjects. In practice it is often difficult to distinguish between the two, as most restrictions took the form of requiring the governor to reserve, or to have a suspending clause inserted in, those acts which the home authorities wished to scrutinize before they were finally put into operation. There were, however, one or two clauses which fall unmistakably into the former category.

Nearly all Royal Instructions, particularly in the earlier part of the period, demanded a detailed explanation of the necessity for passing any particular act. Thus the Instructions to Governor Ross required that the copies of all the acts sent home should be accompanied by a report declaring whether the Act was to introduce a new law, declare a former law, or repeal an old law, and setting out the reasons for passing it, unless this information were readily available in the preamble.[16] It was understood further that the governor's dispatch should be based on, and be accompanied by, a report from the local Attorney-General. But this custom

[14] C.O. 381/1, fol. 251, Instructions to Ross, sec. 27, 15 Oct. 1825.

[15] Ward, J. M., *Empire in the Antipodes* (London, 1966), p. 60.

[16] e.g. C.O. 381/1, fol. 251, Instructions to Ross, sec. 28. Although some changes were made in Instructions to West Indian governors during our period, the Instructions to Ross can often be cited as a typical example of such Instructions.

rapidly fell into desuetude, if indeed it was ever fully adhered to. To begin with, this failure incurred annoyance and criticism on the part of the Colonial Office officials. Stephen objected strongly to an Antigua Act of 1844 to regulate the election of members of the House of Assembly, on the ground that the lack of any inform-ation about the previous situation made it impossible to deduce its effects. Lord Stanley agreed, and declared that, in the circum-stances, sanction was out of the question.[17] As late as 1854 Gairdner complained to Merivale that out of a number of ordin-ances transmitted from British Guiana four were unaccompanied by any report from the local Attorney-General.[18] But by the late fifties the attitude, especially towards the North American Colonies, had changed considerably. A collection of over 200 Canadian Acts sent home in 1858 was accompanied only by a letter from the Attorney-General to explain why the usual form of report had been discontinued. The previous practice, as Rogers reminded Merivale, had been that the governor 'should comment in separate despatches on any act which required the special con-sideration of the Secretary of State, and should transmit with the body of the acts a report from the Law Officers containing an analysis of each separate law'.[19] In the present instance the Attorney-General had simply entered a certificate vouching for the propriety of the Acts. In the large majority of cases the full requirements of the Instructions were, Rogers considered, 'quite useless'. He would be perfectly well satisfied with the new scheme, though it was possible that the manuscript summary served some purposes in the Colonial Office of which he was unaware. But on this point he was assured by Blackwood that it was 'scarcely ever referred to'.[20]

A procedural matter of this kind could scarcely be described as an issue of major importance, but the policy adopted towards it fits in very well with the general pattern. A similar attitude may be discerned towards another of these procedural provisions, whose intention *inter alia* was to maintain control over local finances. In the Instructions to the West Indian governors, a

[17] C.O. 323/59, Antigua; Stephen to Stanley, 18 Sept. 1844; Minute by Stanley.
[18] C.O. 323/70, British Guiana; Rogers to Merivale, 7 Dec. 1854; Minute by Gairdner.
[19] C.O. 323/87, Canada; Rogers to Merivale, 29 May 1858.
[20] Ibid., pencil note by Blackwood.

clause was retained till the late thirties which forbade them to allow any law for constituting a Court of Judicature, establishing the militia, or for imposing customs dues to continue for less than one year.[21] This Instruction was not adhered to, and Stephen felt obliged to call the attention of Sir George Murray to the 'great inconvenience of enacting laws containing peculiar and questionable provisions for so short a period as one year'.[22] If, as frequently happened, the act had expired before it reached Britain, the Government found itself reduced to the alternatives of 'aquiescing in enactments which may be highly objectionable, or of disallowing them at the expense of extreme inconvenience to the local government'. Stephen advised Murray that the Governor 'should be admonished of the necessity of watching, with particular vigilance, these annual enactments'. Otherwise such measures, from the shortness of their duration, would escape all revision whatever. Nevertheless, despite this opinion, by 1837 the direct prohibition against annual acts had been tempered to allow their enactment in certain circumstances, either to provide for some temporary emergency, or where it had 'hitherto been the custom to enact laws for the space of one year only'.[23]

Control over Private Acts [24] was relaxed in much the same way, although not until rather later in our period. Private Acts were generally required to contain a suspending clause, so that they could not come into operation until specially confirmed by the Crown.[25] The original object of the stipulation was no doubt to prevent government being carried on in the interest of private individuals. Yet by the late 1850s it was considered that not only was this rule obsolete, but positively undesirable. As Rogers noted and Merivale agreed, it was important that 'such Acts should not contain any such clause, as the consequent necessity of express confirmation by H.M. seems to impose a special responsibility on the Home Government in matters which it is impossible that the

---

[21] e.g. Instructions to Ross, sec. 14.

[22] C.O. 323/45, Bahamas; Stephen to Murray, 6 Dec. 1828.

[23] Ibid.

[24] A private Bill is 'a Bill to alter the law relating to some particular locality or to confer rights on or relieve from liability some particular person or body of persons'. Wade, E. C. S., and Bradley, A. W., *Wade and Phillips Constitutional Law*, 7th edn., (London, 1965), p. 146.

[25] e.g. C.O. 381/19, fol. 26, Instructions to Sir Benjamin D'Urban (British Guiana), sec. 16, 5 Mar. 1831.

Secretary of State can know anything, and therefore very undesirable that he should even seem to interfere.'[26] It was therefore decided that the clause should be removed from future acts of a private nature, and the Instructions amended.

Another important proviso contained in most Instructions was that which forbade 'tacking', i.e. the passing of acts which combined within themselves provisions on more than one subject or which set out to legislate on a subject other than that contained in the title.[27] The objections to this practice are self-evident. However, these objections appear to have been pressed only when the act in question was considered undesirable for other, political, reasons. For example, in 1829 Stephen brought about the disallowance of a Dominican Act to authorize the appointment of a Rector, because at the same time it authorized the Rector of St. Andrews to solemnize the marriage of slaves 'with the consent or approbation of the Owner or Employer', thus 'establishing a principle of the greatest importance upon a subject altogether remote from the avowed object of the Legislature'. Stephen's real objection was that, by implication, the Act denied to the slaves the right to be married without their owner's consent.[28] His indifference to the evils of tacking is clearly illustrated by his report in April 1840 upon an Act from St. Vincent for the regulation of markets, which also included three sections to do with fisheries.[29] In this instance he was content merely to note the fact, without any suggestion of disallowance. Criticisms of the practice were seldom pressed by his successors. The point was raised by Wood (a lawyer rather than an administrator) in 1852 and 1855, when two Acts, from Nova Scotia and New Brunswick respectively, sought to consolidate and amend a variety of existing statutes. But Merivale, very sensibly, pointed out that the rule had never been intended to apply to such cases.[30] If it had been, then no colony would be able to consolidate its laws. Even when, in 1856, a British Guiana Ordinance was passed to provide both for the registration of the population and for the payment of compensation

[26] C.O. 323/88, Bahamas; Rogers to Merivale, 16 Nov. 1859.
[27] e.g. C.O. 381/8, fol. 158, Western Australia; Instructions to Charles Fitzgerald, sec. 10, 7 Feb. 1848.
[28] C.O. 323/46, Dominica; Stephen to Murray, 14 Jan. 1829.
[29] C.O. 323/55, St. Vincent; Stephen to Russell, 11 Apr. 1840.
[30] C.O. 323/73, Nova Scotia; Wood to Merivale, 21 Feb. 1852; note by Merivale.

to persons whose property had been destroyed in recent riots, no serious objection was raised.[31]

All this should not be taken to suggest that conflict with Royal Instructions even in the later part of our period was never invoked as a justification for disallowance. One rule which was not dispensed with was that which forbade the re-enactment of a law which had previously been disallowed. This occurred on a number of occasions, notably in 1827 (St. Kitts),[32] and in April 1855 when the Legislature of Honduras tried to revive an Act, disallowed in the previous year, which required the Attorney-General to be a member of the English Bar, thus imposing a disability on Scottish, Irish, and colonial barristers.[33] The new Act indeed went further, in that applicants for the post must also have practised for at least three years in the English Courts of Common Law. There was no hesitation in deciding against the enactment. However, this attitude was not extended to the other, similar, Instruction, which required that no Act repealing one already allowed might be passed without a suspending clause. When the Governor of Dominica raised the point in 1825, and refused his assent to an Act reducing the salaries of Public Officers, his action was questioned by Stephen, who no doubt suspected the Governor of some partiality in the matter.[34] Although Stephen had to admit that, technically, the Governor was in the right, he pointed out also that 'during the twelve years that have elapsed since I first had the honour to report on the Acts of the Colonies, no other example has occurred on which this Instruction has been enforced, although in that period several hundred Acts have been passed to which the same objection might have been raised. In truth the rule itself, though always repeated in the Instructions, has been allowed for more than a century to fall into desuetude.'[35]

Something of the inflexibility which may be observed in the case of previously disallowed acts may be seen also in the attitude to acts regulating electoral qualifications, or imposing restrictions upon transient traders. The authorities were evidently concerned to retain a high degree of control over electoral legislation, even with colonies like Canada whose acts were usually treated with

[31] C.O. 323/81, British Guiana; Rogers to Merivale, 23 Dec. 1856.
[32] C.O. 323/44, St. Kitts; Stephen to Goderich, 18 Aug. 1828.
[33] C.O. 323/79, Honduras; Rogers to Merivale, 10 Apr. 1855.
[34] C.O. 323/43, Dominica; Stephen to Bathurst, 6 Jan. 1825.
[35] Ibid.

considerable latitude. The Instruction which required the insertion of a suspending clause in all such acts[36] seems almost invariably to have been insisted on, even where there was no other insuperable objection to the proposed law. One of the first reports which Stephen wrote as legal adviser to the Office was on this subject. In 1813 the Legislature of Grenada passed an Act setting out the qualifications for members of the Assembly. Although this Act did not alter the actual qualifications, it did dispense with the oath, which members had previously been required to take, that they were in fact possessed of the necessary property. Stephen pointed out that this Act conflicted with the clause in the Governor's Instruction which directed him not to give his assent to any act by which the qualifications of the electors or the elected in the Assemblies should be fixed or altered, 'or by which any regulation should be established with respect thereto, until the Draft of such intended Acts should have been transmitted for H.M.'s approbation'.[37] Although the ultimate fate of this particular Act is not clear, it would seem likely, in view of later practice, that it was not sanctioned. In 1832 a Bahamas Act to enable coloured freemen to vote for members of the Assembly was disallowed because it lacked a suspending clause, despite the fact that, as Stephen asserted, it made 'a decided advance towards a more liberal system than has hitherto prevailed in the Colony'. Lord Goderich refused to consider its sanction, and stated firmly that it was 'so important to insist upon this rule re. suspending clauses being adhered to, that I should most certainly disallow the law, even if it were more satisfactory'.[38] It was to be expected therefore that His Lordship would also have accepted Stephen's opinion on a similar unreserved law from Upper Canada, intended to augment the membership of the House of Assembly by giving an additional member to the counties of Lanark and Carlton. 'Your Lordship', Stephen submitted, 'will probably think it inexpedient to establish a precedent which may hereafter reduce the rule itself to entire insignificance.' His Lordship did.[39]

[36] e.g. C.O. 381/10, fol. 149, Bahamas; Instructions to Sir James Smyth, 15 Aug. 1829 (ch. 13).

[37] C.O. 323/39, Grenada; Stephen to Bathurst, 13 Nov. 1813.

[38] C.O. 323/48, Bahamas; Stephen to Goderich, 24 Nov. 1832; Minute by Goderich.

[39] C.O. 323/48, Upper Canada; Stephen to Goderich, 20 Nov. 1832; Minute by Goderich.

Stephen and Lord Goderich were also in accord over the vexed question of the imposition of discriminating duties by the West Indian islands on transient traders. Instructions to the West Indian governors almost invariably placed a restriction upon this class of enactment, while the West Indian Legislatures, undeterred, continued to pass numerous Acts on the subject. These Acts had two objectives: to raise much-needed cash, and to protect the trading interests of local merchants against competition from outside; the local justification for them being that the merchants affected, not being domiciled in the West Indies, enjoyed privileges which the native trader had to pay for. On the other hand, the Home Government repeatedly opposed this view, arguing that transient traders had to pay for facilities in their own countries, and it was unjust to require them to pay twice over. Stephen first raised a serious objection to an Act of this type in 1815, after the wars in Europe were over, though he admitted that there had been many previous examples, upon which he had refrained from commenting. The effect of this particular Act, from St. Vincent, was to impose a tax of £3 per cwt. on all goods sold in the island by any person not domiciled there—which amounted to laying a duty of that amount on all imports from Britain. If this were indeed the case, then, in assenting to it, the Governor had failed to comply with the 26th clause of his Instructions, which forbade him to assent to any law 'whereby duties shall be laid on the Shipping or upon the produce or manufacture of this Kingdom'.

There was a wider issue at stake here than that of mere disobedience to an Instruction. 'It appears also', wrote Stephen, 'to be subversive of the acknowledged rights of Parliament in regulating the general trade of the Empire, that a colonial legislature should exercise a power of imposing duties, without any ascertained limit of restriction, on goods exported from this country by British merchants.' 'That they have in these Acts violated the Royal Instruction', Stephen continued, 'can hardly, I apprehend, be disputed; nor does it seem to me less clear, that it is a usage inconsistent with the Rules by which the constitution of this country has limited the power of all subordinate legislatures: although it must be confessed that there is no subject of law on which exact information is more difficult to be found, than with respect to the conflicting rights of the various Legislative bodies comprehended within the general bounds of the Empire.'[40] Stephen's determination to uphold Britain's trading rights in the West Indies was as strong in the early 1830s as it had been in the years immediately following the Napoleonic Wars. A transient traders Act passed in Jamaica in 1831 was the occasion for a lengthy explanatory report from Stephen to Goderich, in which he pointed out that upon Lord Belmore's appointment to the governorship of Jamaica, 'a clause was introduced into his Instructions for the express purpose of preventing his assent being given to any Act of this description. That instruction however seems to have been disregarded. It is therefore objected to this Act, first that the principle on which it proceeds has been repeatedly condemned by H.M.G.; secondly that Lord Belmore's assent to it was given in contradiction to H.M.'s express command; and thirdly that it is a matter of great moment that all Governors should understand that commands of that nature are not a mere form, but are advisedly intended as the rule for their guidance in the discharge of the duty committed to them.'[41]

It could, of course, be argued that this was something of a special case, in that this was a new Instruction which might be expected to command more obedience than an old, obsolete one. Although this provision occurs again in later Instructions to West Indian governors,[42] the Colonial Office did not continue to insist upon adherence to it, swayed no doubt by the increasing financial difficulties of the plantations. When Jamaica again sought, in 1844, to impose a duty of 10 per cent on goods imported by any transient trader, G. W. Hope, the Parliamentary Under-Secretary, came out in opposition to Stephen's legalistic view, and suggested that 'the necessities and difficulties of the West Indian colonies are now such that the less we interfere with their own mode of raising their own revenue, I think will be the better.'[43]

The lack of any very important examples of objections after Stephen's period of office is suggestive. As we have seen, his successor as Permanent Under-Secretary, Herman Merivale, expressed doubts in 1854 as to whether it was useful or advisable to enforce even the soundest policy upon the colonial legislatures by

[40] C.O. 323/40, St. Vincent; Stephen to Bathurst, 26 June 1815.
[41] C.O. 323/48, Jamaica; Stephen to Goderich, 22 Oct. 1831.
[42] e.g. C.O. 381/11, fol. 306, Bahamas; Instructions to William Rawson, 10 Nov. 1864 (cl. 4).
[43] C.O. 323/59, Jamaica; Stephen to Stanley, 28 June 1844; Minute by Hope.

this means. There had been a few occasions when compliance with Instructions had been insisted upon irrespective of the merits of the act in question. These were exceptional, and the truth was that the Instruction was a useful weapon to hold in reserve. It could provide a technical justification for disallowance of an objectionable act when the home authorities felt reluctant to be too explicit as to their real grounds for disapproval. As Wood remarked on a Barbados Act of 1850, 'the departure from the Royal Instructions would be a sufficient reason for disallowing the Act, if that were a desirable object.'[44] But the Instruction was no more than an instrument of policy, and despite Mr. Justice Boothby's assertion that Royal Instructions had, in some sense, the force of law, informed opinion within the Colonial Office was against him.

[44] C.O. 323/68, Barbados; Wood to Merivale, 7 Mar. 1850.

Part III

IMPERIAL POLICY AND COLONIAL LAWS

8

IMPERIAL AFFAIRS AND
LOCAL AUTONOMY

In dealing with Colonial Office attitudes to rules of procedure or rules of law, we are treading on relatively safe ground. A rule can generally be defined within reasonably precise limits: it is a comparatively simple matter to place the rule against the official action and read off the results. But in dealing with attitudes to laws affecting colonial policies or interests, the case is wholly different. To take policies topic by topic would be meaningless—one cannot equate, for example, the attitude to colonial discriminatory tariffs with the attitude to, say, the extension of a local railway line. Some kind of categorization is necessary.

One obvious distinction to draw would be between laws affecting 'imperial interests' and laws of purely local significance. This is not a historian's abstraction; contemporaries themselves thought in those terms. But one soon comes to suspect that contemporaries were no clearer than we are as to what this distinction really meant. Not only was it extremely difficult to determine, at any particular time, where the dividing line should be drawn, but it was also necessary to take into account both changes in policy over a period and the different stages of political growth of individual colonies.

The question was, of course, particularly relevant to the novel status of 'responsible government' colonies. Lord Durham, in his famous Report, insisted that 'imperial affairs' with regard to these colonies ought still to remain under the control of the Imperial Government. Within this category he included 'the constitution of the form of government; the regulation of foreign relations, and of trade with the mother country, the other British colonies, and foreign nations; and the disposal of public lands'.[1] It is a matter of history that within a generation, imperial control over these matters had been either abandoned or severely curtailed.[2]

[1] Lord Durham, *Report on Affairs in British North America* (3 vols., Oxford, 1912), II. 282.
[2] In Canada, of course, imperial control over public lands was abandoned *before* the introduction of 'responsible government'.

There was one classic example in our period of an attempt to give legislative sanction to some such division. In the early 1850s the Legislatures of New South Wales and Victoria proposed the inclusion in their Constitution Acts of a provision empowering the Governor to give a final assent to laws affecting local matters—only Acts touching imperial interests should be subject to reservation or disallowance.[3] Among the Colonial Reformers, Adderley in particular spoke strongly in favour of the principle. 'It was a monstrous thing', he told the House of Commons in June 1855, 'that British subjects should thus be subject to two sovereigns.'[4] But within the Colonial Office the move did not meet with the same approval. T. F. Elliot, a senior official, denounced the 'efforts of the politicians to reduce almost to a nullity the ties with the mother country';[5] while Sir Frederic Rogers described the clauses as a 'Legislative Declaration of Independence', the result of successive Secretaries of State currying favour with the Australian colonies.[6] Possibly Elliot and Rogers exaggerated the seriousness of the affair. Three years later Herman Merivale adverted to it in a minute to Lord Carnarvon, in which he noted that, in the discussions of a few years back, 'it was pretty generally felt and admitted that it would be better, and really conduce to the maintenance of colonial union, if this power [of disallowing acts of purely local significance] could be legally abolished'. As Merivale saw it, 'the attempt was only abandoned on account of the insuperable difficulty of distinguishing between Imperial and domestic questions.'[7]

The truth was that any attempt to fit colonial laws into the two categories of 'imperial affairs' on the one hand and 'local affairs' on the other could only be made on an empirical basis. This fact enhances rather than diminishes the value of these concepts to the historian. If it could be shown, for example, that certain types of colonial legislation tend to move, through time, from one category to another, this trend could prove a valuable indication of changing attitudes to colonial policy.

[3] Burt, A. L., *The Evolution of the British Empire and Commonwealth*, p. 383.

[4] *Hansard*, 3rd Ser., vol. 138, col. 1758, 21 June 1855.

[5] C.O. 309/25, Hotham to Newcastle, 26 June 1857; Minute by Elliot.

[6] Marindin, G. E., (ed.), *The Letters of Lord Blachford*, p. 157, Rogers to Church, 15 Sept. 1854.

[7] C.O. 323/87, New Brunswick; Rogers to Merivale, 23 Sept. 1858; Minute by Merivale to Carnarvon.

Before we can attempt this, however, we must be clear as to what the two categories mean, and whether they are sufficient to cover between them all colonial laws raising non-legal issues.

It would seem to be fair comment to say that, when contemporaries such as Lord Durham or Gibbon Wakefield spoke of 'imperial affairs', what they really meant was matters in which Britain had a material or political interest. This is certainly true of the particular topics of which Durham spoke, and it is probably true also of others, such as imperial defence. But this definition, if adopted, by no means covers all cases in which the Office felt obliged to intervene. In between this category, and that of local affairs, falls a third—those colonial laws which raised questions not of material interest but of moral obligation.[8]

A. IMPERIAL AFFAIRS

Durham's first 'imperial affair' was the 'constitution of the form of government'. In the context of Canada, with its close proximity to the republican United States, the stipulation was understandable. While Durham was, of course, primarily interested in imperial relations with 'responsible government' colonies, this and his other reservations were even more applicable to colonies at an earlier stage of political maturity. What was to be denied to Canada could hardly be granted to the British West Indies.

It is certainly true that imperial authority over colonial constitutions was maintained in our period, in that imperial acts were passed granting constitutions to the newer colonies.[9] Repeated demands from Cape Colony for a constitution embodying representative institutions were consistently refused by the Colonial Office until 1854, despite the recommendation made by the Commissioners of Enquiry into the Administration of the Cape in 1826 that a legislative assembly should be set up as soon as circumstances allowed.[10] In 1865–6, after the Governor Eyre incident and a discussion lasting many years as to the suitability of even

[8] See Chapters 9 and 10.
[9] e.g. 15 & 16 Vict., c. 72, granting a quasi-federal constitution to New Zealand.
[10] P.P., H.C. 1826–7, XXI (282), pp. 18–19. For an explanation of the Colonial Office attitude see McCracken, J. L., *The Cape Parliament 1854–1910* (Oxford, 1967), pp. 7–9.

representative institutions in the British West Indies, the constitutions of Jamaica, Dominica, Antigua, St. Kitts and Nevis were voluntarily abandoned by the local legislatures, and replaced through Order-in-Council by Crown Colony government.[11]

There are, however, few examples of conflict between the Colonial Office and colonial legislatures over constitution acts enacted by the legislatures themselves. The explanation for this is simple enough—that such acts were passed under the authority of a specific imperial statute, and any likely difficulties were generally ironed out during prior consultation. One obvious exception is that already mentioned above, when certain of the Australasian colonies tried to introduce into their Constitution Acts the provision differentiating between 'local' and 'imperial' affairs. Yet by 1861 the Duke of Newcastle, as Secretary of State, was prepared to take a much more liberal view of the powers of colonial legislature to alter its own constitution. In response to a request from the Governor of South Australia that he be given an Instruction requiring him to reserve or disallow all local acts intended to alter the Constitution Act, Newcastle was unsympathetic. Constitution Acts, in his view, were no more than 'Colonial Laws . . . making provision for matters in which the colonists are exclusively interested' and 'alterable by the usual method of legislation'.[12] This was indeed the doctrine contained in Clause 5 of the Colonial Laws Validity Act, though it should be understood that the clause referred only to colonies with representative institutions. 'Every Representative Legislature', the clause declared, 'shall . . . have and be deemed at all times to have had, full power to make laws respecting the constitution, powers, and procedure of such legislature', provided that the proper forms were observed.

On the subordinate matter of the electoral system, official attitudes were similar to those noted above, and a reasonably clear distinction was made between the politically more advanced colonies of white settlement and the plantation colonies of British Guiana and the West Indies.

With regard to the colonies in British North America, even before the idea of 'responsible government' was ever considered,

[11] On the unsuitability of representative institutions in the West Indies see Henry Taylor's penetrating memorandum of 19 Jan. 1839, P.R.O. 30/48/7, Cardwell Papers.

[12] C.O. 13/102, Newcastle to MacDonnell, 26 Jan. 1861.

the Colonial Office had come to recognize the futility of risking an open conflict in defence of its control over the colonies' electoral structure. As early as 1832 Stephen strongly advised Lord Goderich against interfering with a Lower Canadian Act providing for the vacating of seats in the House of Assembly. Recent events there, he considered, 'have so completely demonstrated the independence of the House of Assembly of His Majesty, that it may perhaps have become a reasonable doubt whether the few and insignificant means which the executive government retains of exercising any species of control over the Members of that House are worth maintaining at the expense of a controversy'.[13] In the case of the North American colonies, the surrender of control in this sphere had evidently gone so far before the alteration in their political status that no change in attitude could be expected in the later years. When Blunt, in July 1848, suggested that the defects in a New Brunswick Act to provide for the election of representatives to the Assembly should at least be pointed out to the colony, Lord Grey emphatically disagreed. It should be confirmed, he instructed, without any remark.[14]

In these cases, it was evidently believed that nothing was to be gained and much could be lost by taking a firmer stand. This was by no means always true with regard to the other colonies. Quite a different attitude was taken when the Legislature of British Guiana sought to alter the existing political structure and introduce 'free institutions', by doing away with the Governor's veto and raising the number of elective members in the Court of Policy to seven. The elective section of the local legislature was at that time dominated by the property owners, who numbered rather less than one per cent of the total population. Rogers realized that, in demanding these changes, the colonists 'desire not so much a *bona fide* representative government, which the nature of the population renders evidently impossible, as the diminution of the influence of the Crown'.[15] In these circumstances the proposal could not be sanctioned. The Colonial Office was constantly on guard to prevent such situations as these where the property interest tried to increase its power by legislative means, at the

[13] C.O. 323/48, Lower Canada; Stephen to Goderich, 27 Apr. 1832.
[14] C.O. 323/64, New Brunswick; Wood to Merivale, 5 July 1854; Minute by Blunt and Grey.
[15] C.O. 323/72, British Guiana; Rogers to Merivale, 13 Aug. 1852.

expense of either the Crown or the underprivileged. This tendency was particularly obvious in the West Indian plantations, where the planter legislatures, after the abolition of slavery, tried either to restore the *status quo ante* by reviving, under new guise, the disabilities 'formerly incident to national origin and colour', or to strengthen their position against the approaching emancipation of the labourers by lowering the property qualification for voting. In both instances, the Secretary of State was persuaded to refuse assent.[16]

Though both these colonial acts might appear at first glance to be legitimate attempts to broaden the base of government in the colonies, it was perfectly clear to the home authorities that this was not their real intention. Ever since Henry Taylor's brilliant analysis of West Indian politics in 1839, it had been accepted by the Office that the racial divisions and extremes of wealth, influence, and education inseparable from the plantation system had made the successful operation of representative institutions there virtually impossible. It was therefore essential that any such attempts to lessen the influence of the Crown be resisted, in the interests especially of the unrepresented and victimized classes.

Attacks upon the prerogative powers of the Crown were frequent and varied. Perhaps the most extreme form adopted by such encroachments were attempts to wrest from the Crown the power to control sessions of the local assemblies. A Tobago Act of 1825 which provided for the calling together of the Assembly 'twice at least in each year' was felt to merit outright disallowance, in that it would deprive the King of the power of convening the Assembly only when he thought fit and thus leave the Assembly largely independent of Crown control.[17] Three years later the Jamaican Legislature employed a subtler approach by trying to retain certain powers for the members of the Assembly beyond the date of its dissolution. Included in an Act appointing Commissioners for Public Buildings was a provision whereby the Members of the dissolved House would continue to exercise the power of superintending public buildings and barracks.[18] It is

[16] C.O. 323/51, Grenada; Stephen to Glenelg, 3 Aug. 1835.
    C.O. 323/53, St. Vincent; Stephen to Glenelg, 18 Apr. 1838.
[17] C.O. 323/43, Tobago; Stephen to Bathurst, 17 Sept. 1825.
[18] C.O. 323/45, Jamaica; Stephen to Huskisson, 25 Jan. 1828.

possible that the legislators had overlooked the implications of this provision, but Stephen did not make the same mistake. However insignificant the point at issue, in this and other cases, he was convinced that 'it can never be unimportant to maintain the established lines of demarcation between the prerogatives of the Crown and the powers of the local legislatures'.[19]

The exact position of these 'lines of demarcation' was generally interpreted by Stephen in terms favourable to royal authority. Indeed at times his indignation at the presumption of a colonial legislature seemed quite out of proportion to the seriousness of their action. Thus he vehemently attacked a St. Lucia Act introducing trial by jury which included a clause declaring that the Act was not to take effect until 'confirmed by Her Majesty with the advice of Her Privy Council'. This was surely an excusable defect, yet he denounced it as 'an encroachment teeming with other encroachments'. 'The legislature of that colony have no right to prescribe to their Sovereign what advice she must take in assenting to any Acts of theirs.'[20]

This outburst may simply have been a fit of bureaucratic petulance. Stephen was in poor health at the time and on the point of retiring from the Office. There were certainly many more serious encroachments on the powers of the Crown than this. Among these were attempts to undermine the control of the Crown over the local militia, and in 1826 Lord Bathurst gave orders for the unfortunate Lieutenant-Governor of Tobago to be censured for assenting to an Act which would make officers in the local militia removable only by court martial, thus establishing a military force on the island virtually independent of the Crown.[21] Huskisson took much the same line in 1828 when the Dominican Legislature tried to remove from the Governor power to proclaim martial law, except with the consent of a Council of War, composed of members from the Council and Assembly.[22]

The one aspect of the prerogative which appears to have suffered the most frequent attacks was that of patronage. The power to appoint certain public officers, especially judges, was

[19] C.O. 323/47, Stephen to Murray, 16 May 1830.
[20] C.O. 323/62, St. Lucia; Rogers to Stephen, 17 Sept. 1847; Minute by Stephen.
[21] C.O. 323/43, Tobago; Stephen to Bathurst, 8 Dec. 1826.
[22] C.O. 323/45, Dominica; Stephen to Huskisson, 31 May 1828; Minute by Huskisson.

clearly important for the preservation of royal authority. Characteristically, Stephen refused to agree that the Jamaican Legislature
had the power to invest the Bishop with ecclesiastical jurisdiction,[23]
and even objected to an Act from Tobago which vested the
appointment of the Public Treasurer in the Governor instead of
the King.[24] Admittedly, he did disagree with Rogers' objection to
an Act from Ceylon which determined the rank and precedence
of the Bishop of Colombo, but only because, as he pointed out,
the local legislature had been empowered to alter the regulations
dealing with precedence by the Letters Patent of June 1844.[25]

Later Secretaries of State do not seem to have shared Stephen's
attitude to this aspect of the prerogative. There was the important
case in 1849 of Governor Mathew whose original Commission of
June 1844 had not empowered him to act as Ordinary (although
his predecessors had been thus empowered). He had, however,
continued to do so, and the consequent illegality of his acts had
called forth a local Act to legalize them by vesting him in the
office. Rogers felt obliged to report to Elliot that, in his opinion,
'this disposition, even in favour of the Queen's representative, is
an infringement of the Crown's Prerogative, in as much as the
Office belongs to the Crown as Head of the Church.' Lord Grey
made no attempt to deny this, but evidently believed that, in the
circumstances, there could be no good reason to withhold confirmation.[26]

Direct encroachments of this kind on the power of appointment
were less common than the subtler approach through the power
of the purse. Where a colonial legislature had the right to vote
money for the salaries of public officers, it could, and frequently
did, wield effective control over the selection of persons to fill these
offices by limiting the grant specifically to certain named persons,
instead of to the office itself.

In passing an Act to provide a salary for the Rev. Thomas
Browne, the Legislature of St. Vincent openly admitted that it was
intended to give them an effective vote on appointments by the
executive government. The colonists excused their action by
declaring that 'gentlemen have not infrequently been selected to

[23] C.O. 323/49, Jamaica; Stephen to Goderich, 14 Mar. 1833.
[24] C.O. 323/51, Tobago; Stephen to Glenelg, 2 Oct. 1835.
[25] C.O. 323/61, Ceylon; Rogers to Grey, 24 Sept. 1846; Minute by Stephen.
[26] C.O. 323/66, Bahamas; Rogers to Elliot, 13 Oct. 1849; Minute by Lord
Grey.

fill offices of a high and important nature in the colonies, who have not possessed the qualifications suited for performing the duties of such offices'.[27]

Stanley decided to confirm the Act with no more than a mild protest against the principle involved. Perhaps he sensed the justice of the colonists' claim; more likely he was well aware of the practical weakness of the Colonial Office position. For when Stephen had reported on two similar St. Vincent Acts six months before, he had made it clear that there was no point in refusing such provision as was to be had for the maintenance of the clergy, just because it was not to be had on the most advantageous terms.[28] The contest between the executive and the Home Government on the one hand and the Assembly on the other continued throughout the period, but with little perceptible gain by either side. Sir William Colebrooke in Tobago did succeed in upholding his objections to an Act granting salaries to the Colonial Secretary and Provost Marshal by name, but this was promptly replaced by another which was to remain in force only during the continuance in office of the present incumbents. Merivale and Blunt could do very little but concur in Rogers' objection to the Act that it unduly controlled the Executive in the selection of candidates for public employment, and suggest that Sir William be sent a copy of Rogers' report. As the Governor was well aware of these arguments and agreed with them, this recommendation cannot have been expected to produce any worthwhile results.[29]

If it was considered important to preserve the royal prerogative and the authority of the Crown in general, then equally it might seem to be desirable to protect the power and position of the governor, as the representative of the Crown in the colonies. But in so far as most colonial acts affecting the governor had to do with finance (except those encroaching upon his powers over the militia noted above) there was often little that the Colonial Office could do to override the wishes of the local legislature. It is true that to begin with the attempts of the local legislature to control the governor's salary were firmly resisted. 'The pecuniary independence of the governor upon the Assembly', Stephen thought,

[27] C.O. 323/57, St. Vincent; Stephen to Stanley, 4 Oct. 1842.
[28] C.O. 323/57, St. Vincent; Stephen to Stanley, 28 Feb. 1842.
[29] C.O. 323/22, Tobago; Rogers to Merivale, 1 July 1852; Minutes by Merivale and Blunt.

'is so essential to the proper conduct of his administration that an innovation entirely destructive of that independence ought . . . to be guarded with peculiar jealousy.'[30] In this connection it is particularly interesting to compare this opinion, put forward in 1828 and referring to the status of the governor of one of the West Indian islands, with that of the officials in 1855 upon an Act from Newfoundland. Newfoundland, by this time, had come to be allowed a great deal of freedom in managing her own affairs. In 1855 the local legislature enacted that the salary of the governor should be reduced from £3,000 to £2,000 at the next appointment. The Governor himself and the Home Government opposed the Act as unjust and impolitic. The Governor pointed out that although he could scarcely refuse his assent, no governor would be able over six years to recover even the cost of his outfit. It would be very difficult, Ball told Merivale, to find a well-qualified governor prepared to accept such meagre terms. Yet neither he nor Merivale could see any way out of the difficulty. 'Even in the case of the Governor's salary,' Ball wrote, 'I should not be disposed to engage in a conflict with the local legislature.' The only consolation was that this was a question 'in which the interest of the Imperial Government is very trifling compared to that of the colony' and might therefore best be decided by 'the matured opinion of the Local Legislature'.[31]

This was not the only way in which the colonial legislatures sought to control the executive, or to avoid its interference. A favourite approach was to enable money to be paid out of the Public Treasury, either in salaries or in grants to public institutions, without the governor's warrant. Stephen was successful in 1826[32] and 1840[33] in having two such enactments rejected, but in the latter case, a Barbados Act to provide for the care of lunatics, there were other cogent reasons why it should not have been confirmed. But from 1842 onwards, if not before, there appears to have been reluctance to enter into conflict with any of the colonial legislatures over the issue. The Home Government officials had begun to recognize the futility, and worse, of such a course. 'As often as we enter into a financial controversy with any one of these

[30] C.O. 323/45, Grenada; Stephen to Murray, 31 Dec. 1828.
[31] C.O. 323/78, Newfoundland; Rogers to Merivale, 4 Oct. 1855; Minutes by Ball (Parliamentary Under-Secretary) and Merivale.
[32] C.O. 323/44, St. Kitts; Stephen to Bathurst, 5 Apr. 1826.
[33] C.O. 323/55, Barbados; Stephen to Russell, 28 Aug. 1840.

colonies', Stephen remarked ruefully, 'so often, or nearly so, it happens that the ground taken against them is abandoned, and that objectionable practices acquire new strength by this show of ineffectual resistance to them.' 'In truth', he concluded, 'these questions are less important in reality than in appearance.' The real strength of the executive government, in St. Vincent at least, lay in its position as arbiter between the rival racial factions.[34] By this time the accumulation of precedents had become so formidable that official disapproval of any further such enactments was confined to allowing them to come into operation without any formal notice being taken of them.

It seems clear then, that with a few exceptions, the Colonial Office was anxious to maintain the authority of the Imperial Government in the colonies, by safeguarding control over their constitutions and electoral systems and by preserving the powers of the representatives of the Crown against legislative encroachments. The exceptions were to be found in the politically more advanced colonies of white settlement; if they were to be found elsewhere, it was as a result of the difficulty of controverting the wishes of a well-entrenched legislature on matters which were not fundamental to the exercise of imperial authority.

If this is indeed an accurate statement of the case, then some convincing explanation for it must be found. Given the current demand at home for economy and disengagement, the logic of Free Trade, and, in the colonies, an obvious desire for further extensions of local autonomy, it is not immediately clear why their claims should be resisted. A full analysis of contemporary thinking on this matter is beyond the scope of the present study, but there are two probable explanations for this attitude. In the first place, it was necessary to avoid having responsibility without power—especially if the misuse of power by the locals might require imperial intervention. Secondly, it was evidently assumed that the continued exercise of imperial authority in the colonies could serve some useful purpose—either to safeguard imperial interests, or to benefit the colonies themselves.

There were relatively few areas of legislation in which the colonial legislatures might have damaged the interests either of the Empire as a whole or of Britain in particular. But one of these— the defence of Britain's control over imperial trade—was not only

[34] C.O. 323/57, St Vincent; Stephen to Stanley, 5 Jan, 1842.

mentioned by Durham in 1839 but was crucial to continued existence of the imperial system.

The British Empire has always been an empire of trade. Whatever qualifications may be made to this statement, the fact remains that the existence, nature, and structure of the British imperial system have always had a close connection with the requirements of Britain's economy. The British in the seventeenth and eighteenth centuries, gripped tight in the strait-jacket of bullionist mercantilism, took it for granted that the colonies existed simply in order to benefit the mother country by supplying her with raw materials, accepting her products, and encouraging her mercantile marine. James I's tirade against the growing use and importation of tobacco from Virginia was only partly a moral outburst; it also displayed his annoyance that fertile colonial land should be put to such unproductive use. Political control over the colonies, if never so inflexible as that exerted by Spain, was nevertheless used in an attempt to shape the colonial economies. The political, as well as economic, importance of such control was well understood by colonial governors. Lord Cornbury, Governor of New York, wrote to the Board of Trade in 1705 to draw attention to the manufacture of woollens and serge in Connecticut and Long Island. 'Now if they begin to make serge, they will in time make course [sic] cloth, and then fine . . . how far will this be for the service of England, I submit to better judgements; but . . . I declare my opinion to be that all these Colloneys, which are but twigs of the main Tree, ought to be kept entirely dependent on and subservient to England, and that can never be if they are suffered to goe on in the notions they have, that as they are Englishmen, soe they may set up the same manufactures here as people say doe in England.'[35] Colonial governors in the 1760s were instructed to report upon the growth of manufacturers in their colonies and to discourage any which might compete with industries at home. But of course the main instruments of economic control remained the Acts of Trade and the Navigation Acts.

The tentative move towards Free Trade principles after the Napoleonic Wars initiated the gradual erosion of the old mercantilist structure. The Ghent Treaty of 1814 and Huskisson's con-

---

[35] Lord Cornbury to Secretary Hedges, quoted in O'Callaghan, E. B. (ed.), *Documents Relating to the Colonial History of New York*, 4 vols. (Albany, 1850–1), IV. 115.

cessions of 1822 and 1825 began the process of opening up British colonial trade to the world (though Huskisson himself was not a Free Trader and insisted upon maintaining Imperial Preference). By the end of our period the main bulwarks of mercantilism in Britain, the Navigation Acts, Corn Laws, West Indian sugar duties, and Canadian timber preferences had all disappeared. For most of this period, however, it remained open to question whether 'Free Trade' meant the freedom of the colonies to regulate their own trade.

Decision-making in a government department, in the Colonial Office or elsewhere, is frequently governed more by pressure than by principle. The breach with the American colonies in the previous century provided a salutary example of the effects of putting policies, accepted by long usage, into reverse. Thus Stephen, commenting unfavourably upon a Barbados Act imposing additional duties on imports of sugar products—an Act which he thought conflicted with the general law of the Empire—felt bound to draw attention to the long list of similar acts from other colonies assented to in the past. 'That the legislature of the United Kingdom possesses a general superintending authority over the whole trade of the Empire', he wrote in 1814, 'is too clear to be questioned. That this superintendence is the prerogative of the Imperial Parliament solely and exclusively, I should have thought equally clear, if the long continued usage of which I have above quoted many examples did not seem to furnish an exception. From these examples I think it appears that the Colonial legislatures have been for a great number of years entrusted with the power of regulating, by the imposition of duties, the trade in Colonial produce amongst themselves.'[36]

However, it has been argued that the adoption of Free Trade principles at home involved not the relaxation, but the strengthening, of metropolitan authority over the commercial policy of the Empire.[37] As Secretary of State, Lord Grey evidently believed that when Parliament adopted Free Trade it did not abdicate the duty and the power of regulating the commercial policy not only of Britain, but of the Empire. 'The common interests of all parts of the Empire require that its commercial policy should be the same

[36] C.O. 323/40, Barbados; Stephen to Bathurst, 8 July 1814.
[37] See Allin, C. D., *Australasian Preferential Tariffs and Imperial Free Trade*. (Minnesota, 1929), p. 35.

throughout its numerous dependencies, nor is this less important than before, because her policy is now directed to the removal, instead of as formerly to the maintenance of artificial restrictions on trade.'[38] These views were reflected in contemporary attitudes to colonial customs acts. In 1828 Stephen reported unfavourably upon a Nova Scotia Revenue Act which granted a drawback, in certain cases, of the duty on imported spirits, because, as he had frequently pointed out before, if such drawbacks were to be allowed in the colonies by acts of the Local Assembly, 'Parliament is virtually deprived of the regulation of Colonial Trade'. The granting of such concessions ought, he considered, to have been forbidden by the British statute; for 'without such a regulation the whole of the elaborate system devised by Parliament for free warehousing Ports in the Colonies, is nugatory'.[39]

With regard to those colonies which had not yet achieved responsible government, the powers of tariff regulation here defended were frequently exercised. As a typical example we might take the disallowance of a St. Kitt's Act of 1830 which imposed a duty of 6s. 9d. per ton on every vessel exporting Island produce, to provide for the salaries of Customs officers; the argument against it being that its effect would be to place the burden of supporting these officers upon British shipping.[40]

This was a comparatively minor objection. The real problem arose over the attitude to be adopted towards colonies which insisted either upon imposing differential duties discriminating against imports of British manufactures or upon imposing tariffs not for revenue purposes, but to protect native industries. On the former point, Stephen for one entertained no doubt. Acts passed on this principle, he considered, offended against the whole conception of the economic empire, and his superiors evidently agreed.[41]

The two points together were at the root of the long-drawn-out controversy after 1846 between the Colonial Office and Canada,

[38] Earl Grey, *The Colonial Policy of Lord John Russell's Administration*, 2 vols. (London, 1853), I. 281.

[39] C.O. 323/45, Nova Scotia; Stephen to Murray, 29 Nov. 1828; Murray ordered disallowance. Of course at this time tariff reform was directed not towards Free Trade as such, but towards the substitution of imperial preference for imperial monopoly.

[40] C.O. 323/48, St. Kitts; Stephen to Goderich, 20 Apr. 1831.

[41] e.g. C.O. 323/50, New Brunswick; Stephen to Stanley, 30 Dec. 1834; and C.O. 323/52, Nevis; Stephen to Glenelg, 26 Mar. 1836.

over the latter's right to manage her own affairs. At no time was it in dispute that the Canadian Government was perfectly free to impose tariffs in order to raise revenue. Lord Grey in 1848 readily acknowledged 'the propriety of leaving to the colonists the task of raising the revenue which they may require by such methods of taxation as may appear to them most expedient', and in considering the Tariff Act No. 479 of 1847 he disclaimed any wish to interfere for the sake of protecting the exclusive interest of British manufacturers.[42] But if it were true, as it appeared to be, that some of the 1847 duties had been imposed not to raise revenue but to protect the Canadian manufacturer, he felt obliged to state his government's opinion that 'such a course is injurious alike to the interests of the mother country and to those of the colony'. Although he would not go so far as to advise disallowance, he did feel that a careful revision of the tariff list was required.

It is interesting to compare this relatively tranquil incident with the furore which broke out a decade later over the customs tariff of 1859. The differences between the two Acts were of degree only (duties on wood, iron, and tin, for example, were raised to 25 per cent). Merivale was convinced that the introduction of differential provisions—'the only reason thought sufficient for interference with the Customs Acts of a colony like Canada'—did not in this case arise.[43] That the matter was not allowed to end here must be explained as being due to the aggressiveness of the Canadian Finance Minister, Galt, the tactlessness of the Board of Trade, and the ineptitude of the Colonial Office officials in accepting, with insufficient scrutiny, the complaints of the Sheffield Chamber of Commerce[44] and the Board of Trade's report.[45] The essence of the complaints of these two bodies was first, that the new tariff introduced differential and discriminatory duties, and second, that it tended to the protection of native manufacturers, which would depend so strongly upon the maintenance of that protection as to prevent any subsequent lowering of the tariff. The Duke of Newcastle in November 1859 transmitted to Governor Head the Board of Trade's report without comment.[46] But he had already

---

[42] C.O. 43/149, Grey to Elgin, 31 Mar. 1848.
[43] C.O. 42/617, Head to Lytton, 26 Mar. 1859; Minute by Merivale to Carnarvon, 12 Apr.
[44] C.O. 43/152, Newcastle to Head, 13 Aug. 1859.
[45] C.O. 42/622, Head to Newcastle, 11 Apr. 1860; Enclosure; Memorandum by A. T. Galt.   [46] C.O. 43/152, Newcastle to Head, 5 Nov. 1859.

made his own attitude plain in August.[47] Although he would probably feel obliged to advise the Queen to assent to the Act, he agreed with the Chamber of Commerce that 'practically, this heavy duty operates differentially in favour of the U.S.', and he felt obliged to warn Head of 'the injurious effect of the protective system, and the advantage of low duties upon manufactures, both as regards trade and revenue'.

The transmission of these views to Canada brought an immediate response from Galt. While unable to agree that the intention of the Customs Act was either to impose differential duties or to protect emergent industries, he did not feel that the latter object was necessarily undesirable. These arguments aside, he was prepared to carry the dispute to a higher constitutional plane: '. . . The government of Canada', he declared, 'acting for its legislature and people cannot, through those feelings of deference which they owe to the Imperial authorities, in any manner waive or diminish the right of the people of Canada to decide for themselves both as to the mode and extent to which taxation shall be imposed . . . . Self government would be utterly annihilated if the views of the Imperial Government were to be preferred to those of the people of Canada.'[48]

D. C. Masters has warned us against exaggerating the importance of this incident in bringing about the recognition by the Home Government of Canada's right to fiscal autonomy.[49] Its significance, he feels, was as a preliminary to the more decisive battle over the establishment of a customs union and the assimilation of tariffs among the provinces of British North America. Certainly it is true that Galt's arguments in the tariff battle had done nothing to change the attitude of the Board of Trade. But the members of the Colonial Office had learnt their lesson. Galt's attack on the memorial of the Sheffield Chamber of Commerce had caused Merivale to study the manufacturers' complaint once more, with the comment that 'when the memorial . . . is attentively read, . . . it will be seen that the whole complaint is general and vague, and has no reference in reality to the present Custom Act

[47] C.O. 43/152, Newcastle to Head, 13 Aug. 1859.

[48] C.O. 42/618, Head to Newcastle, 11 Nov. 1859; Enclosure; Memorandum by A. T. Galt.

[49] D. C. Masters, 'A. T. Galt and Canadian Fiscal Autonomy', *Can. Hist. Rev.* 15 (1934) *passim*.

at all, except as a continuation of former policy.'[50] The Secretary
of State appended a grudging admission that if he had been misled
by the Sheffield Chamber, he intended to tell them so. Thus when
Galt renewed the offensive against imperial control in his proposals for the customs union, all the senior officials in the Office
took care to be more circumspect. T. F. Elliot in particular
indulged in a caustic criticism of the Board of Trade's pedantic
and irrelevant speculations upon the nature of Free Trade. He
agreed that Galt's conception of Free Trade—the absence of all
tariff barriers—did not accord with that of His Majesty's Government, which he defined as being the opposite of protection. But
the question now before the Office was, he felt, one to be decided
not by abstract theorizing but by active statesmanship. 'The
Government of Canada has taken a step in advance to get rid of
the nuisance of internal Customs Houses, and even to procure if
possible an identity of tariffs in British North America. We all
know quite well—the Board of Trade as well as we do—that this
is an object which every enlightened Government must desire to
effect.'[51] Elliot's letter to Booth, of 23 March 1861, was both a
repudiation of the Board of Trade's view of the subject and an
admission that, even though the free interchange of produce
between the provinces might confer a 'character of discrimination
upon their customs duties on similar articles imported from foreign
countries', the Colonial Office did not feel prepared to interfere.

Neither in this case, nor in that of the 1859 tariff, was the Office
disposed to satisfy Galt's demand for a thorough exposition of the
views of the Imperial Government on the whole question of
tariffs and the constitutional relationship between the colonies and
Britain. In practice perhaps this did not greatly matter. The fact
remained that the views of the Canadian authorities on fiscal
autonomy had prevailed, and the Home Government had lost
control over Canadian tariffs.

In view of Durham's expressed desire to maintain control over
imperial trade and thus protect Britain's commercial interests, it
may seem surprising that he was not equally concerned to retain
control over imperial defence. The reason for this neglect possibly

[50] C.O. 42/618, Head to Newcastle, 11 Nov. 1859; Minute by Merivale to
Fortescue, 1 Dec.; Minute by Newcastle.
[51] C.O. 42/626, Sir F. Williams to Newcastle, no. 2, 2 Jan. 1801; attached
memorandum by Elliot.

lies in the fact that few contemporaries thought in terms of an overall imperial strategy, and allowed the purely military aspects of colonial defence to be submerged under demands for economy in government spending. Matters were further complicated after 1854 by the separation of the War Department from the Colonial Office.

Indeed it is not at all clear just what were the long-term plans on this subject on the part of the imperial authorities. One historian has suggested that current opinion in Britain favoured the view that 'self-government begets self defence', and that once a colony had received representative institutions, it should adopt responsibility for its own defence, both on grounds of economy and as a necessary part of political maturity.[52] But the adoption of such responsibility seems to have involved only the responsibility of paying for British garrisons, not the responsibility of controlling the colony's own defence. Of course many colonies welcomed the continued existence of British military garrisons, which not only defended them but also served the interests of colonial retailers.

British policy of reducing garrisons and increasing contributions from the colonies towards their own defence was largely successful in North America and the West Indies. Recognition of the threat to the Empire from Russia during the 1850s produced a rush of acts from Nova Scotia to New South Wales reorganizing the existing militia and increasing the size of volunteer forces.[53] Where trouble arose was mainly in the Cape and New Zealand, both colonies that had formidable problems of internal defence, and in the Australian colonies, which were evidently dissatisfied with the arrangements for maritime defence. What these colonies wanted was to be able to control a small naval force of their own, under local commanders with authority to operate outside colonial territorial waters. Acts passed with this object in view by New South Wales in 1857[54] and Victoria in 1860[55] were disallowed, ostensibly on legal grounds as being *ultra vires*. The Law Officers, when consulted, suggested that the only solution to the colonial problem would be for local vessels to be commanded by officers with commissions from the Crown, and the whole force would

[52] Tunstall, E. B., *Imperial Defence* (*C.H.B.E.*, vol. II), p. 817.
[53] e.g. the Canadian Militia Act of 1855, C.O. 42/598.
[54] C.O. 323/82, New South Wales; Wood to Ball, 15 Apr. 1857.
[55] C.O. 309/51, Barkly to Newcastle, 11 June 1860; Minute by Cox, 16 June.

have to act as part of the Royal Navy.[56] This was a lawyer's solution, and was not welcomed by the Admiralty if it was likely to involve the permanent detachment of part of the Navy to colonial waters, even if supported by colonial contributions. Their alternative suggestion was for a colonial force commanded by officers commissioned by the Queen, but manned and paid for locally, with its task restricted to coastal and harbour protection.[57] To T. F. Elliot in the Colonial Office this was no solution at all; such a force would be as 'helpless as unnatural', though Rogers was less critical.[58] No further move was made for some years, since the readiness of the permanent officials to accept the creation of a colonial navy as a necessary corollary to growing colonial independence was not shared by Newcastle. Something more nearly approaching a solution was eventually achieved by Edward Cardwell, when he hit upon the idea of extending the 1859 Royal Navy Reserve Act to the colonies by the Colonial Naval Act of 1865. Henceforward the colonial naval forces would remain local in peacetime, but in time of war would pass under the control of the Admiralty.

It is difficult, therefore, to draw any very clear conclusions about a subject in which so many interests and departments of government were involved. If any consistent policy was followed, it was that of Earl Grey, who insisted that the colonies should pay for everything beyond their quota of imperial troops. Although the building up of local volunteer forces was permitted in the mid-fifties, it was only towards the end of our period that any substantial relaxation was permitted in the matter of the colonies' control over their own defences.

It is of course understandable that on matters so closely connected with British interests as imperial trade and imperial defence, the authorities at home should be reluctant to make premature concessions. Where the interests involved were less influential and where the colonial governments were in a much stronger position, Colonial Office attitudes were naturally rather different. A good case in point is Durham's last 'imperial affair'—the disposal of public land—where the Colonial Office was ultimately forced to

---

[56] C.O. 309/53, Admiralty to Colonial Office, 25 Dec. 1860; Enclosure; Harding and others to Somerset, 4 Dec. 1860.
[57] C.O. 309/53, Admiralty to Colonial Office, 26 Dec. 1860.
[58] Ibid., Minutes by Elliot and Rogers.

recognize what Wakefield had understood before 1840: that control over land revenues must inevitably lead to control over the lands themselves.[59]

In the case of the less advanced colonies, the Office was very unwilling to allow any diminution of the rights of the Crown over public lands. Stephen objected to Russell in 1839 that the Antigua Legislature, in vesting in certain trustees a portion of land for building a Presbyterian church, was assuming the power to grant away public lands—a power which properly belonged to the Crown. The Act, he suggested, should be repealed and re-enacted in a more satisfactory form.[60] The same principle of the maintenance of the law respecting the rights of the Crown in this matter was behind the Duke of Newcastle's dispatch to the Governor of Sierra Leone in 1861,[61] in which the latter was informed that the Queen's assent would not be given to any more ordinances giving more time to the Crown grantees to register their claims. But there were times when the colony was too small, and the point at issue too insignificant, for serious objections to be maintained. It was decided, in effect, to treat the defects in the Honduras Land Titles Act of 1859 as a matter 'of local concern, which may properly be left to the decision of the local legislature'.[62]

The real problems of land disposal, however, arose mainly among the settlement colonies. Here the issues tended to be more pressing, the colonists more demanding, and the difficulties more complex. In the earlier years of our period there was little doubt that land disposal must remain in the hands of the central government. Although Stephen's objections to a New Brunswick Act of 1840 granting tracts of land to the North American Colonial Association were not upheld to the point of disallowance, nevertheless, the Lieutenant-Governor was forbidden in future to give his assent to similar acts without previous reference to the Queen.[63] In the same year the Governor of the united Canadas soon found that the imperial Act [64] which gave him power to dispose of a portion of the Clergy Reserves was not to be stretched beyond

[59] Wakefield, E. G., *The Art of Colonisation*, p. 438.

[60] C.O. 323/54, Antigua; Stephen to Russell, 21 Nov. 1839.

[61] C.O. 323/90, Sierra Leone; Murdoch to Rogers, 20 Dec. 1860; Draft dispatch no. 156, Newcastle to the Governor of Sierra Leone, 14 Jan. 1861.

[62] C.O. 323/88, Honduras; Rogers to Merivale, 2 June 1859.

[63] C.O. 323/55, New Brunswick; Stephen to Russell, 13 May 1840; Minute by Russell.   [64] 7 & 8 Geo. IV, c. 62.

strict limits. In the opinion of the Law Officers Dodson and Wilde, an act for the disposal of all the reserves, with the proceeds to be invested as the Governor and Council might direct, would be ineffective without a further Act of the Imperial Parliament.[65]

By the late fifties and early sixties, however, the officials had begun to dance to a very different tune. For Canada the 1840 Act of Union, by exchanging territorial as well as other revenues in return for a permanent Civil List, had, in effect, handed over also all control over the disposal of the lands themselves. In the case of Australia there was little positive interference in the matter after the Land Sales Act of 1842. Although the officials might continue to disapprove of the way in which the colonial legislatures dealt with the land, they were seldom disposed to force their opinions upon the colonists. Murdoch and Rogers, writing to Merivale in 1858, strongly criticized a Tasmanian scheme for the free grant of unsettled waste land on the island.[66] Designed to promote new settlement in the colony, the Act provided for the free grant of lots of between 50 and 640 acres. Applicants were to be bound by certain conditions, principally that they must be in possession of capital to the value of £1 for each acre applied for and that they would undertake to remain on the lot for at least five years, during which period they must bring at least one tenth of it under cultivation. Murdoch and Rogers objected that the Act 'resembles very closely the schemes which have been tried with signal failure in other of the British Colonies', and pointed in particular to the lack of provision for the introduction of labourers. Nevertheless, the matter, in their opinion, was one of local concern, and they could suggest no reason why it should not be confirmed.[67] Similar objections, Murdoch felt, might also be raised against the Victorian Land Act of 1865; but nevertheless, as its enactment was clearly within the competence of the Legislature and had been 'the result of long and deliberate consideration on their part', the Secretary of State, he suggested, would probably not feel able to interfere.[68]

One exception to the general rule of non-interference on the public land issue must be noted. The land question in New Zealand had had a complex and confused history ever since the first white

[65] C.O. 42/473, Dodson and Wilde to Russell, 16 Mar. 1840.
[66] C.O. 386/77, fol. 95, Tasmania; Murdoch and Rogers to Merivale, 12 June 1858.   [67] Ibid.   [68] C.O. 386/80, Victoria; Murdoch to Rogers, 2 Aug. 1865.

settlements. The machinations of the New Zealand Company and the problem of protecting native interests had greatly added to the difficulties in the way of equitable administration. The solution favoured by the General Assembly was to delegate their powers to deal with Crown Lands under the Constitution Act to the Provincial Councils. Acts passed to achieve this object in 1856, 1858,[69] and 1864[70] were disallowed with monotonous regularity. Objections were partly political, in that it was considered unsafe to entrust power over native lands to a provincial legislature not directly accountable to the Home Government, and partly legalistic, in that such delegation was beyond the competence of the General Assembly. At the same time it was admitted that the Assembly itself was perfectly capable of making its own regulations for the land disposal.

With this exception, the public land question had virtually ceased to be an issue of imperial concern once a colony had achieved responsible status (and in Canada it had ceased to be of imperial concern even before the colony achieved this status). Of all the 'imperial interests' so far considered, this was the first to have imperial control over it almost wholly abandoned. In view of the long-standing policy on land and emigration supported by Grey, Durham, and others, this was a major surrender on the part of the British Government.

From this survey of attitudes to imperial affairs in the period one or two tentative conclusions may be drawn.

In the first place, we would clearly not be justified in seeing British colonial policy towards laws affecting imperial interests as homogeneous. The degree of control insisted upon, over any one issue, varied markedly—depending upon the degree of political maturity of the colonies concerned, as well as upon particular circumstances. However, while some distinction obviously existed between colonies which had been granted 'responsible' government and the remaining colonies, there was not always a clear dividing line. Attitudes to Canadian legislation, for example, were always comparatively mild even before the 1840s, when responsible government was introduced there by Lord Elgin, on the instructions of Earl Grey.

There was also a second dimension—the time factor. It is

[69] C.O. 386/74, fol. 292, New Zealand; Murdoch to Merivale, 31 Dec. 1858.
[70] C.O. 386/75, fol. 32, New Zealand; Murdoch to Rogers, 7 May 1864.

perfectly clear in all the imperial issues so far considered that a definite relaxation of control over them can be discerned as the period progresses. There were probably several reasons which explain this development. For one thing, the granting of some measure of independence and autonomy to the colonies had a snowballing effect—the more power over their own affairs that was granted to the colonies, the more they came to expect. The decline of the mercantilist structure of empire and the development of informal trade connections outside the formal empire must have had some effect upon the original determination to retain close control over colonial tariff policies. There was undoubtedly a growing feeling in the Office that the more advanced colonies could only develop along sound lines if they were allowed to make their own mistakes. And at the back of all attitudes towards colonial autonomy there was a growing recognition of a practical fact of life: that Britain simply did not have the power to enforce her will in the face of stubborn colonial resistance, without involving herself in commitments which would be out of proportion to the importance of the issues; the only probable effect would be to embitter imperial relationships.

B. LOCAL AFFAIRS

Herman Merivale, writing to Lord Carnarvon in 1858, pointed out that although 'in colonies having responsible government, the power of disallowance is most important to preserve Imperial interests', nevertheless, 'all colonial statesmen have agreed that in merely domestic matters it should be reduced as nearly as possible'.[71] If we substitute for the phrase 'colonies having responsible government' 'colonies of white settlement', then this statement of policy becomes generally true for the whole of our period. At the same time, interference in the local affairs of the other less advanced colonies was relatively more prevalent.

We are, of course, faced once again with the problems of definition. One's view of what constituted a 'local affair' must depend a good deal on whether one looks at the affair as a colonist or as a member of the Colonial Office—most of the cases cited in the previous section would have been considered in a later age to be

[71] C.O. 323/87, New Brunswick; Rogers to Merivale, 23 Sept. 1858; Merivale to Carnarvon.

matters of exclusively local concern. It is of course also true that the vast majority of acts dealing with local affairs were not reported on at all, but allowed to come into operation without remark. We must therefore base our conclusions upon only those acts which were generally agreed to be primarily of local concern, and those which were, for one reason or another, reported on by the legal adviser.

Taken chronologically, the first major concessions to local determination are to be found in reports on acts from the North American Provinces. This was to be expected as the English-speaking population had been derived largely from the American Loyalist camp, and had already, in 1791, been granted considerable constitutional privileges, partly as a reward for their loyalty and partly because, as Americans, they had been used to a representative constitution. On almost all domestic questions the wishes of the colonists, however injudicious, were generally respected. Only a few of the wealth of examples available need be cited. For instance, objections to an Upper Canadian Act of 1828 to provide for the easier recovery of estrays were not pressed, as not being sufficient cause for the disallowance of a provincial law.[72] The Lower Canadian Registry of Deeds Act, though contrary to the recommendations of the 1828 Canada Committee, was not interfered with, 'as this is wholly a matter of internal regulation and local interest'.[73] The political crisis of the thirties caused the officials to be more than usually circumspect. 'In the present aspect of affairs in British North America', wrote Stephen in 1836, 'it would require the most clear and cogent motives to justify the disallowance of any Act which has come into operation in the province of New Brunswick.'[74]

Stephen for one was very well aware of the futility of entering into a 'contest with either of the Canadian Legislatures upon any question which is exclusively of local concern. In any such controversy, their success may be postponed for a little while, but it is ultimately certain. The principle of leaving to the Canadas the regulation of their own local interests must, I conceive, be fully followed out in all its consequences, as the only basis on which the connection between the two countries can now be maintained.'[75]

[72] C.O. 323/45, Upper Canada; Stephen to Huskisson, 19 May 1828.
[73] C.O. 323/47, Lower Canada; Stephen to Murray, 21 Apr. 1830.
[74] C.O. 323/52, New Brunswick; Stephen to Glenelg, 20 Dec. 1836.
[75] C.O. 323/52, Upper Canada; Stephen to Glenelg, 4 Aug. 1837.

As the newer settlement colonies increased in political maturity, so this policy became extended to them also. Murdoch and Wood, writing to Merivale in 1851, expressed grave doubts about a New South Wales Act which would have authorized the building of a tram road from some coal-bearing land belonging to a Dr. Mitchell to the docks at Newcastle, passing through land belonging to the Australian Coal Company. The latter protested, with a good deal of justification, that the powers of the Legislature were here being used for the benefit of a single individual; yet the reviewers suggested that since these objections had been deliberately over-ruled by the Colonial Legislature, supported by the judgement of the Governor and the Law Officers, it was probably not a case in which Lord Grey might think it fit to intervene.[76]

Sometimes objections to injudicious enactments were felt to be so strong that intervention was seriously contemplated. When New South Wales proposed, in 1853, to authorize substantial government assistance to the Sydney Railway Company, which had already got into serious financial difficulties, T. F. Elliot was constrained to wonder whether 'the objections to it are so strong that it should be deemed to form one of those rare cases in which a Veto should be exercised from home'. In the end he suggested that the Act be referred to the Treasury, as being of questionable policy but on a subject which the Duke of Newcastle did not consider suitable for interference.[77]

As a final example, there was the case of the Tasmanian Act to amend the constitution of the Legislative Council. This Act raised a storm of protest in the colony, mainly because the pro-vision that no judge might hold a seat in the Council was felt to be directed against the popular Mr. Justice Horne. Nevertheless, the Duke of Newcastle saw no reason to disagree with Rogers's opinion that on this point the Tasmanian Legislature was the best judge.[78]

Instances of direct interference in the local affairs of the advanced colonies were thus relatively rare, and took place only when some vital principle of justice appeared to be endangered. This was felt to be the case in 1844, when the Canadian Legislature

[76] C.O. 386/69, fol. 150, New South Wales; Murdoch and Wood to Merivale, 23 June 1851.

[77] C.O. 323/75, New South Wales; Rogers to Merivale, 5 Aug. 1853; Minute by Elliot. The Duke of Newcastle concurred.

[78] C.O. 323/90, Tasmania; Rogers to Merivale, 4 Jan, 1860.

sent home a bill for the discouragement of secret societies. Stephen was in no doubt as to the proper course. 'Whatever else may be conceded to the Parliament of Canada,' he warned Lord Stanley, 'concession must of course stop when they ask that the Queen should be advised to participate in the enactment of a law, of which any class of H.M.'s subjects would be entitled to complain, as a violation of their constitutional rights and privileges.' Lord Stanley evidently agreed, and disallowance followed.[79]

On the other hand, less compunction was felt in demanding alterations in the local acts of the less advanced colonies. Of the acts disallowed each year from the colonies as a whole, the majority had been enacted by this class of colony. As we have seen already, this was particularly true in the case of acts from the plantation colonies to do with the status and treatment of slaves, ex-slaves, and immigrant labour. In these instances, the adoption of a strict line could be justified as the maintenance of imperial policy towards the abolition of slavery and the establishment of the apprenticeship scheme, or as the protection of an unrepresented class against victimization and gross injustice. But there were also examples of disallowance upon lesser grounds, where the most serious charge which could be levelled against the local legislature was that of injudicious or impolitic behaviour. In 1826 Lord Bathurst ordered the disallowance of an Act from Lower Canada (which was not, at this time, granted the same licence as its neighbour) because the Act, in incorporating a Fire Insurance Company, committed to the Company itself the entire regulation of its constitution. This scarcely seems to have been a point of great moment, but one which, at a later date, might well have been left to the local legislature to correct on their own account; however, at the time, Stephen inveighed against it, as being 'repugnant to all the maxims of policy by which H.M.G. and Parliament are habitually guided'.[80]

An interesting example of the contrast in attitude towards the more and the less advanced colonies is provided by the decisions on two Acts to do with estrays, the one from Upper Canada, the other from Bermuda. It has been mentioned earlier that in 1828 (i.e. long before 'responsible government' was even thought of in government circles) Stephen quashed objections to an Upper

[79] C.O. 323/59, Canada; Stephen to Stanley, 20 Mar. 1844.
[80] C.O. 323/43, Lower Canada; Stephen to Bathurst, 1 Dec. 1826.

Canadian Act for the recovery of estrays. It had been provided by this Act that persons taking into their charge any stray cattle were to give a description to the Town Clerk, and if no one came forward to claim the strays within six months, they were to be sold. The local Attorney-General had considered that the time limit was too short and that more positive steps should be taken to inform the owner, but his objections had been overruled. The Bermudan Act on the same subject was passed over thirty years later, yet the view taken of it was more, not less, stringent. Admittedly, the provisions of the Act were rather more drastic, in that they authorized the killing of any animal 'permitted to run at large and to do damage' after a warning had been given, this warning to be valid for two months. At the same time, the inconvenience which the Act set out to remedy was also more extreme. However, although this Act was not disallowed, Merivale thoroughly agreed with Rogers that, until amendments were made, it could not be sanctioned.[81]

If, to these few examples, there is added the large number of disallowances during our period of acts from the plantation colonies, directly or indirectly, for the regulation of labour, the general impression gained is that interference in the local affairs of the less advanced colonies was comparatively frequent. This is true, but only up to a point. As our period wore on, a gradual change in attitude towards these colonies also evolved, corresponding in direction, if not in degree, with the lifting of restrictions on acts from the other dependencies. There were numerous occasions when the Secretary of State and his subordinates refrained from imposing their own ideas upon the local legislatures in deference to local opinion. When St. Lucia, in 1851 proposed to substitute an export tax for the *corvée* to provide for the upkeep of roads, Grey made it quite clear that, while he would have preferred a land tax to an export duty for the purpose, he did not intend to press his objections in the face of local feeling.[82] Sir Frederic Rogers, suggesting that a British Guiana Ordinance to regulate the sale of fresh meat would prove troublesome and ineffectual, was satisfied that 'the matter is probably one which

---

[81] C.O. 323/89, Bermuda; Rogers to Merivale, 17 Nov. 1859; Minute by Merivale.

[82] C.O. 323/72, St. Lucia; Wood to Merivale, 27 Aug. 1851; Minute by Lord Grey.

the Duke of Newcastle will leave to be settled by the Colonial Authorities'.[83]

Even where a colonial legislature had adopted a course of action which could only end in disaster, Colonial Office officials confined themselves to giving fatherly advice. In 1856 the Virgin Islands Legislature passed an Ordinance to reduce the current rate of interest to 5 per cent—much below the general colonial rate—an action which Rogers believed would 'put an end almost entirely to the lending of money in the Virgin Islands'. Henry Taylor suggested that the Governor should be advised that 'in this country, the practice of regulating . . . the rate of interest by legislative acts has been long regarded as useless and pernicious, and is so regarded not only by scientific men and writers, but also by practical men.' But beyond this Taylor was not prepared to go. If the Legislature persisted in wishing to have such a law in operation, they should be told that 'H.M. Government will not oppose their wishes, simply on the ground that the question is one of internal economy, in which no principle of justice or public morality is involved but merely a question of policy or expediency.'[84]

Not for the first time, Taylor had put his finger on the vital principle. As the nineteenth century progressed, interference in local colonial affairs, never conspicuous in the case of the white settlement colonies, became increasingly rare. The Colonial Office might occasionally advise against particularly impolitic acts, but provided that such acts did not affect imperial interests or rules of law, and were not manifestly unjust to individuals or classes, there could be no reason to interfere with the proper exercise of its powers by a colonial legislature. On the contrary there was every reason not to interfere unnecessarily. In the first place, such action would only provoke a conflict likely to embitter imperial relations. Secondly, the Colonial Office was well aware of the value of being allowed to make one's own mistakes. Only through experience and a progressive grant of local autonomy could the various colonial dependencies hope to achieve maturity and stability.

[83] C.O. 323/73, British Guiana; Rogers to Merivale, 17 Aug. 1853.
[84] C.O. 323/81, Virgin Islands; Rogers to Merivale, 13 Aug. 1856; Minute by Henry Taylor.

9

TRUSTEESHIP I—HUMANITARIANISM

WHILE the number of 'imperial affairs' covered by colonial laws in our period was diminishing, they by no means included all topics in which the Colonial Office took a positive interest. Henry Taylor's remark, that the Government would not oppose the wishes of the colonists in a particular case because no principle of justice or public morality was involved,[1] implied that the Government might feel obliged to intervene when such principles *were* involved. The members of the Colonial Office evidently believed that they had a function beyond that of protecting British or imperial interests. Humanitarian influences in British politics were as strong or stronger than they had ever been; and several of the senior officials and ministers, like Stephen and Glenelg, were not so much influenced by the humanitarian movement, as part of it. This fact tended to infuse Office policy towards partisan colonial legislation with a paternalism which too often conflicted with the expressed intentions of the local legislatures. In such a struggle of wills the long-term result was probably unavoidable—in the end the colonists usually had their way. It would, however, be both inaccurate and unjust to minimize the achievements, or at least the intentions, of the imperial authorities in this field. Possibly the greatest contribution that the Colonial Office had to make to the colonies in this period, through the medium of law review, was towards the maintenance of humane standards and the protection of weak, unrepresented, and victimized sections of the colonial communities.

The cause of the slaves naturally bulks largest at this time. Stephen played an active part in drawing up the instruments to bring about abolition, his over-zealousness bringing down upon his head an indirect rebuke from the Duke of Wellington.[2] But

[1] C.O. 323/81, Virgin Islands; Rogers to Merivale, 13 Aug. 1856; Minute by Henry Taylor.
[2] Young, D. M., op. cit., p. 130.

the cause of the Negro was not won by 1833, nor yet by 1838. Tight control over subsequent West Indian labour legislation effectively prevented a return to the pre-abolition position. And there were other less spectacular causes which needed champions, causes that were often in conflict with the wishes of the more influential inhabitants of the dependencies. Immigrants, poor persons, even criminals, had to be defended against discrimination and outright cruelty. In very many of these cases the Colonial Office showed itself prepared to maintain its principles, even at the risk of friction with the colonies concerned.

Stephen's period of office more than spanned the whole period from abolition to the ending of the apprenticeship scheme. In the ten years or so before the passing of the Abolition Act itself, the officials tried their hardest to avoid direct intervention in the affairs of the West Indian plantations. It was enough, they felt, to make suitable suggestions, and to interfere only when these suggestions were flagrantly perverted or ignored. The colonies in the Caribbean had for many years enjoyed representative institutions, and the planter interest was solidly supported by influential members of the Commons. The young Gladstone himself, perhaps more out of deference to family interest than personal principle, had felt obliged to defend the institution of slavery against attack in the House. All the acts to do with the treatment of slaves passed before 1833 were scrutinized by Stephen with great care. His reports on each frequently ran to several pages, but in the end he seldom found any insuperable objection that might give cause for disallowance. Even the retention of whipping as a punishment for female slaves was not thought to be a serious defect.[3] Most of these acts followed the pattern of the St. Vincent Act of 1826 which, 'when judged by the ordinary standard of colonial legislation in these subjects . . . does not appear open to many positive objections of real importance'.[4] Some colonies were even congratulated on the way in which they had complied with the recommendations of Lord Bathurst on the subject.[5]

In contrast, however, to these general enactments dealing with various aspects of the treatment of slaves, serious objections were sometimes raised against acts which denied to the slaves certain

[3] C.O. 323/45, St. Kitts; Stephen to Huskisson, 23 Feb. 1828.
[4] C.O. 323/43, St. Vincent; Stephen to Bathurst, 7 Sept. 1826.
[5] e.g. C.O. 323/46, Nevis; Stephen to Murray, 27 Jan. 1829.

rights at law. It is not immediately clear why a firmer line should have been adopted on this point than over the actual treatment of slaves. It may be suggested that Stephen, being a lawyer by training, felt more qualified to object to legal discrimination than to physical repression, but this view does not square very well with his generally humanitarian outlook. The true answer is more probably that no control over the first type of enactment could be effective without revision of the laws covering such subjects as the rights of slaves to give evidence. As one slave-owner, Sir William Young, openly admitted, the law of evidence 'covered the most guilty European with impunity'.[6]

Before launching a direct attack upon the law of evidence in the West Indian plantations, the Colonial Office raised numerous objections to acts dealing with other aspects of the legal status of the slave. Between 1826 and 1833, Jamaica once, and the Bahamas three times, sent home Acts to do with the trial of questions relating to the freedom of Negroes. The Bahamas Legislature began by restricting the trial of questions of freedom to points not raised in any previous hearing in any other court.[7] Undeterred by the disallowance of this Act and by the objection of Lord Bathurst that such a rule might, through some technical error or judicial mistake, keep a slave in bondage for ever, the Legislature passed a similar Act in 1828.[8] This, it is true, removed some of the defects particularly complained of, but it introduced new ones. Disallowance again followed, but within four years it had been re-enacted with only slight modification. This time Stephen felt obliged to be more critical, and raised four major objections, of which 'the capital, and . . . the conclusive objection to the law, is that the claim cannot be revived in a new suit, unless it can be shown that the question is "in every respect precisely" identical with that already decided'. Lord Goderich was prepared to be broad-minded but firm. 'If it really is an amendment upon the whole, though only to a slight degree, of the existing law', he wrote, then he would not disallow it but point out its defects to the Legislature in the hope of having it amended. 'If, however, the last clause is likely to throw greater difficulties in the way of

    [6] Wilberforce, W., *Appeal on Behalf of the Negro Slaves* (1823), p. 12. See also Mathieson, W. L., *British Slavery and its Abolition*, pp. 84–5.
    [7] C.O. 323/43, Bahamas; Stephen to Bathurst, 2 Nov. 1826.
    [8] C.O. 323/45, Bahamas; Stephen to Murray, 6 Dec. 1828.

persons claiming their freedom, than will be removed by other parts of the law, it must be disallowed.'[9]

This was only one of the ways in which the Negro section of the population was discriminated against. A common type of enactment was one that granted certain limited rights to slaves, with the implication that, without such a grant, these rights did not exist. One of these was passed by the Jamaican Legislature in 1827. Stephen agreed that the effect of the Act might well be beneficial, but, in his opinion, the slaves already had far greater privileges, which this Act might then curtail.[10]

The most obvious method by which the slave population might be kept down was through the medium of harsh penal laws. In this respect the record of the West Indian plantations was better than others. When Mauritius passed an Ordinance in 1828 to establish the weight of fetters that might be placed on slaves, Stephen was severely critical that such an act could still be passed in a slave colony, when throughout the West Indian colonies the use of chains had long been discontinued.[11] The local legislature persisted, and Stephen complained to Murray that 'it would be a waste of time to discuss the merits of such a law as this. It appears to me to demonstrate the unfitness of the Governor and his Council to legislate at all on any subject connected with the slave population.'[12]

By 1830 it was becoming increasingly clear that the slave colonies were unlikely to adopt the desired attitude to the slaves without at least the threat of more direct pressure. Stephen wrote to his new chief in 1831 that it had been the intention of Sir George Murray, at the beginning of the current session of Parliament, to introduce a bill declaring the evidence of slaves to be admissible on the same terms as that of free men in all parts of the King's Dominions. There was more to this move than was immediately obvious. As Stephen pointed out, 'the importance of this measure consisted much less in the change of law which it would have effected, than in the assertion it would have made of the right and determination of Parliament to legislate for the internal affairs of the Colonies on the subject of slavery. . . . It

[9] C.O. 323/48, Bahamas; Stephen to Goderich, 24 Nov. 1832; Minute by Goderich.

[10] C.O. 323/44, Jamaica; Stephen to Bathurst, 12 Jan. 1827.

[11] C.O. 323/46, Mauritius; Stephen to Murray, 21 Feb. 1829.

[12] C.O. 323/47, Mauritius; Stephen to Murray, 3 May 1830.

was the conviction of the late Cabinet that the time had at length arrived.' The subject of slave evidence had been chosen advisedly as one on which the greatest concurrence of opinion was to be expected. Murray evidently hoped, mistakenly, that the fear of further interference would cause the colonies to accept all the reforms suggested by the Home Government in 1824.[13]

In 1833 the Act of Abolition was duly passed, and the Colonial Office was then faced with the duty of ensuring that the local legislatures used their powers in accordance with both the letter and the spirit of the Imperial Statute. They cannot have expected it to have been an easy task. Laws poured in from all the plantation colonies with the thinly disguised object of reviving the pre-1833 position. The Bahamas Act of 1834, upon which Stephen refrained from making any recommendation, merely re-established the old authority of the overseer and driver under the new titles of 'Employer' and 'Constable'. Section 48 of the Act authorized the whipping of boys under fourteen and girls under twelve for offences which included that of inadequate work.[14] The Legislature of the Bahamas was guilty of more than one breach of the spirit of the imperial enactment. The intention of Parliament in passing that statute had been to register as apprentices only those who had been slaves on 1 August 1834. By adding other sections of the coloured community to the list, who would then be considered as slaves for the purposes of compensation, the planter interest hoped to extract the maximum amount from the authorized fund.[15]

A favourite legislative manœuvre, designed both to emphasize the continuing distinction between whites and coloureds and to ensure that the former retained their ancient power, was carried out by means of various police and militia laws. As usual, the Bahamas Legislature started the fashion with an Act of 1834 which forbade any Negro, either African or American, from serving in the local militia. In the case of American Negroes, the stipulation, Stephen thought, was just, on account of their alien status. But for its extension to African Negroes, who must be considered as subjects, he felt that the Act must be deprecated 'as calculated to keep alive those distinctions which had their origin in Negro

[13] C.O. 323/213, fol. 70, Stephen to Goderich, 3 Feb. 1831.
[14] C.O. 323/50, Bahamas; Stephen to Goderich, 20 May 1834.
[15] C.O. 323/50, Bahamas; Stephen to Goderich, 4 Dec. 1834.

slavery, and which should disappear with its extinction'.[16] Nevertheless, the Act was not immediately disallowed, but a decision was suspended pending possible amendment. It is interesting also to compare Stephen's views in this case with those on a similar Act from Barbados in the same year establishing a police force in Bridgetown. This Act was objected to by the local Attorney-General because it put control over the police into the hands of a Vestry representing the white interest. Stephen could not agree that this was a serious objection. 'I do not apprehend', he wrote, 'that sound policy requires that the practical equality of the two classes should accompany the overthrow of the theoretical inequality.'[17] The Act was disallowed, but only because, by taking the appointment of the magistracy out of the hands of the Governor and putting it into those of a planter Council, it had infringed upon the royal prerogative. But whatever the attitude may have been towards these Acts in 1834, by 1838 it had hardened considerably. Militia Acts passed by Antigua, Grenada, and St. Vincent in 1838, reviving the old disabilities connected with the status of slave, were peremptorily disallowed.[18]

Tirelessly, the planter-dominated legislatures continued to turn out laws of every kind to maintain their position. With equal persistence Stephen and his superiors blocked every move. In addition to the revival of old powers under new guise, Special Magistrates were given wide authority to deal with intransigent Negroes at their discretion. Under the provision of a Dominion Act of 1838 an offender, in certain circumstances, could be convicted by the 'view' of a single Justice of the Peace—that is, without any actual evidence at all.[19] Other Acts authorized Justices of the Peace to impose penalties upon masters as well as servants, and gave the appearance at least of being more equitable. A St. Kitts Act of 1838 empowered a Justice of the Peace to punish any 'misdemeanour, miscarriage, or ill-behaviour' on the part of servants with a fine of up to £5, or the loss of employment. At the same time fines of £5 could be imposed upon a master found guilty of cruelty. Clearly the fines, though equal in amount,

---

[16] C.O. 323/50, Bahamas; Stephen to Goderich, 23 Oct. 1834.

[17] C.O. 323/50, Barbados; Stephen to Goderich, 1 Dec. 1834.

[18] C.O. 233/53, Antigua; Stephen to Glenelg, 22 Mar. 1838. C.O. 323/53, Grenada; Stephen to Glenelg, 10 Dec. 1838. C.O. 323/54, St. Vincent; Stephen to Normanby, 26 Feb. 1839.

[19] C.O. 323/53, Dominica: Stephen to Glenelg, 27 Mar. 1838.

would be very unequal in effect, while the payment of a £5 fine
by the master would protect him from any further indictment for
the same offence.[20] This sort of enactment, which took away with
the right hand what it had given with the left, was typical. For
instance, a Barbados Act to establish an Assistant Court of Appeal,
ostensibly to give protection to emancipated slaves, in fact prescribed such complicated rules of procedure that this purpose
would have been almost wholly defeated.[21] These Acts would be
unobjectionable, Stephen noted, only 'if credit may be given to
the legislature for honesty of intention, and to the Magistracy for
uprightness of purpose—such credit will in this country be very
generally refused them.'[22] All the Acts cited above were disallowed.

As the time appointed for the ending of the apprenticeship
scheme approached, there was a rush of new legislation to set the
pattern for the new relationship between master and servant. Acts
to end the existing system and make way for the new had to be
closely watched. Stephen objected to the Grenada Act for this
purpose because it gave the apprentice labourers no security, as
they could be dismissed from their homes and their jobs for a
number of vaguely worded offences, and on the decision of two
Justices of the Peace.[23] A similar Act from Dominica in the following year he described as 'directly opposed to the provisions of the
corresponding Order-in-Council', and suggested that the repeal
of the objectionable parts be required.[24]

After 1839 the change in circumstances among the erstwhile
slave-owning colonies led to a change in the nature of their
legislation. Despite compensation, the destruction of the institution of slavery further undermined their already unstable economic
structures. From now on the concern was not so much for the
delineation of the status of their native Negro inhabitants, as for
the encouragement and regulation of labour immigration, and,
conversely, the discouragement of ex-slaves from emigrating.
Acts such as one sent home from St. Vincent in 1839 purposely
multiplied the formalities that had to be gone through before a
prospective emigrant could leave,[25] while a Barbados Amendment

[20] C.O. 323/53, St. Kitts; Stephen to Glenelg, 22 Sept. 1838.
[21] C.O. 323/53, Barbados; Stephen to Glenelg, 13 Sept. 1838.
[22] C.O. 323/53, St. Vincent; Stephen to Glenelg, 20 July 1838.
[23] C.O. 323/53, Grenada; Stephen to Glenelg, 27 Sept. 1838.
[24] C.O. 323/54, Dominica; Stephen to Normanby, 29 May 1839.
[25] C.O. 323/54, St. Vincent; Stephen to Normanby, 10 July 1839.

Act of the following year failed to remove the scale of fees objected to by the Secretary of State. The latter further enacted, in effect, that anyone advising a labourer to emigrate might be severely punished.[26] The kind of obstacle put in the way of would-be emigrants was instanced by a Montserrat Act of 1843. By this Act the unfortunate individual was required to get a certificate from two Justices of the Peace before he could leave even his parish. He had then to wait a further ten days before getting a ticket from the Colonial Secretary, who would grant it only if the emigrant could show that he left behind him no dependents or debts. This requirement alone would have been enough to bar the way to the majority of poor labourers, whose very reason for wanting to leave might be to earn more money elsewhere in order to keep their dependants and pay off their debts. It was further required that all masters of vessels trading with the island had to find sureties of £1,000 that they would not remove any inhabitant without the necessary ticket. This last, Stephen thought, was the most serious defect of all, as it seemed to run counter to the Imperial Inter-Colonial Passengers Act.[27]

These few examples pale into relative insignificance before the plethora of colonial acts to regulate the importation of immigrant labour. Basically there were two types of immigration scheme: those financed and, to some extent, regulated by the Home Government, and those initiated and managed by the colonists either privately or with the help of the colonial treasury. From the outset, the aims and objectives of colonists and Colonial Office conflicted. The policy of the Office was clearly set out by Lord Grey in 1851.[28] The first part of Grey's policy concerned the duration of contracts, and laid down that in the case of liberated Africans, contracts for as long as three years should not be allowed. Even where they were permissible, they were in no case to be compulsory. Rogers and Murdoch pointed out, however, that contracts nominally for five years but determinable at the desire of the immigrant at the end of each year, had been sanctioned in the case of the Chinese, and were authorized by the British Guiana Ordinance No. 22 of 1851 and the Trinidad

[26] C.O. 323/55, Barbados; Stephen to Russell, 26 May 1840.
[27] C.O. 323/58, Montserrat; Stephen to Stanley, 24 July 1843.
[28] Earl Grey to the Governor of Jamaica, Dispatch no. 398 of 1851 quoted in C.O. 386/88, fol. 395, Rogers and Murdoch to Merivale, 29 May 1852.

Ordinance No. 9 of 1850. Secondly, immigrants imported under the government scheme were to be distributed among the planters by the Immigration Agent, not according to priority of application but according to his own judgement of what was best for the immigrants. Adequate provision should be made for government superintendence. Finally, the cost of introduction, if recovered from the liberated Africans, should be applied in providing means for their instruction and civilization.

The principle behind this statement of policy was concern for the economic, social, and moral welfare of the imported labourer. Not unnaturally such considerations in the eyes of the colonists came a very poor second to their overriding need for cheap subservient labour.

The most frequently contested issue was that of the duration of contracts and indentures. The Jamaican Legislature was sharply criticized by Murdoch and Rogers in 1848 for authorizing the indenture of liberated Africans for seven years, and for providing that they might be re-indentured from time to time to any employers. 'The Home Government', they wrote, 'has repeatedly prescribed a shorter term of indenture for this class of persons, and has ever insisted on this shorter term more strenuously in regard to liberated Africans brought to the colony at the expense of the British Treasury, than in regard to labourers introduced at the expense of the Colonists.' The Act was 'so directly at variance with the notorious policy of Her Majesty's Government' that it ought to be disallowed.[29]

It should be understood that Colonial Office policy on contracts was not dictated solely by concern for the individual, but also by a realistic assessment of how the labourer could be induced to work hardest for his employer. To this extent the Secretary of State had the welfare of the colony also in mind. In reporting on a Jamaican Act for the encouragement of immigration in 1851, Wood and Rogers drew Elliot's attention to the three-year contract clause, which also laid down that for the first year the labourer was to have no money wages, but a stipulated amount of food and clothing. 'The imposition of such terms', they felt, 'would be unwise, with reference to the interests of Jamaica', as it was unlikely that any immigrant from America, Europe, or China would agree to accept such conditions.[30] Although the Secretary of State was prepared

[29] C.O. 386/88, Jamaica; Murdoch and Rogers to Merivale, 24 Mar. 1848.
[30] C.O. 386/88, fol. 175, Jamaica; Wood and Rogers to Elliot, 15 Oct. 1851.

to allow five-year contracts for Chinese workers, Murdoch and Rogers regretted that British Guiana should, in 1853, decide to legalize them absolutely for all immigrants other than liberated Africans. The nature of the Chinese, they pointed out, was represented to be such that they 'are extremely ready to work if they are allowed the prospect of indefinitely advancing themselves by their industry—but also as little inclined to give themselves trouble without that stimulus'.[31] Absolute five-year contracts would almost certainly have the latter effect. Henry Taylor described the Ordinance as a 'most unfortunate measure', and the Duke of Newcastle authorized its disallowance.[32]

This policy was ultimately vindicated by the colonists themselves. Commenting on a Trinidad immigration law of 1858, Rogers reminded Merivale how a British Guiana Ordinance of 1856, imposing long terms of indentures on immigrants, had been temporarily suspended as it had been found that such imposition tended to discourage emigration from Madeira. 'This seems to me', he wrote, 'an encouraging circumstance, as it shows that the competition for Immigrants between the different colonies is very likely to secure liberal terms for them, with less of interference on the part of the Home Government which, however hitherto necessary, must always be invidious.'[33] Other plantation colonies, however, did not profit from this example, and continued to enact long-term contract laws.[34]

Earl Grey's second stipulation, that immigrants should be assigned to the most suitable employer, could not of course be supervised through the medium of the review process. To a limited extent, however, it was possible to keep an official eye upon the social welfare and moral improvement of the liberated Africans. The Colonial Land and Emigration Commissioners, whose job it was to report on colonial immigration acts, took exception to two West Indian Acts in 1850 which failed to appropriate to objects of moral or social improvement of liberated Africans the revenue

[31] C.O. 386/89, fol. 447, British Guiana; Murdoch and Rogers to Merivale, 15 Apr. 1853.

[32] C.O. 323/74, British Guiana; Murdoch and Rogers to Merivale, 15 Apr. 1853; Minute by Henry Taylor, 22 Apr.; Minute by the Duke of Newcastle, 5 May.

[33] C.O. 386/98, fol. 111, Trinidad; Rogers to Merivale, 25 Sept. 1857.

[34] e.g. C.O. 386/104, fol. 88, Jamaica; Ordinance no. 5 of 1858, Murdoch and Rogers to Merivale, 24 Mar. 1858.

derived from the stamp duty on their engagements and the monthly tax. Both Acts, from Trinidad and St. Lucia, instead directed that the revenue was to be put to an Immigration Fund.[35] Murdoch and Rogers were strongly supported by the senior members of the Office when they suggested the disallowance of an Act from Grenada which would have authorized the payment of bounties to the importers of immigrants from the Azores, Madeira, Canaries, and Cape Verde islands. Importation by private individuals on bounty would, they feared, risk 'a recurrence of those evils which existed before the Government Agencies were established at Madras and Calcutta'.[36]

The planter interest in the colonies, quite understandably, wanted a labour force which, by means of long and disadvantageous terms of contract, would be both cheap to run and easy to control. In addition, they wanted to be relieved of a substantial part of the financial burden of introduction. To a certain extent, the Home Government was prepared to meet them by financial contributions and loans on the security of special taxes. But there were many financial expedients that they were not prepared to sanction. Writing to the Governor of Trinidad in 1860, the Duke of Newcastle had agreed that, provided that two-thirds of the expense of immigration were defrayed either by individual employers or by sources of revenue paid by the planters as a class, the remaining third might be paid out of the general revenue. The planter-dominated Legislature of Jamaica found in this concession too good an opportunity to miss. Their Act of 1861 made the employer liable for only £1 per annum for each labourer, which would have accounted for only between one third and one half of the total expense. To find the balance the Legislature resorted to a devious expedient, which utterly failed to slip past the home officials. The rest of the money was to be derived from export duties to be levied on a number of home products. Provided that these last were produced exclusively by the employers and that the duties were new ones imposed for the purpose, then clearly the principles laid down by the Duke of Newcastle would have been maintained. This was no doubt the impression which the Legislature intended to give. But in point of fact, less than half of these products derived directly from the employers, and the duties were old

[35] C.O. 386/87, fol. 154, Murdoch and Wood to Merivale, 3 Oct. 1850.
[36] C.O. 323/74, Grenada; Murdoch and Wood to Merivale, 10 Nov. 1853.

duties which already existed to raise money for parochial charges. This money was now to be raised by the imposition of other duties on horses, cattle, and sheep. When examined closely, therefore, the expense of immigration was in reality to be borne by the public revenue, although, as Murdoch pointed out, the public was to benefit only indirectly, if at all.[37]

The attitude adopted by the Colonial Office towards labour legislation in the plantation colonies, both before and after emancipation, appears in many respects to run counter to the general trend noticed with regard to legislation from other colonies and on other subjects. At first the officials hesitated to intervene to any great extent, but as time went on, though they still found interference distasteful, they were forced to exert more and more pressure. This is all the more surprising when one considers that some of the West Indian colonies, if they did not enjoy the freedom of responsible government, had at least possessed representative institutions for a considerable time. The explanation for this attitude is to be found both at home and in the colonies concerned. The British Government had been under pressure from the abolitionist leaders for many years to take positive steps to end slavery and ameliorate the condition of the Negroes. It was evident too that there were other individuals besides Stephen within the Office who sympathized with this view. Government intervention was only delayed so long because of the endemic reluctance to interfere, and because of the powerful representation that the planter interest enjoyed in the British Parliament. Once the irrevocable step of abolition had been taken, it was the responsibility of the home officials to see that the spirit as well as the letter of the Act was faithfully observed. Their determination to do so increased as resistance by the colonists stiffened, and their good faith could no longer be trusted.

As G. R. Mellor has pointed out, the problems of the slaves in the West Indies were related in some ways to those of the aborigine peoples of the Cape.[38] While the general principles of imperial policy towards these peoples were the same, the attitudes manifested towards laws affecting them differed with circumstances.

Slavery in the Cape lacked the viciousness of the West Indian system, nor was it as vital to the provision of a labour supply. In

[37] C.O. 386/104, fol. 218, Jamaica; Murdoch to Rogers, 29 June 1861.
[38] Mellor, G. R., *British Imperial Trusteeship 1783–1850*, ch. 5.

addition to the slaves there were large numbers of free native Africans, many of them Hottentots, whose usefulness as labour was reduced by their ingrained tendency to wander.

The position of the Hottentots in the Cape had been regulated by the codes issued by Governor Caledon in 1809 and 1811. The purpose of these codes was both to encourage among the Hottentots a preference for a life of service and to protect them against over-harsh treatment by their masters. By the proclamation of 1809 were enacted the 'pass laws' which prohibited the movement of a Hottentot from his registered place of abode without a certificate from the appropriate authority.

The system laid down by these two proclamations continued, with minor amendments, until 1828. In that year the Cape Ordinance No. 50 introduced significant changes: the 'pass' system was abolished; Hottentots and other free Africans were not to be subject to any compulsory service to which other of His Majesty's subjects were not liable; coloured people were declared competent to own land; and the legal relationship between master and servant was set out in detail, giving considerable protection to the interests of the latter.

Reactions to the Ordinance were as might be expected. It received the assent of the King-in-Council, after further guarantees of the rights of Hottentots had been added. At the same time the law stirred up a violent controversy in the Cape itself between on the one hand the missionaries and on the other the influential class of farmers and landowners. Complaints that the Ordinance increased Hottentot vagrancy became more vociferous after the abolition of slavery in 1833 had made it imperative that an adequate and reliable supply of labour be found. Just as in the West Indies, the Legislature in the Cape sought to reimpose the authority of the masters by passing the Vagrancy Act of 1834. Even before this Act reached the desk of the legal adviser, it was shot to pieces by the legal authorities at the Cape—mainly on the ground that it repealed part of the 1828 Ordinance without the necessary consent of the Crown and that its provisions conflicted with firmly established principles of personal liberty. The Act was consequently disallowed.[39]

Before 1834 laws passed in the Cape respecting the slaves had, of course, been entirely separate from those to do with the free

[39] C.O. 49/26, Separate; Aberdeen to D'Urban, 11 Mar. 1835.

coloured peoples. Most of this slave legislation was intended to operate to the benefit of the slaves, and there is evidence, despite the complaints of the missionaries, that slaves received much better treatment there than in the West Indies. The registration of slaves, introduced by Governor Somerset in 1816, was itself designed to foil attempts to treat free natives as slaves; and Somerset was also responsible for the enlightened slave proclamation of 1823, intended to protect the person and property of the slave against exploitation.

The terms of the 1823 proclamation were also included in the well-known Ordinance No. 19 of 1826. The most important innovation introduced by the Ordinance was the appointment of the Inspector of the Slave Registry as Registrar and Guardian of the Slaves, with the District Registrars as Assistant Guardians. It was to be the responsibility of these Guardians to watch over the interests of any slave involved in a serious court action either as the victim or the accused, to attend the trial, and to act there on the slave's behalf. In addition the Ordinance laid limits for the punishment of female slaves. The only opposition to certain parts of the Ordinance came not from the imperial authorities, but from the slave-owners. They were particularly annoyed by the system whereby a slave might gain his freedom by 'appraisement', and by the provision which debarred anyone who had been twice convicted of maltreating a slave from owning or managing slaves.

Although the slave element of the Cape labour force had never been as vital to the economy as it had been in the West Indies, nevertheless emancipation in the former colony proved extremely inconvenient. As in the West Indies, emancipated slaves often took the opportunity to leave the farms; while the Hottentots, always prone to wandering, seemed to many to have become even less reliable since the Ordinance No. 50 of 1828. Farmers put their trust, for a solution, in the new vagrancy law of 1834, only to see it disallowed on the grounds we have noted.

For the Boer farmers, the series of slave and free labour enactments since 1823 was bound to have the effect not only of damaging their financial position, but also of upsetting the traditional relationship between owner and slave, master and servant. There is no doubt that dissatisfaction with government policy on these issues was one of the principal causes of the Great Trek. From the point of view of the British Government, the legislative record of the Government of the Cape, culminating in the Masters and Servants Ordinance of 1841, must have been satisfactory. The explanation for this divergence between the achievements of the Cape and the West Indian colonies in slave and labour legislation is simple. Before the establishment of the Cape Parliament in 1854, legislative responsibility there was vested either in the governor or, after 1834, in the legislative council over which the governor exercised almost complete control. Nevertheless, the constitution of 1854 itself contained a 'colour-blind' franchise, and it was in Natal, rather than in the Cape, that native policy came to be based upon a distinction before the law between the European and native populations.

In attempting to deal with the problems of native labour, whether free or slave, the officials at home had been motivated first by concern for the unrepresented classes and secondly by concern for the whole colonial community. Exactly the same motives and priorities can be discerned in their intervention on behalf of other unprivileged classes, the poverty-stricken and the criminal. At times indeed it seemed that their natural desire to protect these groups outweighed their common sense. Stephen's attitude to a Bahamas Act of 1827 bordered on the captious. The purpose of the Act was quite simply to enable the local Vestry to put into effect the will of one Aaron Dixon, deceased; to sell his property, and to apply the proceeds to charitable purposes, as he had directed. Stephen attacked the policy and justice of the measure, as its effect would be to benefit the poor now, but not in the future, once the capital had been used up.[40] Later intervention by other reviewers tended to be both humane and more realistic. Thus Lefevre (one of the Commissioners of Land and Emigration) and Wood drew Stephen's attention to a New Brunswick Act of 1844 for the recovery of small debts due to the Crown. This Act authorized the Governor to appoint Receivers with the duty of collecting Crown debts on a commission basis. The report described the system as a 'necessary and simple scheme', but suggested that it 'should not be enforced aggressively against poor persons by Receivers who are entitled to a percentage on the sums collected'. The Governor, they thought, should be instructed to make proper inquiries into the circumstances of Crown Debtors,

[40] C.O. 323/44, Bahamas; Stephen to Bathurst, 3 Feb. 1827.

before allowing proceedings against them.[41] A close watch was kept upon acts establishing governing bodies to administer poor relief. Rogers and Merivale both criticized a British Guiana Poor Law Amendment Act of 1854, on account of the 'unnecessary and mischievous character of the clauses confining relief to certain classes', and because there was no incentive for the paid Inspectors appointed under it to keep down the expenditure.[42]

From concern for poor persons it was only a short step to the protection of criminals. Indeed, judging by the laws passed by some colonies, the two terms were synonymous. In 1828 the Legislature of Grenada passed an Act to 'ascertain what persons shall be termed Rogues and Vagabonds' which Stephen compared very unfavourably with the English statute.[43] The colonial Act included in the definition anyone who refused to work for fair wages, a provision which drew the eminently sensible, if pedantic, remark from Stephen that 'mere indolence, unattended with positive criminality or direct injury to others is not, I think, an offence properly falling within the cognisance of human laws.' The Act was duly disallowed.

By far the greatest number of objections raised against penal laws were concerned with the over-severity of the punishments prescribed. In this the officials were obviously concerned most with the protection of the individual, but at the same time they did not lose sight of a larger purpose. In particular, as time went on, they became increasingly prepared to leave the operation of harsh penal laws to the discretion of the colonial authorities. The number of such acts to be disallowed was small, and included some West Indian Ordinances that punished minor trespass as a crime[44] and authorized transportation on the mere suspicion of receiving stolen goods.[45] The most usual course was for a decision upon inequitable legislation to be suspended until it could be resubmitted to the offending legislature for amendment. This procedure was followed for Acts which put the onus of proof upon the accused;[46] authorized the use of the cat upon prisoners in the

[41] C.O. 386/82, fol. 126, New Brunswick; Lefevre and Wood to Stephen, 10 Aug. 1844.

[42] C.O. 323/76, British Guiana; Rogers to Merivale, 22 Mar. 1854; Minute by Merivale.   [43] 5 Geo. IV, c. 83.

[44] C.O. 323/54, Barbados; Stephen to Normanby, 10 July 1839.

[45] C.O. 323/52, Virgin Islands; Stephen to Glenelg, 3 May 1837.

[46] C.O. 323/51, Antigua; Stephen to Aberdeen, 14 Feb. 1835.

treadmill;[47] substituted life imprisonment for transportation;[48] and extended to female servants the same severe penalties for breach of contract as for men.[49] But by 1850, and earlier in the case of Canada, even this relatively mild form of censure was seldom used. Stephen strongly disagreed with Rogers in 1846 that the threat of disallowance should be held over the head of the Governor of Canada, unless he secured the amendment of the Registry Act of that year, even although the penal clause of the Act authorized punishments taken from an Elizabethan statute, including ear-lopping and nose-slitting. 'It would be injurious and offensive to the Canadian legislature,' Stephen wrote, 'either to suggest or to entertain any doubt of their willingness to correct such a mistake.' The Act should be confirmed at once.[50]

Restraint towards the affairs of the Canadians is not surprising, but it is interesting to find the same attitude being expressed by Earl Grey towards the criminal laws of British Guiana only five years later. That colony had in 1850 passed an Ordinance for the prevention of wilful trespass. This Ordinance called forth petitions from two local inhabitants, Mr. MacFarlane and Mr. Spooner, with whose views Sir Frederic Rogers partially agreed. In parti-cular he objected to the clauses allowing jurisdiction to ordinary as well as stipendiary magistrates, and denying to the friends and relatives of a labourer access to his cottage unless it had an open path or road leading to it. Earl Grey, however, saw no reason to interfere, basing his opinion upon the economic dependence of the employer in Guiana upon the labourer. 'I think it very inex-pedient', he wrote, 'to interfere more than can possibly be helped with local legislatures, and that the power of urging amendments in laws passed by them should be reserved for cases of consider-able importance. The defects pointed out by Mr. Rogers will no doubt be corrected if in practice they are found to lead to any inconvenience, which I do not much apprehend. In Guiana the employers are so much more dependent on the labourers than the latter upon them that there is little risk of any vexatious abuse by the owners of the plantations of the power of forbidding access

[47] C.O. 323/51, Tobago; Stephen to Glenelg, 2 Oct. 1835.
[48] C.O. 323/58, Canada; Stephen to Stanley, 6 Mar. 1843.
[49] C.O. 386/67, South Australia; Murdoch and Wood to Merivale, 22 Dec. 1849.
[50] C.O. 323/61, Canada; Rogers to Earl Grey, 28 Sept. 1846; Minute by Stephen.

to the labourers' cottages except by the regular paths. Therefore simply confirm the ordinance.'[51] As a statement of general policy, Grey's views in this case were faithfully adopted by his successors and subordinates. Henry Taylor agreed, in 1852, to leave the operation of the Nevis Rabid Animals Act, with its fine of £20 or six months' hard labour for bringing *any* dog to the island, to the discretion of the President;[52] while Lord John Russell, in 1855, refused to interfere with an Ordinance from Honduras that made a servant liable, for certain offences, to pay a fine direct to his master, on the ground that this was already established law in the dependency.[53]

The way in which laws concerned with crime and punishment were dealt with would seem to have been in line with the policy already noticed in the case of local colonial affairs. This does not mean, of course, that the home authorities had become indifferent to the fate of the over-punished criminal. They had always entertained a deep personal sense of responsibility towards all those classes within the colonies whose interests might be subordinated to those of the politically more influential. The change that was taking place as our period advanced was not the outcome of insensibility, but rather of the realization that, for the healthy development of a colonial community, the local authorities must be left free to exercise their own discretion and to assume a fuller responsibility for their own affairs.

It would be historically inaccurate, however, to depict the Colonial Office as making these concessions solely out of a concern for the colonies and their inhabitants. Power begets power, and when the officials took issue with the more autonomous colonies on matters of humanitarian principle, they generally lost in the end. In the 1850s something of a battle royal took place between the Office and the Australian colonies over the problem of time-expired convicts.

On the general question of convict transportation, the home authorities and the Australians were in broad agreement that the system had outlived its usefulness. It was expensive, the annual cost being estimated in the thirties at half a million pounds. There

[51] C.O. 323/70, British Guiana; Rogers to Merivale, 15 Feb. 1851; Minute by Earl Grey.
[52] C.O. 323/72, Nevis; Rogers to Merivale, 3 Feb. 1852; Minute by Taylor.
[53] C.O. 323/79, Honduras; Wood to Merivale, 16 June 1855; Minute by Russell.

was little evidence of its value in reforming criminals—much more of its degrading effects. The colonists themselves found the system increasingly irksome and objectionable; they feared cheap competition from convict labour, and it was felt that there was little prospect of political development while transportation continued. The home authorities therefore took a critical view of colonial legislation that tended to increase the flow of convicts to the convict colonies.[54] Although the recommendations of the Molesworth Commission of 1837 were not carried out immediately, no more convicts were sent to New South Wales after 1840, and transportation, except to Western Australia, was discontinued in 1857.[55]

This was, however, only part of the convict problem. The Australian colonies showed themselves increasingly anxious not only to reduce the existing convict population, but to refuse entry to transportees whose time had expired. The first shot in the battle was fired by New South Wales in 1850, when for the 'prevention of vagrancy' the Legislature enacted that 'everyone transported to or convicted in a British Colony in the Southern Hemisphere shall, if he arrives in New South Wales within seven years of his conviction, be bound to notify the proper authorities of his name, occupation, and intended residence'.[56] Failure to do so could incur a penalty of up to two years' hard labour. Sir William Denison, the Governor of Van Diemen's Land, to which convicts were still being sent, complained bitterly against the Act, largely because it deprived the conditional pardon of much of its value. The tendency of the law, he thought, would be to throw back on Van Diemen's Land persons who might otherwise have quitted their old associates and re-established their character in a new country. Rogers took a different line. Indeed, he felt that Denison had over-estimated the disadvantages. To him, the question arose 'whether Colonial Legislatures not expressly authorized to do so can be allowed to interfere, . . . with the graduated scale of restraint; through which it has been determined by

---

[54] e.g. C.O. 323/52, Montserrat; Stephen to Glenelg, 25 Mar. 1837. Stephen objected to a Montserrat Act authorizing transportation as a punishment for cattle stealing, on the ground that the augmentation of the convict population was undesirable, especially in the case of Negroes, who would suffer from the change in climate.

[55] Woodward, E. L., *The Age of Reform*, pp. 369–70, 450–2.

[56] C.O. 323/69, New South Wales; Rogers to Merivale, 18 May 1850; Minute by Merivale, 24 May; Minute by Earl Grey, 27 May.

Government that the convicts should be restored to entire liberty.'
Merivale agreed that the real question was not that the regulations
themselves were oppressive, but rather 'whether they do not constitute an interference with a course of policy determined on with
reference to the Empire generally'. Earl Grey took an even
stronger line. 'As I read the act, it is a distinct infringement of
H.M.'s prerogative of mercy . . . It is also unjust to persons who
have been sentenced to punishment for a limited time by subject-
ing them to an additional punishment after that time has expired.
If so, it clearly must be disallowed.'[57]

By taking a stand upon principle in this way, the home authorities were committing a tactical error. Should they eventually be
obliged to change their attitude, the consequent loss of face and
the size of the colonial victory would be all the greater.

Rogers had feared that, if allowed, the Act would provide a
precedent which the other Australian colonies would follow. His
fears were fully justified, despite its disallowance. Late in 1852
Superintendent Latrobe of Victoria sent home an Act to prevent
the introduction into the colony of offenders 'illegally at large'.
The provisions of the law were exceedingly harsh, the onus being
placed on the accused to prove his own innocence. It was quite
clear, moreover, that, although said to be confined only to offenders
'illegally at large', it applied equally to holders of a conditional
pardon. The Superintendent urged, in justification, the necessity
of preserving life and property in Victoria, pointing out that of all
prisoners, less seamen, admitted to Melbourne Jail over the past
six months, 63 per cent were ex-convicts. But in spite of all the
Superintendent's arguments, the Duke of Newcastle felt unable
to recommend anything but disallowance. 'I am reluctant', he
wrote, 'to disallow an Act of the Victoria Legislature to which in
present circumstances so much importance seems to be attached,
but I fear it must be done. Many of the provisions are most unjust, and that which invalidates the conditional pardon of the
Sovereign cannot be confirmed by Her Government.' The most
that he was prepared to do was to adopt Mr. Peel's suggestion that
the Victorian Government should be warned of the impending
disallowance by a dispatch, to give them time to amend the Act
(already in operation) and that disallowance by Order-in-Council

[57] C.O. 323/69, New South Wales; Rogers to Merivale, 18 May 1850; Minute
by Merivale 24 May; Minute by Earl Grey, 27 May.

should be from a definite date 'as it will leave no hope to the legislature of any change of decision at home if the time for disallowance is peremptorily fixed'.[58]

In the event Latrobe took it upon himself not to publish the disallowance, and the Act continued in force until 1854. Governor Hotham was instructed to produce a more moderate scheme, and at the same time he was to release men imprisoned under the first Victorian Act. But the answer of the Victorian Legislature was to pass an even more stringent Act. Again the Colonial Office decided on disallowance. But they could not afford to ignore Hotham's warning that 'Victoria possesses the wealth and strength to stand unaided, she does not lack the pretensions to walk alone'.[59] It was agreed that sufficient time should be allowed for the colony to enact a new law which would contain heavier penalties for crimes committed by a former convict.[60] This concession proved no more satisfactory than before, and a third Act was passed, continuing the second Act (passed for one year only) for a further year. The Office was beaten. Merivale advised Labouchere to give in, as it was evident that 'the colonies are absolutely determined to have their own way. No reasoning with them, or suggestion of milder courses has been or will be of any effect whatever.'[61]

The victory was now almost complete, the final seal being put upon it by the enactment of Act No. 68 of 1859 which rendered the temporary act permanent. In the previous year South Australia had joined the lists with a similar Act, which invoked a recapitulation of the arguments in the Victorian case. Carnarvon found it 'open to very great objection', but considered that the renewal of the agitation over the convict question which had elsewhere died away, 'would probably be the worst evil'. Lord Stanley felt able to be more magnanimous. Having, he confessed, taken some days to consider the subject, he was satisfied that the Act should be assented to. 'It seems to me that a colony, professedly free from convictism, has a right to make that immunity real as well as nominal. But it is not real if facilities are afforded for convicts whose sentences have expired to pour in, these convicts being

[58] C.O. 323/75, Victoria; Wood to Merivale, 5 Apr. 1853; Minute by the Duke of Newcastle.
[59] C.O. 309/27, Hotham to Newcastle, 18 Nov. 1854.
[60] Ibid., draft dispatch from Russell to Hotham, 4 June 1855.
[61] C.O. 309/30, McArthur to Labouchere, 15 Apr. 1856; Minute by Merivale, 4 Aug. C.O. 323/89, Victoria; Rogers to Merivale, 10 June 1859.

prohibited from returning to England.'[62] It had taken eight years, and the opinions of four Secretaries of State, for the attitude of the Colonial Office in this affair to be softened from strict disallowance to tolerant, if cautious, support.

The ex-convicts were only one class of undesirables which the Australian colonies were anxious to exclude. The battle they had fought over the convict question was almost re-enacted over the very similar problem of Chinese immigration. But it too ended with an ultimate vindication of the principle that it was the colonists, and not the Home Government, who were the final arbiters of who should or should not be admitted to their colonies.

By the mid-fifties, the number of Chinese in the Australian colonies was comparatively large.[63] They were attracted by the recent gold discoveries in the continent, and their coming gave rise to serious opposition on the part of the colonial community. The situation was very similar to that in the Pacific states of the United States, which brought about the Immigration Act of 1882. The Chinese, it was felt, had nothing to contribute to the colony but their passage money. They did not bring their wives with them, and evidently had no intention of settling permanently. 'They merely pick up gold, the property of the Crown, and carry it away with them to their own country.' In the circumstances, no objection was raised to the Victorian Act of 1855 passed to limit, or even to end, Chinese immigration by imposing an immigration tax of £10 per head on all Chinese coming to the colony, and a further tax of £10 per head on each immigrant over the proportion of one to every ten tons burden of the immigrant ship.[64] Given this precedent, it would have been illogical to contest the right of South Australia to pass similar legislation with the object of preventing the Chinese from evading the Victorian law by landing in the adjoining colony. Lord Stanley, it is true, agreed to sanction it only with the greatest reluctance. To impose a prohibitive tax on the landing within a British colony of persons of a certain race 'is a measure questionable in policy, and harsh as regards those whom it affects'. He was persuaded, however, partly by the Victorian precedent, and partly the consideration that it was inexpedient, except in extreme cases, to interfere with the internal

[62] C.O. 323/87, South Australia; Rogers to Merivale, 27 Feb. 1858.
[63] 19,000 in Victoria by 1855.
[64] C.O. 386/80, Murdoch and Rogers to Merivale, 21 Sept. 1855.

affairs of colonies such as those in Australia. 'Such interference', he wrote, 'creates jealousy and obstinate persistence in error, while a contrary policy gives a better chance of hasty decisions, founded on prejudice, being reconsidered at leisure.'[65]

Up to this point there might be good reason to suppose that this question was one of local importance only. But the situation was evidently different by 1859. By this time a new treaty had been concluded with the Chinese Emperor by which 'extensive privileges of ingress into the Chinese Empire are conceded to British subjects'. This circumstance lifted the affair out of mere local importance, and caused the Colonial Office to consider the situation, and two more Chinese Immigration Acts from New South Wales and Victoria, more strictly. As Murdoch remarked, 'the exceptional obstruction of Chinese immigration is contrary to the principles of this country, and peculiarly inopportune at the present time.' Nevertheless, the attitude of the Australian colonies was understandable, and in view of the precedents set, these Acts could hardly be disallowed. Murdoch's only solution to the practical problem was to suggest that a certain proportion of Chinese women be required to accompany the males.[66]

[65] C.O. 323/87, South Australia; Rogers to Merivale, 20 Feb. 1858; Minute by Lord Stanley.

[66] C.O. 386/80, fol. 152, Victoria; Murdoch and Rogers to Merivale, 10 June 1859; Also C.O. 386/76, fol. 242, New South Wales; Murdoch to Elliot, 5 Feb. 1862.

TRUSTEESHIP II—VESTED INTERESTS

SLAVES, apprentices, immigrants, criminals, and ex-convicts were from their status in colonial society, and their lack of political influence, the classes most in need of a champion. The Colonial Office fulfilled this function to the best of its ability and within the limits of its powers. But there were other groups in colonial society, public officials, certain private individuals, and the colonial Churches, which found themselves being victimized, or their interests endangered, by the dominant element in the local legislature.

If, as we have seen, the Colonial Office found it unrewarding to take issue with the dependencies over their control of official appointments through the regulation of salaries, its members were nevertheless anxious that no injustice should be done to individuals. As was so often the case, Stephen and his colleagues based their policy upon a double consideration: on the one hand, basic principles of equity and justice, on the other a concern for the healthy development of the colony involved. Thus Stephen, objecting in 1834 to a Bill from Lower Canada which would deprive the Attorney-General of his customary fees, looked beyond the question of the individual to a hypothetical future. If this principle were carried further, he warned, it might 'impair the stability of all civil rights'.[1] A decision should be delayed until the Assembly should be able to consider compensation.

Injustices of this kind, either intentional or inadvertent, were likely to arise at the transfer of territorial or general revenues from the Crown to a colonial government. In his instructions to the Governor of Nova Scotia in November 1846, Lord Grey had made it clear that no such transfer would be allowed except under certain conditions—in particular, that all public officers must be retained at the same salary. But when, in 1848, Nova Scotia passed an Act effecting such a transfer, it was found that these instructions had not been fully complied with, and that the salaries of the judges

[1] C.O. 323/50, Lower Canada; Stephen to Stanley, 30 June 1834.

had been reduced. Wood, in his report on the Act, felt obliged to advise against its confirmation.[2] And when in 1852 the same colony was guilty of similar injustices to certain holders of judicial and legal office, Merivale reiterated the objections of his government with an exquisite combination of tact and firmness.[3]

In the same year Nova Scotia had passed an Act to revise and consolidate the general statutes of the colony. The officials appointed to carry out the revision, however, exceeded their authority in changing the substance as well as the wording of some laws. The judges in particular complained that the effect of the Act was to repeal two previous local statutes, which had secured them permanent salaries independent of the Civil List and had provided for the appointment of an additional judge, with a similar permanent salary, and for the travelling expense of judges when on circuit. Merivale noted these defects, but suggested that 'these alterations would have been of little consequence here (Nova Scotia being in full possession of the right to legislate for itself) were it not that they appear, or are alleged, to affect the interests of parties to whom the faith of this country seems in some degree pledged, namely the present judges and Sir Rupert George'. Although he felt obliged to advise the withholding of assent for the time being, Merivale was careful to suggest that the colony should be informed that such action was taken at the Governor's own suggestion. The sole reason for delay was to enable the Legislature to 'reconsider enactments which it is not clear that they intended to pass'.[4]

There were other occasions when peculiar circumstances did not permit even this degree of firmness. Wood pointed out in 1852 that however objectionable the principle behind a Montserrat Act reducing the salaries of a large number of public officers, the fact that without this Act the officials would be wholly unprovided for, made disallowance all but impossible.[5]

By 1853 attacks upon the salaries and fees of public officers had become sufficiently common for the Duke of Newcastle to lay down a specific rule for the guidance of colonial governors. Writing to Sir H. Barkly on 16 August, the Duke declared that

---

[2] C.O. 323/64, Nova Scotia; Wood to Merivale, 24 May 1848.
[3] C.O. 323/73, Nova Scotia; Wood to Merivale, 21 Feb. 1852.
[4] Ibid.
[5] C.O. 323/72, Montserrat; Wood to Merivale, 6 Oct. 1852.

'when permanent Acts have been passed by the Legislature assigning specific salaries to particular Officers, and the Crown, having, by its assent to such Acts, become a party to their enactment, has appointed persons to the offices without any intimation that the Salaries so secured by law were to be reduced or withdrawn, the Crown has thereby contracted an obligation, which forbids it to be a party to any enactment which would take away the right to the salary, without obtaining the consent of the Officer, or providing such a fair and reasonable equivalent as ought to command that assent'.[6] These principles, the dispatch continued, would be *prima facie* conclusive against an exceptional tax that was a virtual reduction in salary.

The rules laid down here were obviously very similar to the principles followed in the past and that were to be applied again three years later. In 1856 Rogers reported on a Grenada Act which imposed a tax, ostensibly on 'all trades, professions and callings', but in fact directed especially at the incomes of public officers. The Lieutenant-Governor, the Legislative Council, and the Local Attorney-General all protested against the Act as a virtual reduction of salary, basing their objections upon the Duke of Newcastle's previous dispatch. In defence of the measure it was urged that the effect of the Act would be small (only some £300 p.a. would be received from government officers); that it had a precedent in a previous Act from Tobago; and that a recent Act establishing an Executive Council had only been passed in expectation of the Tax Act becoming law. Rogers, however, disposed of two of these arguments by pointing out that the Tobago Act had been only temporary and that the public officers had given their consent to it.[7] Further, if the Executive Council Act were not confirmed, but were enacted by a prerogative instrument, one of the problems would be avoided. Merivale and Labouchere accepted his recommendations, and agreed on disallowance.

Towards the 'responsible government' colonies, however, an increasingly less stringent attitude may be discerned. The best illustration of this trend is provided by an Act passed, also in 1856, by the Legislature of Jamaica, which, although not generally included in the 'responsible' category of this period, was evidently considered by Merivale virtually to have achieved this status.

[6] C.O. 138/70, Newcastle to Barkly, 16 Aug. 1853.
[7] C.O. 323/81, Grenada; Rogers to Merivale, 26 July 1856.

In 1855 the colony had passed a Judicial Amendment Act which remodelled the Supreme Court and abolished the system of local Quarter Sessions. This had had the effect of replacing the existing Vice Chancellor, three Judges, and six Chairmen by one Chief Justice and three Puisne Judges. The present Act was passed to provide for the compensation of those who had lost office as a result of the previous enactment. Basing his opinion of the Act on the rules laid down by the Treasury for compensation to officials in this country, and also upon the Duke of Newcastle's dispatch on the subject written in 1853,[8] Wood felt obliged to report that the wide difference between the Treasury rule and the actual compensation offered here was 'scarcely equitable'. He admitted the desirability of avoiding a collision with the local legislature, but recommended nevertheless that the claims of the three complainants (two assistant judges and one chairman) should be met. Unless fair compensation were made for these three officers, he felt unable to report that 'the terms prescribed by the Duke of Newcastle as the condition on which the Royal Assent would be given to laws affecting the rights of parties to whom the faith of the Crown is pledged, have been fulfilled'.[9]

Henry Taylor in an attached minute examined the claims in detail, but came to the opposite conclusion. By neglecting to petition the Assembly against the passage of the Acts, he felt the complainants had forfeited the right to petition against their confirmation. In any case, the fact that the judges had been prepared to retire some years previously on only one quarter of their salaries afforded a strong presumption that they were not really aggrieved by the present offer of compensation. Nor was it realistic to compare the colonial compensation scheme with the Treasury rules—English practice, he felt, should not be accepted in a colony 'as being of authority to overthrow an important Act of the Legislature'. The Acts should therefore be confirmed. Merivale, however, could not agree. He was evidently prepared to to incur 'all the evils and annoyance involved in a contest with a colonial legislature, rather than assent to a measure of spoliation towards officers holding judicial appointments'. If the Acts were to be confirmed, it could 'only be on the broader ground that

---

[8] C.O. 138/70, Newcastle to Barkly, no. 1, 16 Aug. 1853.
[9] C.O. 323/81, Jamaica; Wood to Merivale, 26 Mar. 1856; Minutes by Taylor, Merivale and Labouchere.

after the concession of responsible government, which in Jamaica has practically taken place, all further interference with measures affecting individual interest is at an end, and the Crown is no longer guilty of a 'breach of faith', such as the Duke of Newcastle admitted it might commit, writing in 1853. This 'broader ground' was evidently enough to satisfy Labouchere. In authorizing confirmation, he declared that 'there ought to be a very clear case of injustice or disregard of good faith towards the holders of existing officers to justify the refusal of the assent of the Crown'. Such a case, in his opinion, had not been made out.[10]

Interference with acts on this subject from the more advanced colonies was evidently to be kept to a minimum. This attitude was accurately summed up by Merivale in 1858, when he declared that 'it is . . . no reason for disallowance that an Act was unjust to individuals, or interfered with a Royal Charter, or with some vested interest. . . . The only exception is where certain existing vested interests were secured by the Crown at the grant of responsible government—on this ground alone is disallowance justified.'[11]

From this point of view there was no real distinction between the vested interests of public officers and those of private persons. Stephen in 1843 objected to a St. Vincent Act authorizing the town wardens of Kingston to lease certain vacant lands, because it allowed them to do so for twenty-one years, without any reservation of the rights of private individuals.[12] Yet twelve years later Labouchere refused to intervene on behalf of the creditors of plantation-owners in Mauritius when their rights as creditors were set aside in favour of those merchants who had supplied provisions for the plantation employees. The Secretary of State was content to state his objections, but otherwise to leave the responsibility for a decision, in the best interests of the colony, to the Governor.[13] There were even cases where a Crown obligation existed, yet was not adhered to, as when Rogers refused to disallow the Victorian Land Act of 1860 at the request of the squatters, whose rights under an Order-in-Council of 1847 had been terminated by it. Rogers pointed out that when the Order

[10] C.O. 323/81, Jamaica; Wood to Merivale, 26 Mar. 1856; Minutes by Labouchere.

[11] C.O. 323/87, New Brunswick; Rogers to Merivale, 23 Sept. 1858; Minutes by Merivale.   [12] C.O. 323/58, St. Vincent; Stephen to Stanley, 11 July 1843.

[13] C.O. 323/79, Mauritius; Rogers to Merivale, 18 Oct. 1855; Minutes by Labouchere.

had been promulgated, the subsequent political change in the colony had not been foreseen, and in any case the squatters had been allowed to occupy the runs without interference for fourteen years, and had purchased a large part of them. Nevertheless, where an interest had been guaranteed by the Crown, it was usual for it to be respected.[14] Rogers and Murdoch recommended an amendment to the South Australian Waste Land Sales Act of 1857 because it abolished the usual privileges granted to naval and military officers on retirement and reserved only those promises which might have been made before the repeal of the Land Sales Act. The reviewers objected that many such officers might have made plans for taking up land in South Australia after the repeal of that Act. 'The disappointment of these expectations would, under the circumstances, almost involve a breach of faith on the part of the Crown.'[15]

There was, however, one important exception to the general rule of non-interference except where a specific Crown obligation was involved: the protection of non-resident proprietors. This subject occurs so often in the period that the attitude of the officials towards it cannot be ignored or explained away as a minor deviation from established practice. It must be taken as a measure of the great reluctance to meddle with Canadian affairs that Canada alone was allowed, in 1863, to pass an Act which encroached to some extent upon the rights of absentees.[16] This was the only instance of such leniency in the period, and the fact that the Colonial Office consistently refused to allow even other 'responsible government' colonies, such as Prince Edward Island, to pass legislation prejudicial to the non-resident interest suggests that it is dangerous to divide the Empire too rigidly into 'responsible' and 'non-responsible' categories.

As early in the period as December 1834, Stephen had to advise that confirmation should be withheld from a New Brunswick Act which provided for different rules of assessment for resident and non-resident owners.[17] Similarly, Murdoch and Rogers recommended disallowance for a Natal Ordinance imposing a tax upon

[14] Clarke, D. P., op. cit., pp. 286–7.
[15] C.O. 386/79, fol. 131, South Australia; Murdoch and Rogers to Merivale, 18 Feb. 1858.
[16] C.O. 42/625, Monck to Newcastle, 24 Dec. 1862; Minute by Rogers, 27 Jan. 1863.
[17] C.O. 323/50, New Brunswick; Stephen to Aberdeen, 26 Dec. 1834.

alienated lands. There was no objection to the imposition of a tax *per se*, but it was assessed very unequally (a distinction being made between occupied and unoccupied land, between unoccupied land owned by resident and by non-residents, and between large and small holdings); the thinly disguised object was 'to press with much greater severity on the absentee than on the resident, and on the owner of a large than on the owner of a small estate'.[18] If money were required for the upkeep of roads, it should be raised equitably, not 'by singling out for penal taxation classes of property which, though assumed to be the least advantageous to the community, have been acquired in accordance with the established law and custom'. The Legislature of Newfoundland came up against the same attitude when they tried to levy a tax to pay for the land upon which the new town of St. John had been built after the great fire of 1846. The mode of assessment would effectively have exempted resident owners and placed almost the entire burden upon the shoulders of the absentees.[19]

It must have been obvious to all concerned that the colonial legislatures, in framing such proposals, had more in mind than the raising of revenue. They wished to avoid the evils of a situation, prevalent in so many of the British colonies, of speculation in land by financiers who had no intention of settling upon or working the land they had bought. Their attitude is understandable; and the Colonial Office may perhaps be criticized for keeping so closely to the letter of the law.

In no case is this better illustrated than by the running battle waged between the Home Government and the Legislature of Prince Edward Island, though, to be fair, the home officials were aware of the problems of the colonists and did try to find some satisfactory alternative solution.

The antagonism between tenant and proprietor in Prince Edward Island had a long history. In 1767 the land had been divided up into sixty-seven lots of about 20,000 acres each, which were then allotted to various proprietors who were to colonize it and hold it upon certain conditions. These conditions were never in fact fulfilled, but the Home Government had acquiesced in their remission, with the exception of two townships, forfeited in

[18] C.O. 386/107, fol. 288, Natal; Murdoch and Rogers to Merivale, 31 Oct. 1857.

[19] C.O. 323/87, Newfoundland; Rogers to Merivale, 21 Sept. 1858.

1818. Most of the large proprietors were non-resident, and the tenants mostly held leases of 999 years. A popular movement directed against the landlords increased in intensity with the introduction of responsible government and universal suffrage. Repeated attempts were made to induce the government to escheat the lands on the ground of non-performance of the original conditions, but these attempts had no success. Government policy was expressed by Lord Grey in a dispatch to the Governor in 1851, in which he ordered Bannerman to adhere to the decisions of his predecessors in the matter, though he was to try to get the tenants and proprietors to come to some amicable agreement. Above all the Governor was to 'impress upon the Legislature the necessity of abstaining from the introduction into . . . Laws of any provisions which may infringe upon the rights of property'.[20]

To begin with, the Colonial Office was not disposed to be overcritical. Earl Grey accepted Wood's suggestion that the Distress Act of 1851 should not be disallowed, in spite of the objections of Lord Selkirk and others that it unduly favoured the tenants by preventing the removal of distrained property to any greater distance than five miles, unless at the request of the tenant. The object, Lord Selkirk alleged, was to keep property within those districts in which there was a disposition forcibly to resist the payment of rent. There was, however, a precedent to be found in the imperial statute book, and the Lieutenant-Governor had approved the measure. The most Grey was prepared to do as yet was to call the Lieutenant-Governor's attention to 'the necessity of taking effective measures to defeat any attempts to resist by violence the enforcement of the legal claims of the owners of property'.[21]

After some hesitation Sir John Pakington also refrained from interference in the Small Debts Recovery Act of the following year, although, as Merivale informed him, it was clearly drawn up in a spirit hostile to the landowners (who had again protested) and would be an additional difficulty thrown purposely in the way of recovery of rent. Sir John was evidently persuaded in his decision by the fact that the Act was 'clearly within the province of

[20] Grey to Bannerman, 12 Feb. 1851; quoted by Wood and Rogers to Merivale. C.O. 323/78, Prince Edward Island; 28 July 1855.
[21] C.O. 323/71, Prince Edward Island; Wood to Merivale, 16 Aug. 1851; Minute by Lord Grey.

a local legislature'.[22] The next two Acts in the series, however, the one imposing a tax on the rent rolls (rather than the receipts) of proprietors having more than five hundred acres out on lease, and the other requiring compensation for improvements before a tenant could be ejected for non-payment of rent, as Merivale declared, tried 'the principle of allowing all purely local legislation to pass unquestioned, to the uttermost'. Ball agreed. 'I presume', he wrote, 'that there are *some* limits to the practical application of this as well as every other principle of government.' The real faults, he pointed out, lay with Her Majesty's Government for not facing the question before granting responsible government. There was no point in having done so if the desires of the local legislature were to be continually thwarted. In the long run their interests were bound to prevail. His original plan, approved by Molesworth, had been to assent to the Compensation Act, but Lord Palmerston interposed his veto.[23] Her Majesty's Government could not 'take upon themselves the responsibility of advising the Crown to give its assent to Colonial Acts which are at variance with the principles of justice and put aside the rights of property which are the Foundation of social organization'. Ball then suggested a compulsory purchase scheme, backed by a loan, which Labouchere, coming to office in the middle of the controversy, agreed to support.[24]

In the event, the land purchase scheme fell through owing to the increasing instability of the island's finances. Suspicion in the island of the influence on the Home Government of the absentee landowners was intensified, and both Houses of the local legislature submitted addresses declaring that the Government's attitude had caused the people of Prince Edward Island to 'feel degraded below their fellow subjects'.[25]

These representations had little effect upon the home officials. The Governor was informed in 1858 that the Crown could not

[22] C.O. 323/73, Prince Edward Island; Wood to Merivale, 23 Sept. 1852; Minute by Merivale and Pakington.

[23] Palmerston had taken over responsibility for the conduct of colonial affairs during the temporary absence of Lord John Russell and the illness of Sir George Grey.

[24] C.O. 323/78, Prince Edward Island; Wood and Rogers to Merivale, 28 July 1855; Minutes by Merivale, Ball, Palmerston, and Labouchere.

[25] C.O. 226/87, Daly to Labouchere, 18 Apr. 1856; enclosure, 14 Apr. 1856.

assent to the Fishery Reserves Act of that year. This Act referred
to certain areas of land on the sea-shore to which the Crown had
reserved fishing and building rights. In practice, the landowners
had treated the strip as their own, and had paid taxes on it. The
present Act provided that no tenant should be liable to pay rent
to his landlord for any such fishery reserve. The proprietors protested with reason that the effect of the Act was to abrogate by an
ex post facto law distinct agreements between themselves and their
tenants. Rogers called it a 'prostitution of legislative power'. 'I
scarcely know how far it may be deemed proper to apply the
doctrines of non-interference to a case of this kind.'[26]

A further attempt by the Office to find an equitable solution by
appointing a commission of inquiry was sabotaged by the colonists
who tried, in a new enactment, to give the decisions of the Commission the force of law, and to revive the old controversy over
escheat. Murdoch was 'well aware that it is almost impossible to
exaggerate the inconvenience of withholding H.M.'s assent from
this Act. It will be represented that the interests of the Land
Owners in this country have again prevailed with Her Majesty's
Government against those of the Tenants', with a consequent
incitement to the tenants to take the law into their own hands.
But these grave disadvantages, he felt, had to be faced, 'rather
than assent to an Act the principle of which is fraught with so
much injustice to individuals, and such entire disregard to the
rights of property'.[27] A further ten years were to pass before a
final settlement was achieved.

This whole affair provides us with a warning against too glib
an acceptance of the view that once the grant of responsible
government had been given, the colonial legislatures were allowed
to deal as they wished with interests not specifically guaranteed
by the Crown. In this case, the guarantee had been implied only,
in the acquiescence of the Government in the non-compliance by
the proprietors with the original conditions on which they held
their lands. Even so, it was not upon this ground, but upon the
principle of the defence of property, that Palmerston, Labouchere,
and others had acted.

In addition, the attitude of the Colonial Office in this instance

[26] C.O. 323/87, Prince Edward Island; Rogers to Merivale; draft dispatch
from Labouchere to Daly, 20 Oct. 1858.

[27] C.O. 386/85, Prince Edward Island; Murdoch to Rogers, 17 Nov. 1860.

may be open to the criticism that it failed to deal with a potentially explosive situation with sufficient realism. As Ball had foreseen, the wishes of the tenants were bound to prevail, and it was in the interest of the progressive development of the colony that they should. A satisfactory solution should have been found before, not after, the grant of responsible government.

There are good reasons for supposing that this was not a typical case. As we have seen, the attitude towards all vested interests, from those of the Crown to those of private persons, underwent a gradual change. To begin with, these interests were jealously guarded, but as time went on the Home Government showed itself less and less willing to interfere, especially with responsible government colonies, unless a very clear case could be made out that non-intervention would amount to a definite breach of faith.

There is one other interest which the imperial authorities might well have felt themselves under obligation to protect—the Church. Naturally enough, the Colonial Office was not called upon to decide any question relating to theology. The nearest to this that it ever came was over the questions of marriage and divorce already mentioned; matters of ecclesiastical law were generally referred direct to the Queen's Advocate. The kind of questions which the Office was concerned with, however, were the position of dissenting congregations in the colonies and the political rights of members of the clergy.

One of the problems that emerged was how to distinguish between what were and were not 'respectable' religious groups. It was one thing to permit to the ministers of certain dissenting congregations the power of solemnizing marriages, quite another to advance this power to all minority sects. Then there was the problem of allowing dissenters to dispense with certain oaths on grounds of religious scruple.

Stephen criticized an Upper Canada Act of 1826 allowing certain sects to give evidence without oath as a 'very serious and important innovation'. Evidently he had no objection to the English practice of allowing Quakers to give an affirmation, but he saw no reason why this privilege should be extended to Menonists or Junkers. In the interest of the administration of justice his protest was perhaps understandable. Such an extension might, as he said, enable 'the most profligate of mankind' to claim a similar privilege by 'assuming to themselves some barbarous appellation,

and asserting that they feel religious scruples respecting oaths'.[28]
This Act was disallowed, but later legislation by the North American colonies which, directly or indirectly, gave legislative sanction to certain dissenting sects was not interfered with. The important point to note here was that there was little change of attitude at home to the position of these congregations, but rather it began to be felt that, in these colonies at least, the matter was best left to the discretion of the local authorities. Even as early as 1832, the furthest that the Colonial Office was prepared to go was to call the attention of the Governor by means of a confidential dispatch to the difficulties under which such legislation placed the government at home. To risk, by a disallowance, entering into a dispute with the colonial legislatures on topics of this kind would, it was felt, be 'extremely dangerous'.[29] By 1841 even Stephen had become resigned to the fact that, 'it is utterly impossible to stem, on the North American continent, the current of popular opinion in favour of an absolute equality amongst all Christian Societies'.[30]

The Colonial Office did not confine this attitude to Canada. It was with the greatest reluctance that the Crown's assent was withheld from a Tasmanian Act providing for the abolition of state aid to religion. This Act authorized the substitution of a lump sum in lieu of a yearly subsidy, to be paid by the Tasmanian Government to the three local Churches, and was therefore in line with the contents of Lord John Russell's letter to the Society for the Propagation of the Gospel in December 1839. It was felt, however, that the particular Act would be unjust to certain individual interests which had been guaranteed by Her Majesty's Government, and could not therefore be sanctioned. Both Rogers and Merivale regretted the necessity of disallowance. The Act was, said Merivale, 'very near the mark'.[31] Rogers suggested that, in palliation, the Governor be assured that the general question of state aid to religion 'was a subject for the exclusive consideration of the Local Legislature'.

There were instances, however, when the Colonial Office felt that it had a duty to intervene in colonial regulation of religious

[28] C.O. 323/43, Upper Canada; Stephen to Bathurst, 13 Nov. 1826.
[29] C.O. 323/48, Nova Scotia; Stephen to Goderich, 21 Sept. 1832; unsigned pencil note.
[30] C.O. 323/56, Nova Scotia; Stephen to Stanley, 7 Oct. 1841.
[31] C.O. 323/90, Tasmania; Rogers to Merivale, 4 Jan. 1860. Minute by Merivale.

matters. This situation arose when certain colonies sought to exclude members of the clergy from political office. New South Wales in 1851 and New Brunswick in the following year both passed Acts to this effect, and both Acts were promptly disallowed.[32] Admittedly, in New Brunswick, the Bishop of Fredericton had a claim under the Royal Instructions of 23 August 1848 to sit in the Legislative Council, and to deprive him of this right, Rogers asserted, 'interferes directly with the Royal Prerogative'. But the Office's action cannot be explained only in terms of a defence of the prerogative. They were determined also to uphold a political principle, and to exclude the clergy of all denominations from political power and privileges was contrary to the policy that had hitherto been sanctioned by the Imperial Government. As Lord Grey had told the Governor of New South Wales in 1851 'very strong reasons should be adduced for excluding from political power . . . any specific class of persons not evidently disqualified from it properly, especially when the excluded class possess education, character and influence'. It should be left to the electorate to choose whom it wished to represent it in the Council.[33]

The policy of the Government towards these two Acts appears to have been determined by its solicitude for the welfare of the colonists, rather than for the privileges of the clergy. Some confirmation for this view is to be found in the refusal to interfere in South Australia's policy of excluding ministers of religion from sitting upon the Education Board. Merivale contented himself with remarking, as in extenuation of its eccentricity, that 'South Australia was a colony founded by persons of peculiar sentiments, and its history has been marked by a steady objection on the part of the principal people to any interference by the legislature in religious matters'. It was, so it appeared to him, 'a subject on which I think the will of the local legislature ought to be followed and the Act confirmed, whatever the opinion of the government here may be as to its policy'.[34]

In approaching the whole question of the protection of various interests within the colonies, the Colonial Office was obviously acting in accordance with general principles of humanity and

[32] C.O. 323/73, New Brunswick; Rogers to Merivale, 22 May 1852.
[33] Ibid.
[34] C.O. 323/73, South Australia; Rogers to Merivale, 7 July 1852; Minute by Merivale.

justice. It was only to be expected, then, that the officials would take a keen interest in the administration of justice itself, and that they would examine critically all colonial proposals for changes in the law that might affect the judges and the courts. Reforms connected with the judicial systems of both Britain and her dependencies were in the air. The Commissions of Enquiry into the Administration of Justice in New South Wales and the West Indies demonstrated both the interest of the imperial authorities in this matter and the great need for improvements and reorganization.

In point of fact, there was remarkably little opposition raised to colonial laws that affected the jurisdiction, structure, or procedures of the colonial courts. As we shall see in a later chapter, the argument that representative colonial legislatures did not have the power to erect or change the constitution of local courts did not commend itself to the home officials. The fact that the series of British Guiana Ordinances of 1846 which reformed legal procedure had aroused considerable controversy within the colony was not allowed to stand in the way of their confirmation unaltered.[35] Even the infringement of the prerogative implicit in the transfer to a new Court by the Legislature of Nevis of jurisdiction over some of the matters rightly belonging to the Office of Ordinary was not taken to be an insuperable obstacle.[36] Jurisdiction was in any case limited to the probate of wills and the administration of estates—matters in which the decrees of the Ordinary, when issued under the authority of the Governor's Commission, could not, in any case, be enforced. Drastic changes in the administration of justice in New Brunswick in 1854, involving the abolition of the Court of Chancery, the transference of jurisdiction in equity to the Supreme Court, and even the extinguishing of the office of the Master of the Rolls, received whole-hearted support from Merivale and Grey. This exception to the general rule of defending the interests of judicial officers may perhaps be explained by the degree of responsible government by then enjoyed by the colony. Stipulations were made that the present holder of the office should receive adequate compensation.[37]

[35] C.O. 323/61, British Guiana; Rogers to Grey, 7 Oct. 1846.
[36] C.O. 323/70, Nevis; Wood to Merivale, 16 May 1851.
[37] C.O. 323/77, New Brunswick; Wood to Merivale, 3 Aug. 1854; Minutes by Merivale and Grey.

Innovations in legal procedure in advance of the practice prevailing in Britain were often encouraged and even suggested by the home officials. A good example of this was the unusual practice followed in jury trials by Van Diemen's Land and some other colonies. Stephen had always been conscious of the difficulty of giving advice to colonies on the subject. 'The principles of legislation on such a matter as Jury Trials', he felt, 'could not be stated in any one universal and inflexible form of words. All the world over these arrangements must be matters of compromise and of adaptation to the particular condition, character, wants and resources of the place.'[38] This diffidence did not prevent him from making the novel suggestion, adopted first by Van Diemen's Land and later, in a modified form, by Barbados, that unanimity from a jury would be required for the first hour only. For the second hour, unanimity less one would be sufficient; less two for the third hour; three for the fourth. If there were no agreement then, a fresh trial should be ordered.[39] Where the system was tried it was found to work well. Official support for this scheme did not mean, however, that new schemes for the administration of justice unacceptable to the local population would be imposed upon them. Hope and Stanley were very ready, in 1842, to fall in with the wishes of the united Canadian Legislature when they demanded the repeal of many of Lord Sydenham's measures for the anglicization of the judicial system. Although Stanley, for one, was in sympathy with the object of Sydenham's programme, he did not see how the Home Government could refuse to defer to the opinions of the United Legislature, if only because a refusal to sanction the repeal of the Ordinances would 'rather impede than accelerate the consummation desired of introducing English institutions and English habits of thinking in the Canadian population'.[40]

Where the officials were prepared to intervene more forcibly, was in cases of colonial laws that tended to undermine the impartiality or the independence of the judges.

Strong objections were raised against the clause in a St. Lucia

[38] C.O. 323/63, South Australia; Wood and Rogers to Stephen, 9 June 1847; Minute by Stephen.

[39] C.O. 323/78, Barbados; Wood to Merivale, 28 June 1855; Minute by Taylor.

[40] C.O. 323/58, Canada; Stephen to Stanley, 6 Mar. 1842; Minutes by Hope and Stanley.

Ordinance which allowed the judges a fee of 10 per cent on all sums recovered in their courts. An enactment of this kind was bound to lay all the judges open to the temptation or at least the charge of partiality. Stephen restated the old legal maxim that justice must not only be done—it must also be seen to be done, by asserting that 'it is scarcely less important that a Judge should have credit for uprightness, than that he should be upright in reality'.[41] The same principle was followed with regard to another Ordinance from the same colony which revived an old French law rendering the judges liable to penalties for improper judicial acts. Nor were laws of like character from 'responsible government' colonies immune. The Legislature of Nova Scotia in 1850 transferred by local enactment the judicial and administrative functions of the Justices of the Peace to elective Wardens and Counsellors, who were to remain in office for one year only. The effect of this would no doubt have been, as Rogers told Earl Grey, to put them 'under a strong temptation to take, in all the questions which may come before them, the popular view, and that of the party by which they are supported. I should fear therefore that the proposed measures would not tend to ensure either the election of the persons most competent to discharge the peculiar duties of a magistrate, their gradual improvement by experience, or the un-biased administration of justice.'[42] In the event, a decision was suspended in order to allow the local legislature to reconsider.

The judges were among the few public officials whose salaries were consistently defended against reduction, even if their other rights, such as pensions or compensation for loss of office, were not so faithfully protected. In 1860 Rogers refused to waive the right of reservation of bills altering the salaries of judges,[43] and when Queensland attempted such an alteration in the case of the unpopular Mr. Justice Lutwyche, Merivale advised that the proposal should be resisted '*à outrance*'.[44] The reluctance to move in the case of Mr. Justice Boothby may, in part, be explained in terms of the same principle; though it is interesting to note that when he was at last removed from office, it was by the Governor and the Executive Council, with the concurrence, even the support, of the Home Government.

[41] C.O. 323/48, St. Lucia; Stephen to Goderich, 18 Sept. 1832.
[42] C.O. 323/69, Nova Scotia; Rogers to Merivale, 4 July 1850.
[43] C.O. 234/1, Bowen to Newcastle, 3 Feb. 1860; Minute by Rogers.
[44] C.O. 234/2, Bowen to Newcastle, 4 Oct. 1860.

Stephen's remark in 1843 that the function of government was 'to consult for the permanent interests of Society, as opposed to the immediate interests of the most active and powerful of its members', was more than the personal belief of one man—it was a principle followed by the Office as a whole in the mid-nineteenth century. It was only to be expected that the Office would oppose the intentions of the colonial legislatures when such intentions ran counter to particular British interests or general imperial interests. What is remarkable about British policy towards colonial laws in this period is the extent to which the appropriate officials were ready to take responsibility for the well-being of the colonial communities under their care.

Such an attitude lays itself open to the charge of being paternalistic and undemocratic; but to make this charge is to judge contemporary British policy in wholly anachronistic terms. The members of the Office were not over-impressed by the claims of the 'populace' to rule, and their experience of the workings of representative institutions in the West Indies, admittedly with a high property franchise, had not been particularly happy. However, their determination to protect the interests of certain underprivileged groups was subject to a number of qualifications in practice. The first of these was the belief, which came to be acted upon more frequently as time went on, that the colonies must, in the interests of their future stability, be granted a growing measure of control over their own affairs. Naturally enough this attitude was more noticeable with regard to the colonies of white settlement, especially those with no very deep-seated racial problems and whose inhabitants had come to expect as their right the existence of liberal political institutions. Of course, it might be argued that just as the humanitarian aspects of Colonial Office policy were the outcome of pressures brought to bear from outside, so also was the policy of the gradual devolution of power. In other words, the Office felt obliged to relax its hold on the colonies, not as a matter of principle, but in response to demands from pressure groups at home and in the colonies.

This argument contains at least some truth. The Colonial Reformers believed it to be inequitable that the colonies should have to obey two masters—their own government and the Imperial Parliament. Those of them who, like Wakefield, were connected with contemporary schemes of systematic colonization, were indeed anxious that their new colonies should be allowed to develop unhindered along individual lines. But to suggest that Stephen and his colleagues were directly influenced by the Colonial Reformers in their attitudes to colonial laws is not only unwarranted by the evidence, but is inherently unlikely. The strained relations between Stephen and Wakefield over the affairs of the New Zealand Company, and the bitter attacks by the latter and Charles Buller on 'Mr. Mother-Country' do not suggest that there was any very free interchange of opinions between them

There is, however, considerably more evidence as to the effect of pressures from the colonies themselves. The Colonial Office was again and again forced to recognize the weakness of its position and the futility or worse of engaging in a conflict with the colonial legislatures. The Colonial Office, either because it was looking back to the European experience in America or, more probably, because it was looking forward to some looser form of imperial union, was anxious not to push its authority to the point of provoking a serious breach in intra-imperial relations. If, as some believed, the ultimate disintegration of the Empire was inevitable, then the parting when it came should be without bitterness or recrimination.

Part IV

THE COLONIAL OFFICE AND THE COLONIAL LAWS VALIDITY ACT

II

THE MAKING OF THE COLONIAL
LAWS VALIDITY ACT

THE passing of the Colonial Laws Validity Act in June 1865 provides us with a particularly appropriate conclusion to the study
of official attitudes to colonial laws over the period. Although, in
the twentieth century, it was the restrictive character of the Act
which received the most attention and was a significant factor in
the demand for a re-definition of Dominion status in 1926,[1] in its
original conception the Act had been not restrictive but emanci-
patory. In both letter and spirit it conformed closely to the ideas
and opinions upon colonial laws expressed by Colonial Office
officials from Stephen onwards, and in one aspect in particular
—the restriction of 'repugnancy' to conflict only with imperial
statutes applicable to the colony—it went further in the direction
of colonial emancipation than had hitherto been accepted. But
in its general conception the Act was very much the product of
official experience over the previous half century.

This is not to say, however, that the Colonial Office, left to itself,
would necessarily have been anxious to see such an Act pass on
to the statute books. The last statute to attempt a definition of the
legal relationship between Britain and her plantations had been
passed in 1696, although the 1840 Canada Act of Union had
anticipated (for one colony only) the definition of repugnancy
which was, by the Colonial Laws Validity Act, extended to all
the British colonies to which the latter Act applied. If more positive evidence of official reluctance to accept statutory definitions
is required, it is to be found in the battle between the Office and

---

[1] See Wheare, K. C., *The Statute of Westminster and Dominion Status*, pp.
127–31; also Madden, A. F. McC., *Imperial Constitutional Documents 1765–1952,
A Supplement* (Oxford, 1953), p. 47, where it is pointed out that the restrictions
on the powers of the Dominion Legislature arising out of s. 2 of the 1865 Act,
as revealed by *Nadan* v. *The King* (1926), 'threw Canada unequivocally on the
side of these Dominions . . . which at the Imperial Conference of 1926 wanted
a precise definition of Dominion rights'.

the Australian colonies in the late 1840s and early 1850s.[2] The point at issue here was the proposal that, in the constitution acts of the more advanced settlement colonies, a distinction should be made between colonial acts dealing with 'local' and those dealing with 'imperial' affairs. In the case of the former, it was suggested, such 'local' acts should not be sent home for ratification by the Crown.

Although there was, of course, no connection between this proposal and the details of the 1865 Act, there was a similarity of principle, in that both involved some definition of the ambit of colonial autonomy. Yet the Australian proposal, put forward by Wentworth, the New South Wales statesman, only eleven years before the passing of the 1865 Act, evoked a strongly antagonistic response from the Colonial Office. One senior official, T. F. Elliot, denounced the 'efforts of the politicians to reduce almost to a nullity the ties with the mother country'.[3] Rogers described the clauses as a 'Legislative Declaration of Independence'—the result of successive Secretaries of State currying favour with the Australian colonies.[4]

Tempers on both sides soon cooled down and the question was not raised again—partly perhaps because the avoidance of this kind of distinction ultimately worked out to the benefit of the colonists. But the incident does show a more than passive resistance by the Colonial Office to the statutory recognition of encroachments on the imperial power.

There existed, then, within the Colonial Office a built-in resistance to statutory definition unless circumstances made such action imperative. This attitude is easily understandable. Colonial affairs were not popular in Parliament in this period, and unless they involved questions of economy, debates on colonial matters were generally sparsely attended. From the point of view of the Colonial Office this was probably a desirable state of affairs, and they had no wish to draw attention to themselves unnecessarily. When in 1863 the crisis in South Australia forced the Home Government into passing a second validating Act, Newcastle, the Secretary of State, complained petulantly to the South Australian

[2] See Burt, A. L., *The Evolution of the British Empire and Commonwealth*, pp. 383-4.
[3] C.O. 309/25, Hotham to Newcastle, 26 June 1854; Minute by Elliot.
[4] Marindin, G. E. (ed.), *The Letters of Lord Blachford*, p. 157, Rogers to Church, 15 Sept. 1854.

Governor, Sir Dominic Daly, about the cluttering up of the Imperial Statute Book with enactments 'required to extricate Colonial Governments and Legislatures from the consequences of their own irregularity or inadvertence'.[5] The *amour-propre* of both the Office and the colonial governments had to be considered —both should appear to be capable of managing their own affairs without Parliamentary assistance. In any case, as far as the Colonial Office was concerned, such legislation was unnecessary: the law was already clear, and when doubts arose, they could best be dealt with by the existing procedures of review.

The fact remains that, in the early sixties, the British Government *did* interfere, by legislation, in the affairs of the colonies— twice (in 1862 and 1863) to rescue the Legislature of South Australia from the embarrassment of having many of its most vital laws declared invalid, and again (in 1865) with the Colonial Laws Validity Act.

Given the obvious reluctance on the part of the British Government to legislate for the colonies (and especially for those colonies enjoying 'responsible government') before 1860, one would expect to find some really compelling reason for this change of heart. There can be no doubt that by far the most influential factor in this process was the occurrence of the so-called 'Boothby crisis' in South Australia, which took place between 1859 and 1867. The link between the judgements of Mr. Justice Boothby, Second Puisne Judge of the South Australian Supreme Court, and the passing of the 1865 Act, has not been overlooked by historians. At least one has been led to ascribe to Boothby entire responsibility for the passing of the Act. 'The only great statute of general imperial constitutional law passed in the nineteenth century', writes R. T. E. Latham, was 'occasioned not by any desire to clarify or amend, but by the necessity of upsetting the eccentric decision of a colonial judge.'[6]

This statement is both accurate and misleading. It is almost certainly true that without Boothby the Act would not have been formulated and passed. But it would be unfair to describe all of his opinions and decisions as 'eccentric'. It must be significant that, of the various points of law covered by the Act, all but one

[5] *S.A.P.P.* 130 H.A., Newcastle to Daly, 25 July 1863.
[6] Latham, R. T. E., 'The Law and the Commonwealth' in Hancock, Sir W. K., *Survey of British Commonwealth Affairs* (London, 1937), p. 512.

can be shown to have been raised by Boothby at one time or another during his career as a Judge. Boothby, as Latham asserts, provided the *occasion* for the passing of the Act.

To go no further than this, however, would be to ignore the long experience which the Colonial Office had had, in operating the review process, with the legal relationship between the mother country and her dependent colonies. For our purposes the 1865 Act should be seen as something more than a pragmatic solution to an isolated crisis.

The Act of 1865 contained seven clauses.[7] Working backwards, the seventh clause dealt specifically with South Australian legislation, and was just another attempt, following the Acts of 1862 and 1863, to put the statutory law of that colony back on a firm basis. Clause six was concerned exclusively with the authenticity of certain documents, and although no evidence has come to light to connect it directly with Boothby's opinions, some kind of connection may very well have existed. Clause five had a more general significance, covering the power of colonial legislatures to erect courts and alter their constitutions. Again, these were points raised by Boothby, though obviously related also to accepted opinion on these matters. The really important clauses were the first four. Clauses one to three laid down a clear definition of the repugnancy doctrine, limiting the circumstances when repugnancy between colonial and English law might arise to one only: where the colonial law conflicted with an imperial statute, extending 'by express words or necessary intendment' to the colony in question or to colonies generally. The important point to note here is the omission of any mention of English common law or those 'fundamental principles' of English law adverted to, at various times, by Stephen, Rogers, and the Crown Law Officers. Finally clause four of the Act dealt with Royal Instructions. In brief, this clause stated that no colonial law could be held invalid by reason of any Instructions given to the Governor, unless such Instructions were included in (and not merely referred to by) Letters Patent, the Governor's Commission, or Orders-in-Council.

There is ample evidence to connect all but the most minor of these clauses with points raised by Boothby at various times between 1859 and 1865.

As far as the doctrine of repugnancy is concerned, Boothby at

[7] See Appendix for the full text of the Colonial Laws Validity Act.

no time attempted an express definition of the concept, but his judgements and dicta indicate that his view of it was extremely wide. Looking upon himself perhaps as the champion of the rule of English law in an immature colonial society, he appears to have been concerned that, where possible, English law should control that enacted by the local legislature. His judgement in the case of *McEllister* v. *Fenn*, for example, convinced the Select Committee of the South Australian House of Assembly that to him repugnancy meant more than conflict with imperial acts extending to the colony or with fundamental principles of English law. It meant also the mere alteration of the forms of legal procedure, and the substitution of one species of remedy for another.[8]

His judgements in this and later cases bear out this impression. The Real Property Act he considered repugnant because 'it saps the fundamental principles of the Constitution of the British Empire in that "it removes trial by jury in matters relating to the ownership of land" '.[9]

He raised similar objections to the Grand Jury Act of 1852. In *Liebelt* v. *Hunt* Boothby went so far as to declare that 'the Parliament of this colony had no power to override the common law of England'[10]—a dictum which deserves to rank, in imperial legal history, with that of Sir Edward Coke in *Bonham's Case*.

This reading of the repugnancy doctrine would probably have been too extreme for most contemporary authorities, but it is clear that Boothby's interpretation went still further. Instances of this may be found in the minutes of evidence before the Select Committee of the House of Assembly, in which the judge asserted that 'there is no offence possible in this colony which is not an offence by the law of England';[11] and in his petty objections to the Constitution Act. This last he declared repugnant because by it (contrary to practice in Britain) the Crown was restrained from dissolving the Legislative Council, and (in accord with practice, but not law, at home) the Crown was limited to choosing certain government officers from among the members of the two Houses. As Boothby was evidently also of the opinion that the repugnancy of one section of an act must invalidate the whole,[12]

[8] *S.A.P.P.* 154 H.A. (1861).   [9] Ibid., para. 68.
[10] *S.A.P.P.* 141 L.C. (1861).
[11] Ibid., para. 257.
[12] C.O. 13/110, Law Officers' Report, 25 Mar. 1862.

these objections cast doubt upon all the acts of the local legislature passed under the authority of the Constitution Act.

Sir Frederic Rogers, as we have seen,[13] had already made his position on repugnancy, and that of the Office for which he spoke, as clear as possible. In his view, any colonial statute would be illegal which was contrary to an imperial act which the imperial legislature has expressly or by implication intended to be binding upon the colony. This much was common ground. He had also suggested that repugnancy might arise if colonial statutes failed to conform to 'certain fundamental enactments of statute or principles of common law'. To Rogers, however, this was only a theoretical possibility. In practice, the powers of colonial legislatures to pass laws were limited only by the first consideration, or, in cases where the fundamental principles of English law had manifestly been violated, by the operation of the Crown's power of disallowance.[14] For their part, the Law Officers of the Crown, when appealed to during the Boothby affair, substantially re-iterated Rogers's view. While they agreed that conflict with fundamental principles of English law would constitute repugnancy, they were unable to lay down any sure legal test to distinguish between fundamental and non-fundamental principles. In addition, they were satisfied that the repugnancy of a single provision of a colonial act *did not* invalidate the whole.[15]

Between them, therefore, Rogers and the Law Officers had rejected Boothby's wide interpretation of the repugnancy doctrine, and restated principles of law and practice which had been long accepted by the Colonial Office. Yet there is an interesting and highly significant discrepancy between the actual provisions of the 1865 Act (on this subject) and the official opinions expressed above.

To begin with, the Act firmly restates the generally accepted position on repugnancy between a colonial law and an imperial act 'by express words or necessary intendment' binding on the colony. This statement is contained in the first two clauses, read in conjunction with the preamble, and was modelled, in accordance with the advice of the Law Officers, upon the similar provisions

---

[13] See pp. 62–3.

[14] C.O. 323/87, South Australia; Rogers to Merivale, 5 May 1858.

[15] C.O. 13/110, fol. 456 et seq., Law Officers' Reports, i, 25 Mar. 1862, ii, 12 Apr. 1862.

in the Canadian Act of Union of 1840.[16] Indeed it was at their suggestion that these provisions were not to be confined only to the Canadian and Australian colonies, on the ground that 'the balance of reason and practical convenience is in favour of extending such provisions to all Her Majesty's colonial possessions'.[17]

This much was to be expected—the point of real interest is simply that the definition of repugnancy here stated goes no further. There is no mention in the Act of 'fundamental principles of English law'; no mention at all of the English common law. On the contrary, the third clause of the Act, inserted at Rogers's own suggestion,[18] clearly affirmed that no act passed by any representative legislature should be void on account of any alleged repugnancy to English law unless it were repugnant to an actual act of Parliament, as already stated.

In setting out the limits of the repugnancy doctrine in this way, the drafters of the Act were, perhaps, doing no more than making explicit what was already current practice. Colonial acts conflicting with fundamental principles could still in the future, as in the past, be disallowed. But if this was all that the Colonial Office intended, why then did Rogers suggest the inclusion of clause 3? There are two possible answers to this question, not necessarily mutually exclusive. The first is that Rogers was especially concerned 'to cut the ground from under such objectors as Mr. Boothby'[19]—in particular to reject the latter's contention that the colonial legislatures had no power to override the English common law. Secondly, it is tempting, in the light of what we already know on the subject, to interpret clause 3 as evidence of a more positive and progressive attitude. In other words, clause 3 was included in the Act out of a desire for certainty. It established a clear and easy test for repugnancy so that the right of representative legislatures to pass whatever laws they liked, subject only to the one reservation, might now be clearly and explicitly recognized.

Another point of major imperial significance raised by Boothby was that of the legal status and effect of Royal Instructions to colonial governors. Boothby's argument on the point was that failure on the part of the governor to respect his Instructions

---

[16] 3 & 4 Vict., c. 35, s. 3.
[17] C.O. 13/115, Law Officers' Report, 28 Sept. 1864.
[18] C.O. 13/113, Law Officers' Report, 13 May 1863; Minute by Rogers.
[19] Ibid.

requiring him to reserve an act for the royal assent would automatically invalidate the law *ab initio*: that is, such Instructions must be taken as not directory only, but as having the full force of law.

The crucial case was that of *McEllister* v. *Fenn*, in which the point at issue was the validity or otherwise of the local Real Property Act of 1860. It was during this case that Boothby remarked: 'we cannot take any notice of the Real Property Act of 1860, as it has not received the assent of Her Majesty. The Governor was not empowered under his Instructions to give assent to that Act.'[20] The Instruction to which the judge referred was contained in the eleventh paragraph of clause 11 of the Instructions to Governor MacDonnell, and was to the effect that certain classes of Bills were to be reserved for the Royal Assent, including 'any Bill of an extraordinary nature and importance, whereby our prerogative, or the rights and property of our subjects not residing in the colony or the trade and shipping of the United Kingdom and its dependencies may be prejudiced.'[21] Boothby was claiming, therefore, that since the Real Property Act did affect the rights and property of British subjects not residing in the colony, it should have been reserved by the Governor for the Royal Assent. Failure to do so had, in effect, rendered the Act invalid and of no effect.

Boothby countered the arguments against his opinion with customary skill. On the one hand he was prepared to accept that the Governor had a discretion in deciding which Bills he should or should not reserve; obviously there were some which could not wait until 'Her Majesty's pleasure be known'. But he claimed that, under the terms of 5 & 6 Vict., c. 76, s. 31, such discretion was limited to a 'temporary law, necessary to be forthwith assented to by reason of some public and pressing emergency', and that the Act in question could not be considered in this light. He conceded that a governor's original Instructions might be modified by later Instructions, but claimed that it was the duty of the governor to communicate any such modification to the legislature. He was in no doubt as to the legally binding nature of Instructions, and quoted section 11 of 5 & 6 Vict., c. 76, by which it was enacted

---

[20] *S.A.P.P.* 48 H.A. (1862), Encl. 1. Boothby further declared that even the Queen-in-Council could not confirm an Act which had been wrongly assented to by the Governor.

[21] *S.A.P.P.* 17 H.A. (1858).

that 'it shall be the duty of the Governor to act in obedience to such instructions'.[22]

Boothby's opinions upon the legal status and binding nature of the Instructions were doubly distasteful to the Colonial Office. In the first place, they were in direct conflict with the rules and precedents generally followed by members of the Office in past years. Stephen had been contemptuous of Instructions. At most, failure to observe them might incur disallowance if this were considered politically desirable. At no time were they accorded any superior legal status which might involve the automatic invalidation of a law assented to contrary to their provisions.

Secondly, Boothby's attitude to Instructions, as had been the case with his attitude to repugnancy, implied a restriction upon the powers of the local legislature, a restriction totally out of line with current imperial policy. Once again, Boothby was being more British than the British—an attitude which might have been acceptable in the later eighteenth century, but was no longer so in the mid-nineteenth.

The official answer to Boothby's claims had both legal and political overtones. In their report on the matter, a report with which the Colonial Office thoroughly agreed, the Law Officers asserted that 'we consider such Instructions to be a matter between the Crown and the Governor, and to be, to the latter, directory only'.[23] If Instructions were indeed a private matter between the Crown and the governor, to be divulged to no one except perhaps the Executive Council, then it was difficult to see how they could in effect be legally binding. They could hardly have been produced in a court of law, or considered in the same light as, say, a public statute. Moreover, by emphasizing the 'directory' nature of the Instruction, the authorities at home were reiterating their support for a liberal attitude to the management of colonial affairs. Thus the fourth clause of the Colonial Laws Validity Act spelt out in detail the state of the law concerning Royal Instructions. No colonial law, it ran, was to be held invalid, by reason of any Instruction given to the governor by any instrument other than Letters Patent or the governor's Commission,[24] even though such

---

[22] *S.A.P.P.* 48 H.A. (1862), Encl. 1.

[23] C.O. 13/110, Law Officers' Report, 12 Apr. 1862.

[24] This is my interpretation of the phrase in Clause 4: 'Instrument authorising such Governor to concur in passing or to assent to laws for the peace, order, or good government of the colony'.

Instructions may be referred to in such Letters Patent or Commission.[25]

Boothby's attacks upon the powers of the local legislatures were not confined to their powers to pass laws. He also cast serious doubts both upon their ability to erect their own courts of judicature and to alter their own constitution.

On the first of these points Boothby had made his own opinions clear in his evidence before the Select Committee of the House of Assembly in 1861.[26] His contention was that although such a power had been included in the two statutes 4 & 5 Will. IV, c. 95, s. 2 and 1 & 2 Vict., c. 60, it had been omitted in 5 & 6 Vict., c. 61— this omission having the effect of removing the power. Again, in 13 & 14 Vict., c. 59 the power to erect courts had been extended to New South Wales, Van Diemen's Land, and Victoria, but not to South Australia—presumably because it was felt that enough in the way of erection of courts had already been accomplished.

In the case of *Payne* v. *Dench*,[27] a majority of the Full Court (Boothby and his colleague Mr. Justice Gwynne) had decided that the local Court of Appeals did not exist. Among the many reasons given for this decision was the argument that since the passing of the Constitution Act, the Executive Council, which had previously acted as a Court of Appeal, had become composed of elected members. To have appeal judges elected by the people was surely contrary to the principles of the British constitution and to the provisions of the Supreme Court Act.

Having decided then, in this case, that no local Court of Appeal existed Boothby and Gwynne together made good use of Boothby's earlier argument, in *Dawes* v. *Quarrell* (1864),[28] to prevent the Legislature from setting up a new court. At the same time they denied the validity of the Local Courts Act, casting doubts upon the legality of existing local courts.

The Home Government, however, was quite convinced that the Legislature in South Australia had always been able to set up courts, and that such an ability should be understood in the

[25] Presumably Acts assented to by the Governor in disregard of his Instructions, *contained in Letters Patent*, would still have been invalid after this clause passed into law. See Keith, A. B., *Responsible Government in the Dominions*, vol. II, p. 783, and also Palley, C., *The Constitutional History and Law of Southern Rhodesia, 1888–1965* (Oxford, 1966), p. 236.

[26] *S.A.P.P.* 154 H.A., 27 Aug. 1861.   [27] *S.A.P.P.* 100 H.A. (1863).

[28] C.O. 13/115, Daly to Cardwell, 26 July 1864.

phrase 'power to make laws . . . for the peace, order, and good government of the colony'. The Law Officers concurred, and, in answer to Boothby's objection, pointed out that express mention of the other three Australian colonies in 13 & 14 Vict., c. 59 had been made necessary by reason of their previous disabilities in this respect.[29]

Any doubts that may have remained on the point were firmly dealt with by the fifth section of the Colonial Laws Validity Act. This section emphasized the full power of every representative colonial legislature to establish courts of judicature, to establish or reconstitute them, or to alter their constitutions.

In addition, section five of the Act confirmed the powers of all representative legislatures to make laws 'respecting the Constitution powers and procedures of such legislature'. Boothby had begun not by denying that the South Australia Legislature had this power, but by effectively thwarting its operation. In *Driffield* v. *The Registrar-General*[30] he held that the new Registration Act was invalid because it had indirectly affected the qualification of electors and, therefore, the constitution. Acts affecting the constitution were required to achieve a majority in both Houses, which the Act in question had not done. The attempt made by the Home Government in 26 & 27 Vict., c. 84 to validate colonial acts that had been passed with the intention of altering the constitution he dealt with extremely neatly. In *Re Ware; ex parte Bayne* (1864)[31] Boothby and Gwynne agreed that since the Registration Act had altered the constitution, not by intention but by accident, it remained unaffected by the terms of 26 & 27 Vict., c. 84.

Boothby's even more remarkable judgement in *Auld* v. *Murray* (1864)[32] for the first time cast serious doubts upon the power of the local legislature, as then constituted, to pass a Constitution Act at all. When this Act had come into force, he pointed out, the Ordinance No. 1 of 1851, which had created the Legislative Council, which, in turn, had passed the Constitution Act, had automatically been repealed.[33] Hence the Constitution Act was

[29] C.O. 13/110, Law Officers' Report, 12 Apr. 1802.

[30] *S.A.P.P.* 142 H.A. (1864); Appendix B.

[31] O'Donoghue, K. K., 'The Constitutional and Administrative Development of South Australia, 1855–68', M.A. thesis, Adelaide (1950), p. 257.

[32] *S.A.P.P.* 53 L.C. (1864).

[33] 'Like the conjuror who ate himself', marginal note by Rogers in C.O. 13/114, fol. 20.

the creation of an institution without legal existence or authority, and could not itself exist. While Mr. Justice Gwynne was not prepared to identify himself with this doctrine, he did consider that section 34 of the Constitution Act was invalid, on the ground that it was beyond the powers of the legislature to change the laws regarding the election of members.[34] In view of these arguments, however well founded, it was clearly desirable that the validity of the South Australian Constitution Act, and of other Acts passed by the legislature established under it, should be confirmed. This the second part of clause 5 of the Colonial Laws Validity Act duly accomplished, though it was couched in general terms, applying to all representative colonial legislatures.

Of the points covered by the remaining two sections of the 1865 Act, little more need be said. No evidence has come to light to connect the sixth clause, which established the *prima facie* authenticity of certified copies of colonial acts, directly with the Boothby affair. There may perhaps have been some connection here with Boothby's dictum in *McEllister* v. *Fenn* that all 'proposed' acts of legislature ought to be enrolled in the Supreme Court, under the terms of 9 Geo. IV, c. 83. In any case, in view of Boothby's general attitude, it was important to lay down how the colonial judges were to identify the 'Act copy' (on the analogy in Britain of certification, followed by incorporation in the Parliament Roll).

Finally section 7, the only section to make specific mention of South Australia, is largely self-explanatory. Two previous imperial Acts had been passed, in 1862 and 1863, to settle doubts about the validity of South Australian legislation. Section 7 of the 1865 Act asserted yet again the validity of laws passed by the South Australian Legislatures, and was clearly intended to quiet any remaining doubts with which the first six sections had failed to deal.

If one considered the attitude of the Colonial Office to the Boothby affair from the point of view only of the legal points which emerged from it, that attitude appears on the whole to have been liberal and progressive. In contrast to Boothby's determination to limit the powers of the local legislature, to impose upon it a strict adherence to the law of England, and to undermine its efforts to deal relatively unaided with its own problems, the Colonial Office appeared equally determined to support,

[34] *S.A.P.P.* 53 L.C. (1864); Appendix B.

within limits, local autonomy. It is therefore rather surprising to find that the Colonial Office has been criticized, both by contemporaries and by at least one recent commentator, for adopting an attitude to the affair in general designed to retard the political development of the colony.

Criticism of the Colonial Office has centred around two points. Brother K. K. O'Donoghue's complaint is directed at the failure of the Colonial Office to advise the Queen to have Boothby removed from office, in accordance with the Addresses sent by both Houses of the Legislature.[35] This incident he described as a 'set back in the constitutional development of the state'.

The colonists themselves had evidently been convinced that their petition would be successful. The Legislative Council in particular, in choosing the 'more dignified' course of attaching no reason to their Address, was confident that the mere fact that such a petition had been presented would be enough to cause the Home Government to comply with its demands.

The British Government was unprepared, at this stage, to allow the Crown to act as the passive instrument of a colonial legislature, and there were other compelling reasons for refusing the colonists' request. Rogers pointed out, for one thing, that since no detailed reasons for the request had been given in the Addresses, Boothby was being given no chance to answer the charges against him.[36] There was also the question of setting a precedent—what might happen if both Houses, supported by popular opinion, decided that colonial law should not be affected in any way by imperial law, and demanded the removal of all judges who failed to agree? 'The defence of the Judicial independence', Rogers wrote, 'is the defence of (among others) Imperial interests—and the right of dismissing a Judge, on address, is properly given to the Crown, not as a mere unmeaning form but as recognizing the right to exercise certain discretion.'[37]

The Crown Law Officers, in their turn, produced a more immediately cogent reason for refusing the request. It was their opinion that although Boothby's interpretation of the law was in many ways mistaken, he had been correct in declaring invalid the Electoral Act of 1855, and that therefore the legality of the

[35] O'Donoghue, op. cit., p. 178.
[36] C.O. 13/106, MacDonnell to Newcastle, 25 Oct. 1861; Minute by Rogers.
[37] Ibid.

Parliament which had been elected under it, and all its actions, was open to doubt. To accede to a request made by a technically illegal legislature would be to throw the whole question of invalidity into even greater relief.[38]

To refuse to remove Boothby in these circumstances was therefore understandable, and not necessarily part of a policy to retard the colony's constitutional development. Indeed what the Colonial Office would clearly have preferred would have been for the colonial government itself to shoulder the responsibility.

It was against this *laissez-faire* attitude, rather than against a policy of restriction, that contemporaries in South Australia complained most bitterly. Discontent with the attitude of the Home Government rose to its height in 1864. Governor Daly, writing to the Secretary of State in May, enclosed several extracts from local newspapers in which the latter was vehemently attacked for his refusal to pass 'some sweeping measure'. The Duke of Newcastle, it was claimed, had 'wholly failed to realize our actual position in this colony'.[39] At the same time, both Houses sent new addresses to the Queen, to complain of the effect of the Judge's obstructionism, and proposed a draft Act designed to provide a final settlement.

In view of the fact that the Imperial Parliament had already passed two Acts to deal with the matter, even if these had not been very effective, this criticism was hardly fair. But it is true that the Secretary of State and his senior officials were not very anxious to get involved in the matter. This was partly a matter of political principle, and partly the reflection of a more personal attitude in which one can discern a faint tinge of contempt. Rogers, for one, appears to have believed, in the early stages of the affair, that this was just another incident that had been exaggerated by Governor MacDonnell's customary tactlessness. The Governor, Rogers asserted, was 'one of those people to whom someone is always being discourteous'.[40]

But over and above this personal attitude, was the assumption on the part of the Colonial Office that a colony in the position of South Australia should be responsible for dealing with its own problems, without intervention from outside.

In January 1861 the Duke of Newcastle refused the Governor's

[38] C.O. 13/110, Law Officers' Report, 12 Apr. 1862.
[39] C.O. 13/114, Daly to Newcastle, 23 May 1864.
[40] C.O. 13/103, MacDonnell to Newcastle, 20 Dec. 1860; note by Rogers.

request that he should be given an Instruction to reserve or disallow all acts intending to alter the constitution. Throwing the
responsibility back on the colonial legislature, the Duke expressed
his view that constitution acts were no more than 'colonial laws . . .
making provision for matters in which the colonists are exclusively
interested' and 'alterable by the usual methods of legislation'.[41]
It was Newcastle also who objected, in 1863, to the cluttering up
of the imperial statute book with enactments 'required to extricate Colonial Governments and Legislatures from the consequences of their irregularity or inadvertence'.[42] Throughout the
affair, the Colonial Office supported the claim by the Colonial
Supreme Court to the power of judicial review. It was evidently
both the hope and the expectation at home that the current legal
problems of the colony should be settled within it. In a note on the
Governor's dispatch relating to the matter of the local Court of
Appeal, Rogers pointed out that the questions 'What is the law?'
and 'What ought to be the law?' could be determined only by the
colonial judges and legislature. The Colonial Office, he thought,
'would do well to keep rather pointedly clear of it'.[43]

As it happened, of course, the Colonial Office found itself quite
unable to keep clear of the incident. By 1863 two Imperial Acts
had been passed in an effort to deal with the situation, both had
proved ineffective. The reason for their ineffectiveness was simply
that they did not go far enough—so that from this point of view
the colonists were justified in their demand for 'some sweeping
measure'. But it must be remembered that the Colonial Office had
to deal, not only with the demands of the colonists, but also with
the British Parliament. As early as 1861 Rogers had considered
the passing of an Imperial Act, only to dismiss it as impracticable.
He evidently feared, at this stage, that Parliament would be unwilling to accept the definition of repugnancy which was later
to be written into the Colonial Laws Validity Act. 'Unless Parliament is prepared', he wrote, 'to go the whole length of declaring
that no Colonial Act shall be invalid for repugnancy to English
law unless it is repugnant to some Act of Parliament binding in
the colonies (a line which I am not at all prepared to call unreasonable, but which I should think Parliament would hesitate

---

[41] C.O. 13/102, Newcastle to MacDonnell, 26 Jan. 1861.
[42] *S.A.P.P.* 130 H.A., Newcastle to Daly, 25 July 1863.
[43] C.O. 13/105, MacDonnell to Newcastle, 15 June 1861; Minute by Rogers.

to adopt) I do not see how a statutory distinction could be drawn between the fundamental principles (a violation of which is to avoid a law) and the practical or semi-fundamental principles (a violation of which is *not* to avoid a law).'[44]

By 1865 the Colonial Office was ready to disregard any possible objections by Parliament on this point, though no such opposition appears to have arisen. In any case it had already become clear to Rogers that his main consideration must be for the colonies, rather than for the probable wishes of the Imperial Parliament. By May 1863 both he and the Law Officers were agreed that 'the legislative powers of the Assemblies should be more clearly defined'. His reasons for this opinion are highly significant. 'I think', he wrote, 'these powers should, if possible, be so large and clear as to cut the ground from under such objectors as Mr. Boothby, and to enable Parliament to throw back on the Colonial Legislature the task of curing mistakes and removing doubts.'[45]

Boothby was therefore uppermost in Rogers's mind. His solution to the problem, however, was not to increase the power of the Imperial Parliament to intervene in such matters, but, on the contrary, to free the colonial legislatures from certain supposed disabilities, so as to leave *them* with the responsibility for dealing with the situation.

To emphasize this point, Rogers took care to consult the views of all the Australian colonies, and to incorporate in the final draft some of their recommendations. Thus the words 'notwithstanding such Instructions may be referred to in such Letters Patent or last named instrument' were added to clause 4 at the suggestion of R. D. Hanson, the Chief Justice of South Australia.[46]

The attitude adopted by the Colonial Office throughout was therefore consistent. Initially, they were reluctant to intervene at all in a matter which appeared to be of exclusively domestic concern. As time went on, and it became clear not only that the colonial legislature was failing to control the situation, but also that the issues involved were taking on a wider imperial significance, positive action was taken. The real significance of this incident is to be found not in the fact that the Home Government decided,

[44] C.O. 13/106, MacDonnell to Newcastle, 25 Sept. 1861; Minute by Rogers.
[45] C.O. 13/113, Law Officers' Report, 13 May 1863; Minute by Rogers.
[46] C.O. 13/115, Law Officers' Report, 28 Sept. 1864, fol. 507, Memo of colonial criticism of the proposed Bill.

however reluctantly, to intervene, but in the nature of that intervention. What Mr. Justice Boothby had tried to do was to erect (or strictly 'discover') severe limitations on the power of the legislature in self-governing colonies. By passing the Colonial Laws Validity Act the Imperial Parliament firmly rejected these limitations, and lent its support to the Colonial Office policy of developing upon the colonial legislatures the responsibility for managing their own affairs.

APPENDIX A

The Colonial Laws Validity Act,
28 & 29 Vict., c. 63

'An Act to remove Doubts as to the Validity of Colonial Laws'.

Whereas doubts have been entertained respecting the Validity of divers Laws enacted, or purporting to have been enacted by the Legislatures of certain of Her Majesty's colonies, and respecting the Powers of such Legislatures, and it is expedient that such doubts be removed;

Be it hereby enacted by the Queen's most excellent Majesty, by and with the Advice and Consent of the Lords Spiritual and Temporal, and Commons, in this present Parliament assembled, and by the Authority of the same, as follows:

I   The term 'Colony' shall in this Act include all of Her Majesty's possessions abroad in which there shall exist a Legislature, as hereinafter defined, except the Channel Islands, the Isle of Man, and such Territories as may for the Time being be vested in Her Majesty under or by virtue of any Act of Parliament for the Government of India.

The terms 'Legislature', and 'Colonial Legislature' shall severally signify the authority, other than the Imperial Parliament, or Her Majesty in Council, competent to make laws for any Colony:

The term 'Representative Legislature' shall signify any colonial Legislature which shall comprise a legislative body of which one half are elected by inhabitants of the colony:

The term 'Colonial Law' shall include laws made for any colony, either by such Legislature as aforesaid, or by Her Majesty in Council:

An Act of Parliament, or any provision thereof, shall, in construing this Act, be said to extend to any colony, when it is made applicable to such colony by the express words or necessary intendment of any Act of Parliament:

The term 'Governor' shall mean the officer lawfully administering the Government of any Colony:

The term 'Letters Patent' shall mean Letters Patent under the Great Seal of the United Kingdom of Great Britain and Ireland.

II   Any colonial law, which is, or shall be in any respect repugnant to the provisions of any Act of Parliament extending to the colony to which such law may relate, or repugnant to any order or regulation made under authority of such Act of Parliament, or having in the colony the force and effect of such Act, shall be read subject to such Act, order, or regulation, and shall, to the extent of such repugnancy, but not otherwise, be and remain absolutely void and inoperative.

III No colonial law shall be, or be deemed to have been, void or inoperative on the ground of repugnancy to the law of England, unless the same shall be repugnant to the provisions of some such Act of Parliament, order, or regulation, as aforesaid.

IV No colonial law, passed with the concurrence of or assented to by the Governor of any colony, or to be hereafter so passed or assented to, shall be, or be deemed to have been, void or inoperative by reason only of any Instructions with reference to such law or the subject thereof, which may have been given to such Governor, by or on behalf of Her Majesty, by any Instrument other than the Letters Patent, or Instrument authorising such Governor to concur in passing or to assent to laws for the peace order and good government of such colony, even though such Instructions may be referred to in such Letters Patent or last named Instrument.

V Every colonial Legislature shall have, and be deemed at all times to have had, full power within its jurisdiction to establish courts of judicature, and to abolish and reconstitute the same, and to alter the constitution thereof, and to make provision for the administration of justice therein; and every Representative Legislature shall, in respect to the colony under its jurisdiction have, and be deemed at all times to have had, full power to make laws respecting the constitution powers and procedure of such Legislature, provided that such laws shall have been passed in such manner and form as may from time to time be required, by any Act of Parliament, Letters Patent, Order in Council, or colonial law for the time being in force in the said colony.

VI The certificate of the clerk, or other proper officer of a legislative body in any colony, to the effect that the document to which it is attached is a true copy of any colonial law assented to by the Governor of such colony, or of any bill reserved for the signification of Her Majesty's pleasure by the said Governor, shall be *prima facie* evidence that the document so certified is a true copy of such law or bill, and, as the case may be, that such law has been duly and properly passed and assented to, or that such bill has been duly and properly passed and presented to the Governor, and any proclamation purporting to be published by authority of the Governor, in any newspaper in the colony to which such law or bill shall relate, and signifying Her Majesty's disallowance of any such reserved bill as aforesaid, shall be *prima facie* evidence of such disallowance or assent.

And whereas doubts are entertained respecting the validity of certain Acts enacted, or reputed to be enacted by the Legislature of South Australia: Be it further enacted as follows:

VII All laws or reputed laws enacted, or purporting to have been enacted by the said Legislature, or by persons or bodies of persons for the time being acting as such Legislature, which have received the assent of Her Majesty in Council, or which have received the assent of the Governor of the said Colony in the name, and on behalf of Her Majesty, shall be and be deemed to have been valid and effectual from the date of such assent for all purposes whatever; Provided that nothing herein contained shall be deemed to give effect to any law or reputed law which has been disallowed by Her Majesty, or has expired, or has been lawfully repealed, or to prevent the lawful disallowance or repeal of any law.

APPENDIX B

Statistical Table of Colonial Acts
1813–1865

THIS table has been compiled from entries in the Privy Council Register (P.C. 2/194–262). Record of acts 'left to their operation' were not kept consistently, especially after 1842. It may be assumed from what records there are, that the great majority of acts not either 'specially confirmed' or 'disallowed' were so left.

Year	Referred to P.C.	Specially Confirmed	Disallowed
1813	112	3	0
1814	102	0	0
1815	103	1	0
1816	74	16	1
1817	167	1	4
1818	246	1	6
1819	251	0	2
1820	169	1	2
1821	191	11	16
1822	196	6	6
1823	89	2	3
1824	243	4	4
1825	158	0	11
1826	265	5	2
1827	35	9	21
1828	125	2	1
1829	440	2	32
1830	212	7	7
1831	300	9	8
1832	459	18	4
1833	150	4	10
1834	405	27	5
1835	522	14	14
1836	387	27	21
1837	393	13	10
1838	468	12	38
1839	368	8	19

APPENDIX B

Year	Referred to P.C.	Specially Confirmed	Disallowed
1840	561	9	20
1841	281	14	18
1842	504	30	6
1843	381	11	3
1844	374	23	0
1845	575	22	3
1846	480	19	3
1847	331	20	4
1848	487	27	3
1849	390	25	1
1850	483	15	0
1851	410	11	2
1852	610	17	3
1853	340	14	2
1854	582	13	1
1855	532	8	2
1856	549	17	1
1857	375	12	0
1858	649	9	4
1859	534	15	2
1860	427	10	3
1861	717	11	2
1862	385	14	0
1863	669	10	2
1864	417	12	1
1865	772	12	3

APPENDIX C

Colonies whose Acts passed through the Privy Council 1813–1865

Anguilla
Antigua
Bahamas
Barbados
Berbice
Bermuda
British Honduras
Canada (and Upper and Lower Canada pre-1842)
Demerara
Dominica
Grenada
Guernsey
Jamaica
Jersey
Mauritius
Montserrat
Nevis

New Brunswick
Newfoundland
New South Wales
New Zealand
Nova Scotia
Prince Edward Island
Prince of Wales Island
St. Kitts
St. Lucia
St. Vincent
Sierra Leone
South Australia
Tobago
Tortola
Vancouver Island
Van Diemen's Land
Victoria
Virgin Islands

BIBLIOGRAPHY

PRIMARY SOURCES

I. MANUSCRIPT

All manuscript sources except the Murray Papers are to be found in the Public Record Office in London.

C.O. 323   'Law Officers' Reports'. These reports were written in fact not by the Law Officers of the Crown, as their title would imply, but by legal counsel to the C.O. These reports on colonial laws were continued till 1860. Thereafter material on the review process is to be found in the general C.O. correspondence with individual colonies.

C.O. 324   C.O. miscellaneous correspondence, especially the file in each volume before 1847 marked 'Stephen'.

C.O. 381   Collected Royal Instructions; Commissions to Governors, etc.

C.O. 386   Papers of the Colonial Land and Emigration Board. Also C.O. correspondence arranged by geographical regions, especially C.O. 13 (South Australia) and C.O. 280 (Van Diemen's Land).

P.C. 2.   Privy Council Register.

Murray Papers   National Library of Scotland.

II. PRINTED

All printed sources are generally available except the *South Australian Parliamentary Papers* AND *Debates*, to be found in Rhodes House, Oxford.

Hansard   Parliamentary Debates.

[English] *Parliamentary Papers*   the most useful of these being:

P.P. 1825, XV (157), p. 233   Report of Commission of Enquiry into the Administration of Justice in the West Indies.

P.P. 1847/8, XLII (42), p. 1   Grey to Treasury *re* Stephen's replacement.

P.P. 1847/8, (371), p. 5   Grey on co-operation between C.O. and Committee for Trade and Plantation.

P.P. 1847/8 XVIII pt. 1, p. 528   Report of Committee of Enquiry into C.O. establishment.

P.P. 1836 XI, p. 823   Evidence before Committee on Waste Lands.

P.P. 1847/8 XLIII, p. 60   on *Symons* v. *Morgan*.

Privy Council Appeal Cases   mainly in *English Reports* (Moore, P. C. and Knapp). These have occasionally been supplemented by the much fuller accounts of cases to be found in the Privy Council Office in London. Much of the value of the latter is lost however, by the failure to record the judgements of the Judicial Committee before the mid-1850s.

[English] *Parliamentary Statutes*
South Australian Parliamentary Debates
South Australian Parliamentary Papers

SELECTED LIST OF SECONDARY SOURCES

Allin, C. D., *Australasian Preferential Tariffs and Imperial Free Trade* (Minnesota, 1929).

Andrews, C. M., 'The Royal Disallowance', *Proc. of Am. Antiquarian Soc.* (1914).

Beaglehole, J. C., 'The Colonial Office 1782–1854', *Hist. Studies of Austr. and N.Z.*, vol. 1 (1943).

Beaglehole, J. C., 'Royal Instructions to Governors', London Ph.D. thesis (1929).

Blackmore, E. G., *The Law of the Constitution of South Australia* (Adelaide, 1887).

Blackstone, Sir W., *Commentaries on the Laws of England*, 23rd edn. (London, 1854).

Borrow, T. C., 'South Australia and N.S.W.—the supposed legal nexus', *Pioneer Ass. of S.A.* (1948).

Brown, G. P., *The Judicial Committee of the Privy Council and the British North American Act* (Univ. of Toronto Press, 1967).

Burn, W. L., *Emancipation and Apprenticeship in the British West Indies* (London, 1937).

Burt, A. L., *The Evolution of the British Empire from the American Revolution* (Massachusetts, 1956).

Cambridge History of the British Empire, 8 vols. (Cambridge, 1929–63).

Cannon, L., 'Some Data relating to the Appeal to the Privy Council', *Can. Bar Rev.* (1925).

Chalmers, G., *Opinions of Eminent Lawyers on various points of English Jurisprudence*, 2 vols. (London, 1914).

Clark, C., *A Summary of Colonial Law* (London, 1834).

Clarke, D. P., 'The Attitude of the Colonial Office to the Workings of Responsible Government. 1854–68', London Ph.D. thesis (1953).

Dicey, A. V., *The Privy Council* (London, 1887).

Dicey, A. V., *The Law of the Constitution*, 10th edn. (London, 1959).

Dictionary of National Biography (Oxford, 1921).

Durham, Lord, *Report on Affairs in British North America*, 3 vols., ed. Sir C. P. Lucas (Oxford, 1912).

Edwards, B., *The History of the British Colonies in the West Indies* (Dublin, 1793).

Egerton, H. E., *A Short History of British Colonial Policy 1606–1909* (London, 1932).

Fitzroy, Sir A. M., *The History of the Privy Council* (London, 1928).

Forsyth, W., *Cases and Opinions on Constitutional Law* (London, 1869).

Grey, 3rd Earl, *The Colonial Policy of Lord John Russell's Administration*, 2 vols. (London, 1853).

Haldane, Lord, 'The Judicial Committee of the Privy Council', *Cambridge Law Journal* (1922).

Hall, H. L., *The Colonial Office* (London, 1937).

Hancock, Sir W. K., *Survey of Commonwealth Affairs*, vol. 1 (Oxford, 1937).

Hannan, A. J., 'Mr. Justice Boothby', *Proc. of Royal Geog. Soc. of Austr.* (S. Austr. Branch) (1957).

Hargreaves, J. D., 'C.O. Opinions on the Constitution of 1863', *Sierra Leone Studies* (1955).

Hitchins, F. H., *The Colonial Land and Emigration Commission* (Philadelphia, 1931).

Holdsworth, W. S., *History of English Law*, 13 vols. (London, 1922–56).

Hood Phillips, O., *Leading Cases in Constitutional Law* (London, 1952).

Hughes, H., *Judicial Autonomy in the Dominions* (London, 1931).

Keir, D. L., and Lawson, F. H., *Cases in Constitutional Law*, 4th edn. (Oxford, 1954).

Keith, B., *The Constitution, Administration and Laws of the Empire* (London, 1924).

Keith, B., *Responsible Government in the Dominions*, 2nd edn., 3 vols. (Oxford, 1928).

Knaplund, P., *Sir James Stephen and the British Colonial System* (Madison, 1953).

Knaplund, P., *The British Empire 1815–1939* (London, 1942).

Knox, B. A., 'The Provision of Legal Advice, and C.O. Reorganization, 1866–7', *Bull. of Inst. of Hist. Res.* (1962).

Labaree, L. W., *Royal Government in America* (New Haven, 1930).

Labaree, L. W., *Royal Instructions to British Colonial Governors, 1670–1776*, Am. Hist. Ass. (New York, 1935).

Lucas, Sir C., *Introduction to a Historical Geography of the British Colonies* (Oxford, 1887).

Lucas, S. (ed.), *Charters of Old English Colonies in America* (London, 1850).

McCracken, J. L., *The Cape Parliament 1854–1910* (Oxford, 1967).

Macdonald, V. C., 'The Privy Council and the Canadian Constitution', *Can. Bar Rev.* (1951).

McGovney, D. O., 'The British Origin of Judicial Review', *Univ. of Penn. Law Rev.* (1944–5).

McWhinney, E., *Judicial Review in the English Speaking World*, 2nd edn. (Toronto, 1960).

Madden, F., *Imperial Constitutional Documents, 1765–1952: A Supplement* (Oxford, 1953).

Manning, H. T., *British Colonial Government after the American Revolution* (Yale Univ. Press, 1935).

Marindin, G. E. (ed.), *Letters of Frederic Lord Blachford* (London, 1896).

Marshall, G., *Parliamentary Sovereignty and the Commonwealth* (Oxford, 1962).

Masters, D. C., 'A. T. Galt and Canadian Fiscal Autonomy', *Can. Hist. Rev.*, vol. 15 (1934).

Mathieson, W. L., *British Slavery and its Abolition* (London, 1926).

Melbourne, A. C. V., *Early Constitutional Developments in Australia*, vol. 1 (London, 1934).

Mellor, G. R., *British Imperial Trusteeship 1783–1850* (London, 1951).

Merivale, H., *Lectures on Colonisation and the Colonies* (London, 1861).

Mew's Digest of English Case Law to 1924, 2nd edn. (London, 1925).

Minty, L. le M., 'The Judicial Committee of the Privy Council', *Bermuda Police Magazine* (Dec. 1957).

Moore, Sir W. H., 'A Century of Victorian Law', *Journal of Comparative Legislation* (1934).

O'Callaghan, E. B. (ed.), *Documents Relating to the Colonial History of New York*, 4 vols. (Albany, 1850–1).

O'Donoghue, K. K., 'Constitutional Developments in South Australia, 1855–68', Adelaide, M.A. thesis (1955).

Palley, C., *The Constitutional History and Law of Southern Rhodesia 1888–1965* (Oxford, 1966).

Parnell, Sir H., *Financial Reform* (London, 1830).

Pike, D., *A Paradise of Dissent—South Australia. 1829–57* (London, 1957).

Pollard, A. F., *The Commonwealth at War* (London, 1917).

Rankin, Sir G., 'The Judicial Committee of the Privy Council', *Camb. Univ. Law Soc. Journal* (1938).

Roberts-Wray, Sir K., *Commonwealth and Colonial Law* (London, 1966).

Robinson, R., and Gallacher, J. A., 'The Imperialism of Free Trade', *Economic Hist. Rev.* (1953).

Russell, E. B., *The Review of American Colonial Legislation* (New York, 1915).

Schlesinger, A. M., 'Colonial Appeals to the Privy Council', *Political Science Quarterly*, vol. 28 (1913).

Schuyler, R., *Parliament and the British Empire* (New York, 1929).

Sellers, G., 'Edward Cardwell', B.Litt. thesis, Oxford (1959).

Shortt, A., and Doughty, A. G., *Documents relating to the Constitutional History of Canada 1759–1791*, 2nd edn. (Ottawa, 1918).

Sioussant, St. G. L., 'The English Statutes in Maryland', *Johns Hopkins University Studies* (1903).

Smith, H. A., 'Judicial Control of Legislation in the British Empire', *Yale Law Journal* (1925).

Smith, J. H., *Appeals to the Privy Council from the American Plantations* (New York, 1950).

Snow, A. H., *The Administration of Dependencies* (New York, 1902).

Swinfen, D. B., 'Geneses of the Colonial Laws Validity Act', *Juridical Review* (1967).

Swinfen, D. B., 'Legal Status of Royal Instructions to Colonial Governors', *Juridical Review* (1968).

Tarring, A., *The Law relating to the Colonies*, 4th edn. (London, 1913).

Todd, A., *Parliamentary Government in the British Colonies*, 2nd edn. (London, 1894).

Turner, E. R., *The Privy Council of England*, 2 vols. (Baltimore, 1927–8).

Wade, E. C. S., and Phillips, G. G., *Constitutional Law*, 7th edn. (London, 1965).

Wakefield, E. G., *The Art of Colonisation* (London, 1849).

Walker, E. A., *The British Empire—its Structure and Spirit*, 2nd edn. (Cambridge, 1953).

Ward, J. M., *Empire in the Antipodes* (London, 1966).

Wheare, K. C., *The Statue of Westminster and Dominion Status*, 5th edn. (London, 1953).

Williamson, J. A., *A Short History of the British Empire*, 3rd edn., 2 vols. (London, 1945).

Woodcock, H. I., *Laws and Constitution of the British Colonies in the West Indies*, 2nd edn. (London, 1938).

Woodward, E. L., *The Age of Reform 1815–70*, Oxford History Series, vol. 13, 2nd edn. (1962).

Young, D. M., 'The Workings of the C.O. 1825–30', Ph.D. thesis, London (1955).

Young, D. M., *The Colonial Office in the early Nineteenth Century*, Imperial Studies, No. XXII (London, 1961).

INDEX